The Origins and Deve
of the Dutch Revolt

The Dutch revolt against Spanish rule in the sixteenth century was a formative event in European history. *The Origins and Development of the Dutch Revolt* brings together in one volume the latest scholarship from leading experts in the field, to illuminate why the Dutch revolted, the way events unfolded and how the people emerged fully independent.

Beginning with a useful narrative of events and overview of recent historiography, the book goes on to examine the current state of research, focusing on:

- the role of the aristocracy
- religion
- the towns and provinces
- the Spanish perspective
- finance and ideology

As well as making the most recent research available in English for the first time, this book provides a useful introduction to the topic for sixth-formers, teachers and undergraduates.

Graham Darby is Head of History at King Edward VI School, Southampton. He has published a number of books including *Spain in the Seventeenth Century* (1994) and *The Thirty Years' War* (2001).

Contributors: Martin van Gelderen, Fernando González de León, Guido Marnef, Henk van Nierop, Geoffrey Parker, Andrew Pettegree, James D. Tracy.

The Origins and Development of the Dutch Revolt

Edited by
Graham Darby

London and New York

First published 2001
by Routledge
2 Park Square, Milton Park, Abingdon, Oxon, OX14 4RN

Simultaneously published in the USA and Canada
by Routledge
270 Madison Ave, New York NY 10016

Routledge is an imprint of the Taylor & Francis Group

Transferred to Digital Printing 2010

Typeset in Garamond by
BOOK NOW Ltd

British Library Cataloguing in Publication Data
A catalogue record for this book is available from the British Library

Library of Congress Cataloging in Publication Data
The origins and development of the Dutch revolt / Graham Darby [editor].
    p. cm.
    Includes index.
    1. Netherlands–Politics and government–1556–1648. 2. Netherlands–History–Wars
of Independence, 1556–1648. I. Darby, Graham.

DH186.5.O75 2001
249.2'03–dc21   00–066492

ISBN 0-415-25378-0 (hbk)
ISBN 0-415-25379-9 (pbk)

Contents

Figures, tables and maps

Notes on contributors

Graham Darby was born in London and educated at the University of Hull where he obtained a First in History; Pembroke College, Cambridge; and the Queen's College, Oxford. After working for soccer entrepreneur Jimmy Hill in London, Saudi Arabia and the USA, he became an assistant master at King Edward VI School, Southampton where he is currently Head of History. He is the author of a number of books and articles including *Spain in the Seventeenth Century* (1994) and *The Thirty Years' War* (2001).

Martin van Gelderen is Professor of Intellectual History at the University of Sussex. His books include *The Political Thought of the Dutch Revolt 1555–1590* (1992) and the *The Dutch Revolt* (1993). He is currently preparing a new translation and edition of Hugo Grotius's *De iure belli ac pacis*. Two volumes on *Republicanism: A Shared European Heritage,* edited with Quentin Skinner, will appear in 2001.

Fernando González de León obtained his Ph.D. in early modern European history with an Iberian focus from the Johns Hopkins University in 1992 and is currently Associate Professor of History at Springfield College in Springfield, Massachusetts. He has presented papers at numerous international conferences and is author of various articles and contributions on Golden Age Spanish history in American and European journals, among them *The Sixteenth Century Journal* and *The Journal of Modern History.* He has just finished a monograph on Spanish military policy in the Netherlands entitled *The Road to Rocroi: The Duke of Alba, the Count Duke of Olivares and the High Command of the Spanish Army of Flanders in the Eighty Years War (1567–1659)* which will soon be published.

Guido Marnef is lecturer in early modern history at the University of Antwerp – UFSIA. He is the author of three books, including *Antwerp* *in the Age of Reformation. Underground Protestantism in a Commercial Metropolis 1550–1577* (1996). He has written many articles dealing with Reformation and Revolt in the Low Countries, most recently 'The Netherlands', in A. Pettegree (ed.), *The Reformation World* (2000), pp. 344–64.

Henk van Nierop is Professor of Early Modern History at the University of Amsterdam. He is the author of several books on the Dutch Revolt and the Golden Age, including *The Nobility of Holland: From Knights to Regents* (1993) and *Het verraad van het Noorderkwartier. Oorlog, terreur en recht in de Nederlandse Opstand* (1999).

Geoffrey Parker was born in Nottingham and educated at the University of Cambridge where he obtained a First in History and his Ph.D. After teaching at Christ's College, he went to St Andrews where he became Professor of Early Modern History. He has subsequently held professorships at the University of Illinois, Urbana-Champaign, and at Yale, and he is currently Andreas Dorpalen Professor of History at Ohio State University. He has published – as author, co-author or editor – over sixty articles and twenty-seven books including *The Army of Flanders and the Spanish Road* (1972 and 1990); *The Dutch Revolt* (1977 and 1985); *Philip II* (1978 and 1994), *The Military Revolution* (1988 and 1996); and the *Grand Strategy of Philip II* (1998). He is a Fellow of the British Academy, a corresponding fellow of the Royal Spanish Academy and has been conferred with the rank of Knight Grand Cross of two Orders by the king of Spain.

Andrew Pettegree is Professor of Modern History at the University of St Andrews and Director of the St Andrews Reformation Studies Institute. A specialist on Reformation history and particularly the history of European Calvinist movements he has published several books including *Emden and the Dutch Revolt* (1992), *Marian Protestantism* (1996) and (with Alastair Duke and Gillian Lewis) *Calvinism in Europe, 1540–1610. A Collection of Documents* (1992). His edited survey collection *The Reformation World* was published in 2000.

James D. Tracy is Professor of History at the University of Minnesota, and author of *Erasmus: The Growth of a Mind* (1972), *The Politics of Erasmus: A Pacifist Intellectual and his Political Milieu* (1978), *A Financial Revolution in the Habsburg Netherlands: 'Renten' and 'Renteniers' in the County of Holland, 1515–1566* (1985), *Formation of a Body Politic: Holland under Habsburg Rule 1506–1655* (1990), *Erasmus of the Low Countries* (1996), and *Europe's Reformations, 1450–1650* (1999).

Acknowledgements

I would like to begin by thanking Professor Jeremy Black for initially suggesting that I should edit this book. At the beginning I worked with a number of people at UCL Press but after the imprint came under the direction of Routledge I have had the good fortune to work with Victoria Peters and Helen Brocklehurst; I owe them both a great debt of thanks. Thanks are also due to all my contributors who so readily participated in the venture; particular thanks are due to Henk van Nierop who very kindly agreed to a second contribution at short notice. My greatest debt of thanks goes to Alastair Duke whose expertise in this subject guided me through and saved me from a number of errors. Those that remain are my responsibility alone.

Finally I should like to thank my wife Rose for her keyboard skills and my daughters Natalie, Charlotte and Daniella for allowing their father to disappear into the study far too often.

Graham Darby
Bournemouth
September 2000

Chronology

1384 Philip 'the Bold', duke of Burgundy succeeds as count of Flanders

1477 Charles 'the Bold' killed in battle: Mary of Burgundy succeeds

1496 Philip 'the Fair' (son of Mary and Maximilian of Habsburg) marries Joanna (daughter of Ferdinand II of Aragon and Isabella of Castile)

1515 Charles (son of Philip and Joanna) declared 'of age' to rule Netherlands

1516 Charles proclaimed king of Spain

1519 Charles elected Holy Roman Emperor

1548 The 'seventeen Netherlands' united in Burgundian Circle (Treaty of Augsburg)

1549 Pragmatic Sanction declares the 'seventeen Netherlands' to be indivisible: henceforth provinces will recognise the same prince

1555 Charles renounces his titles in the Netherlands in favour of his son Philip

1559 May: Margaret of Parma appointed Governor-General
12 May: Bull *Super universas*: Pope Paul IV authorised re-organisation of bishoprics
July–August: States General at Ghent demanded withdrawal of Spanish troops and more participation by nobility in government
31 July: Promulgation of bull *Super universas* for new bishoprics
9 August: Orange appointed stadholder of Holland, Zeeland and Utrecht; Egmont made governor of Flanders and Artois
25 August: Philip II departed from Netherlands

1561 10 January: Spanish troops withdrew from Netherlands
26 February: Anthoine de Perronet, bishop of Arras, designated archbishop of Mechelen, made Cardinal (Granvelle)
July: Orange refused to participate in installation of new magistracy of Antwerp

23 July: Orange and Egmont complained to Philip about not being consulted on important matters

25 August: Marriage of Orange to Anna of Saxony

1562 May–June: Formation of anti-Granvelle League

1563 11 March: William of Orange, Egmont and Hornes write to king to complain about Granvelle: on receiving unsatisfactory reply in June, they withdrew from Council of State

26 April: First 'synod' of reformed churches held at Antwerp

August: Margaret of Parma sent Armenteros to persuade king to drop Granvelle

1564 13 March: King recalled Granvelle from the Netherlands

18 March: Egmont, Hornes and Orange returned to Council of State

31 December: William of Orange spoke in Council of State in favour of freedom of conscience

1565 20 February: Egmont arrived in Madrid

30 April: Egmont returned to Brussels

24 June: Council of State agreed to publication of Tridentine decrees in the Netherlands

July–August: Protestant nobles met at Spa to devise campaign against persecution

17–20 October: King's letters sent from Segovia Woods

5 November: Letters from Segovia Woods arrived at Brussels

14 November: Council of State informed about Segovian letters

December: Formation of Compromise of Nobility

18 December: Margaret of Parma demanded implementation of anti-heresy edicts

1566 5 April: Lesser nobility presented petition to Margaret of Parma

Late May: Calvinists resumed open-air services in Flanders

3 July: Edict against return of Protestant exiles

mid-July: Members of Compromise met with Calvinist leaders

30 July: Presentation of second petition for religious freedom

31 July: King, on news of Calvinist services, agreed to rescind Inquisition, but soon after he went back on promise, arguing he had acted under duress

10 August: Start of iconoclasm in Westkwartier (Steenvoorde)

13 August: King authorised Margaret of Parma to levy troops and sent 300,000 ducats

19 August: Orange left Antwerp for Brussels

20 August: Iconoclasm at Antwerp

23 August: Iconoclasm at Amsterdam, Breda, 's Hertogenbosch and Tournai

23–25 August: Negotiations leading to accord; limited religious freedom, dissolution of Compromise; high nobility to provinces to implement terms of accord

2 September: William of Orange brokered religious peace at Antwerp

3 September: News of image-breaking reached king

29 November: Alva reluctantly accepted command of troops to be sent to Netherlands

27 December: Calvinist rebels defeated in Flanders

1567 13 March: Rebel forces massacred at Oosterweel outside Antwerp

23 March: Valenciennes surrendered; Calvinist leaders hanged

11 April: Orange left Antwerp en route for Dillenberg

27 April: Bishops met to discuss implementation of Tridentine reforms

18 June: Alva began march along 'Spanish Road' to Netherlands

22 August: Alva entered Brussels as captain general

29 August: Margaret of Parma asked king leave to withdraw

5 September: Patent issued for Council of Troubles

9 September: Egmont and Hornes arrested

30 December: Margaret left Brussels; Alva succeeded as governor general

1568 12 February: Brederode died

May: Sea Beggars began to operate

23 May: Louis of Nassau invaded Groningen; defeated Aremberg at Heiligerlee

5 June: Egmont and Hornes executed at Brussels

21 July: Alva defeated Louis of Nassau at Jemmingen

5–6 October: Orange crossed Maas

17 November: Orange withdrew across French border

1569 20 February: Orange first granted letters of marque to Sea Beggars

20–21 March: Alva announced fiscal reforms to States General

1570 5 and 9 July: Alva published his Criminal Ordinances

16 July: Alva published General Pardon

1571 31 July: Alva moved to implement 'tenth penny' forthwith

4 October: First 'national' synod of reformed churches held at Emden

1572 1 March: Sea Beggars expelled from England

20 March: Alva warned that Lumey has planned raid on Brill

1 April: Sea Beggars seized Brill

7 April: Flushing refused to accept Spanish garrison

8 April: So-called massacre of Rotterdam
9 April: Riots at Gouda
22 April: Flushing reinforced from Brill
2 May: Sea Beggars opened negotiations with Dordrecht
21 May: Enkhuizen declared for Orange
24 May: Louis of Nassau captured Mons
11 June: Medina-Celi arrived in the Netherlands
15 June: Alva decided to withdraw all Spanish troops from Holland
25 June: Dordrecht agreed to admit Beggars
26 June: Leiden agreed to admit Beggars
4 July: Haarlem agreed to admit Beggars
9 July: Execution of Catholic clergy at Brill (Gorcum martyrs)
19–23 July: First 'free assembly' of States of Holland
26 July: Delft agreed to admit Beggars
26 July: Philip agreed to suspend tenth penny
21 August: Amsterdam reinforced; Beggars abandoned siege
24 August: Massacre of St Bartholomew's Day in Paris
27 August: Orange invaded Brabant
30 August: Orange entered Mechelen
19 September: Louis of Nassau surrendered Mons to Alva

1573   February–April: Prohibition of Catholic mass in Holland
13 July: Haarlem capitulated to Alva after siege of six months
8 October: Spanish abandoned siege of Alkmaar
11 October   Beggars defeated fleet in Zuiderzee; Bossu captured
19 October: Requesens appointed as governor
6 November: Medina-Celi returned to Spain
29 November: Requesens sworn in as governor
18 December: Alva returned to Spain

1574   27 January: Spanish fleet defeated at Reimerswaal
9–18 February: Middelburg surrendered to Orange
14 April: Battle of Mokerheide
7 June: Abolition of Council of Troubles and tenth penny
10 July: Alva's statue removed from Antwerp
3 October: Orange relieved Leiden

1575   8 February: University of Leiden inaugurated
March–July: Peace negotiations continued at Breda
4 June: Holland and Zeeland united under Orange
11 July: Orange recognised as '*souverain ende overhooft*' by States of Holland for duration of war
25 August: Holland issued *leeuwendaalder* without reference to royal authority

1 September: Spain suspended interest payments on public debt
9 October: States of Holland allegedly resolved 'for ever to sejoyne themselves from the Crowne of Spayne'
13 October: States of Holland decided to forsake king and seek foreign help
November: Rebels offered title of Countess of Holland and Zeeland to Elizabeth of England

1576   5 March: Death of Requesens
24 March: Council of State entrusted with government
April: States of Holland reportedly felt no obligation to Philip since he 'has violated his oath'
25 April: Union of Delft: Orange recognised as 'chief and highest authority' in Holland and Zeeland for duration of war
6 May: Title of count of Holland offered to Alençon (Anjou)
29 June: Mondragon captured Zierikzee
25 July: Spanish mutineers sacked Aalst in Flanders
26 July: Council of State declared mutineers to be rebels; States of Brabant decided to recruit troops to oppose mutineers
1 September: Don Juan received his commission
4 September: Council of State arrested in Brussels
6 September: States of Brabant summoned States General on own authority
25 September: States General decided to negotiate with rebel provinces
19 October: Negotiations with Holland and Zeeland began at Ghent
28 October: Negotiations at Ghent concluded
3 November: Don Juan arrived in Luxemburg
4–7 November: 'Spanish fury' at Antwerp
5 November: States General agreed to Pacification of Ghent
8 November: Pacification of Ghent signed
11 November: Spanish garrison at Ghent surrendered

1577   9 January: Union of Brussels
17 February: States General published Perpetual Edict with Don Juan without consultation of Holland and Zeeland whose representatives withdrew in protest
6 April: King reluctantly approved Pacification
28 April: Withdrawal of Spanish troops
12 May: Don Juan entered Brussels
15 June: Protestants executed at Mechelen in contravention of Pacification
24 July: Don Juan seized castle at Namur

19 August: Delegates of Holland and Zeeland rejoined States General

6 September: States General invited Orange to Brussels

11 September: Philip ordered return of Spanish troops

23 September: Orange entered Brussels in triumph

3–4 October: Archduke Matthias left Vienna secretly for the Netherlands

9 October: Utrecht agreed terms with Orange (Satisfactie)

18 October: Privileges restored to Ghent

22 October: Orange appointed *ruwaard* of Brabant (i.e. governor)

28 October: Aerschot and bishops of Bruges and Ypres arrested at Ghent

1 November: Committee of Eighteen established at Ghent

7 December: States declared Don Juan to be enemy of country; no longer recognised as governor general

8 December: States General offered government to Archduke Matthias

10 December: Second Union of Brussels

29 December: Orange entered Ghent

1578   18 January: Matthias made state entry into Brussels

20 January: Matthias accepted government with Orange as his lieutenant

31 January: States army defeated at Gembloers (Gembloux)

February: Protestant preaching began secretly at Ghent

16 February: Ghent seized control of Oudenaarde

16 March: Protestant services began at Antwerp

20 March: Ghent seized control of Bruges

24 April: States General issued edict forbidding Calvinist services

18–22 May: Mendicant houses attacked at Ghent

22 May: John of Nassau appointed stadholder of Gelderland

26 May: *Coup d'état* (Alteratie) at Amsterdam

29 June: Catholic services at Haarlem disrupted

1 June: Calvinists at Ghent preached in public

3–18 June: National synod of reformed churches at Dordrecht

7 June: Calvinists at Ghent rejected Orange's demand to stop services

9 June: Orange proposed *religievrede* to States General (i.e. religious peace)

18 June: Jesuits expelled from Antwerp

12 July: Anjou arrived at Mons; Antwerp, Friesland and Ommelanden accepted *religievrede*

15 July: Pope Gregory XIII warned bishops and clergy to remain loyal to king

13 August: Anjou recognised by States General as 'Defender of the Liberties of the Low Countries'

late August: Calvinist services held in all Ghent parish churches

29 August: *Religievrede* accepted in Antwerp

1 October: Malcontents seized Menen; Don Juan died

10 October: John Casimir arrived in Ghent; Farnese opened negotiations with Walloon provinces

29 December: Orange in Ghent to enforce *religievrede*

1579   6 January: Union of Arras (Hainaut, Artois and Douai)

19 January: Orange left Ghent

23 January: Union of Utrecht (Holland, Zeeland, Utrecht, Gelderland, Ommelanden, Friesland)

4 February: Ghent signed Union of Utrecht

10 March: Amersfoort (Utrecht) compelled to recognise Union of Utrecht

10–11 March: Second iconoclastic outburst at Ghent

3 May: Orange reluctantly signed Union of Utrecht (or 3 June)

7 May: Negotiations between States General and King began at Cologne

17 May: Peace treaty of Arras (Hainaut, Artois and French Flanders)

29 June: Farnese captured Maastricht

29 July: Antwerp signed Union of Utrecht

13 September: Definitive Treaty of Arras signed; reconciliation of Walloon provinces

13 November: Granvelle advised king to outlaw Orange

22 November: King ratified Treaty of Arras

1580   3 March: 'Treason' of Rennenberg in Groningen

15 March: Orange outlawed by Philip II

31 March: States of Holland offered Orange *ed hoge overheid* (supreme authority)

May: Spanish troops left Luxemburg for Lombardy

7 July: Orange accepted *hooge overigheid en regeringe* (*la souveraineté et gouvernement*) of Holland and Zeeland

29 September: Treaty of Plessis-les-Tours: Anjou accepted as prince

13 December: Orange offered *Apology* to States General

1581   23 January: States General took oath of loyalty to Anjou

February: *Apology* published

June: Government forces recaptured Breda

26 July: Act of Abjuration
August: French troops of Anjou entered Netherlands
29 November: Farnese captured Tournai (last Walloon city in States' hands)

1582   February: Spanish troops returned to the Netherlands
18 February: Anjou received as duke of Brabant in Antwerp
7 March: Decided to record resolutions of States General in Dutch
18 March: Attempt on life of Orange by Jean Jauregui at Antwerp
6 July: Farnese captured Oudenaarde
20–31: Anjou received at Ghent as count of Flanders

1583   15–17 January: French fury
27 May: Farnese captured Diest
18 June: States of Flanders repudiated Anjou
16 July: Farnese captured Dunkirk
22 July: Orange left Antwerp for Holland
2 August: Farnese captured Nieuwpoort
August: States General and College of Union of Utrecht merged

1584   24 March: Hembyze arrested
7 April: Ypres surrendered to Farnese
20 May: Bruges surrendered to Farnese
10 June: Anjou died
23 June: Henry III offered '*la souveraineté et protection*' of Netherlands
3 July: Farnese encircled Antwerp
10 July: Orange assassinated at Delft
17 September: Ghent surrendered to Farnese

1585   28 March: English Privy Council discussed intervention in Low Countries
12 August: Agreement of 'provisional succour'
17 August: Fall of Antwerp
20 August: Treaty of Nonsuch
20 October: Act of Ampliation: Elizabeth to send army 6000 strong
1 November: Maurice installed as stadholder of Holland

1586   1 February: Act of Authority: Leicester appointed as governor general
8 March: Oldenbarnevelt appointed *landsadvokaat* (i.e. Advocate of Holland)
7 June: Grave surrendered to Farnese
28 June: Venlo surrendered to Farnese

4 August: Neuss surrendered to Farnese

25 November: Leicester returned to England

1587 29 January: Stanley and Yorke delivered Deventer and Zutphen 'sconce' to enemy

5 February: Dutch embassy met Elizabeth

18 February: Execution of Mary of Scots

8 March: Critical report of Leicester's government received in London

23 March: Lord Buckhurst sent to United Provinces

20 June: Leicester's instructions issued

5 August: Sluis surrendered to Farnese

11 October: *Coup d'état* at Leiden thwarted

17 November: Leicester recalled

6 December: Leicester left Netherlands

1588 Summer: Armada to England; Parma (Farnese) diverted; Armada failed

Autumn: Parma failed to take Bergen-op-Zoom

1589 August: Henry III of France assassinated; mutinies in Spanish army

Late August: Maurice of Nassau became stadholder of Utrecht, Gelderland and Overijssel

1590 4 March: Maurice recaptured Breda – beginning of Dutch reconquest campaign

Summer: Parma diverted to France (till late summer 1591)

25 July: States General made a declaration of sovereignty

1592 Death of Parma

1594 Maurice conquered Groningen

1598 Death of Philip II

1602 Dutch East India Company founded

1609 Twelve-Year Truce of Antwerp between Spain and the United Provinces

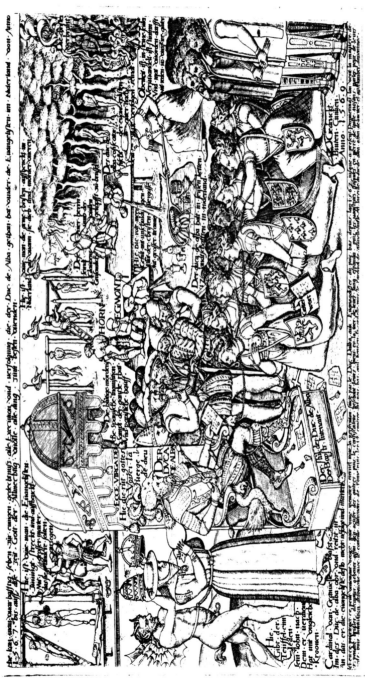

Frontispiece: German woodcut of c.1569 entitled the Tyranny of Alva or Alva's Throne. Alva sits on a throne with Cardinal Granvelle and the devil behind. All around there are scenes of persecution including the executions of Egmont and Hornes. In the foreground the 'seventeen Netherlands' kneel in chains before the Duke with their privileges torn to shreds. (Stichting Altas van Stolk, Rotterdam.)

Introduction

Graham Darby

If you asked a group of history students for the dates of the start of, say, the Reformation, or the French Revolution, or the First World War, hopefully you would be told 1517, 1789 and 1914 respectively. However, if you asked them the same question about the Dutch Revolt you would be much less likely to achieve a consensus. Moreover, if you asked a group of experts you might get even less. Did the revolt begin in 1566 with the iconclastic riots? Or in 1568 with the execution of Egmont and Hornes (the 'Eighty Years War')? Or perhaps in 1572 with the capture of Brill by the 'Sea Beggars'? Or was there no real revolt until 1579 with the Union of Utrecht, or 1581 with the abjuration of Philip II? The problem with the Dutch Revolt is that it is a highly complex series of events, or even episodes, some of which are self-contained. Indeed in many ways the single title 'Dutch Revolt' is deceptive, as it is an umbrella term covering a number of different uprisings in different places at different times which only rarely coincided.[1] When they did coincide, as they did from 1576, what we observe is a number of different elements – the northern provinces' rebellion, noble discontents in the south, urban bourgeois *coups d'état* and the ambitions of the House of Orange – co-existing in a fragile and what proved to be short-lived alliance.

Thus the Dutch Revolt did not just happen at one moment; it evolved over a period of time and underwent numerous changes before eventually coalescing into a conscious desire among some provinces to achieve independence from Spanish rule. Because of this, it is very difficult to pick a date and state categorically that it began at this point. The journey to independence was not a straightforward one.[2] Similarly it is equally difficult to decide a date for its successful conclusion. At what point can we say that the Dutch Republic had emerged as an independent entity? In 1579, 1581, 1590, 1609? Not until 1648 did Spain recognise Dutch independence, though it had been implicit in the truce of 1609, and had been a reality for some time before that.

It is now over twenty years since Geoffrey Parker brought out his book on the Dutch Revolt and in that time a great deal of new work has been done analysing how the revolt originated and unfolded – in the provinces, in the towns, among the aristocracy, and in terms of religious, financial, commercial and ideological developments: so much so that the time is almost right for a new synthesis. This book is not that new synthesis but it does aim to give the reader a clearer idea about the current state of scholarship and is written by many of the experts who have been responsible for that scholarship. Hitherto much of this work has been published only in Dutch, or if in English in article form in academic journals or in rather expensive monographs and often on fairly narrow subjects.

One of the common criticisms of an anthology of essays from a variety to authors is that the contributions seem to be aimed at different audiences, implying that the editor does not seem to know what his intended audience should be. Is the book for specialists or for undergraduates; or for teachers and those sixth-formers who still find the time to read? Well the answer of course is that an editor would like his audience to be as wide as possible. Consequently I hope that parts of this book will find favour with all of the above. Naturally some chapters are quite general and may therefore have little to say to the specialist; on the other hand, some are quite specialised and would initially perplex the sixth-former. Moreover, because the book might well be used by students with little prior knowledge, it has been decided to include, as Chapter 1, a straightforward narrative of events, tracing the formation of Valois Burgundy, the development of the Habsburg Netherlands and the course of the revolt down to *c.* 1590.

This introduction is preceded by a full chronology which readers may wish to refer to now and again, and in Chapter 1 there are four maps which should be consulted by all on a regular basis. A good grasp of the political geography of the Netherlands is essential for even a rudimentary understanding of the revolt. Some will find Chapter 1 superfluous, but others will find it useful to place the specialist articles in some sort of context. Another common criticism of a collection of this nature is that there is some overlap and repetition between the chapters. Given that they are all on different aspects of the same subject, some overlap would appear to be unavoidable, but this should not disconcert the reader.

Chapter 2, *'Alva's Throne'*,[3] was originally given as an address in November 1994 to a joint meeting of the Historisch Genootschap (Historical Society) and the Vereniging van Gescheidenisleraren in

Nederland (Association of Teachers of History in the Netherlands). Since the Dutch Revolt had been placed on the Dutch school curriculum after an interval of many years, it was thought necessary to provide teachers with a survey of recent research on the subject. When Professor van Nierop wrote this piece he had in mind teachers preparing their students for the *eindeexam*, the rough equivalent of Britain's 'A' level examination. It was originally published in 1995[4] and appears here in English for the first time, updated to take account of recent publications.

In this chapter we are given a broad historiographical overview of the subject. Professor van Nierop begins by looking at the traditional reasons for the revolt cited by contemporaries (political oppression, Catholic oppression, etc.) before going on to point out the whiggish nature of historiography that held sway until the 1960s. By this interpretation everything had inevitably been leading up to a Protestant north and a Catholic south. However, in the early years the revolt was open and malleable and, more recently, analysis of single provinces and towns has presented us with a much more complex picture in which 'different groups strove for different goals, which in turn shifted during different phases': the conflict was never the same in two places at the same time. This section also takes account of Jonathan Israel's major work *The Dutch Republic – Its Rise, Greatness and Fall 1477–1806* (1995) in which the author to some extent reverts to the old view that there were fundamental differences between north and south. However, this is not a return to whiggish inevitability but an altogether more sophisticated argument contending that the two regions had had different political and economic interests for some considerable time prior to the 'Troubles'. The chapter continues with a look at the political organisation and political geography of the provinces and goes on to the question of religion, the nature of opposition to Philip II, the role of the economy, the role of the towns, and the role of the nobles, and concludes that the anonymous creator of the print which is known as 'Alva's Throne' got it about right: the revolt was a struggle for both freedom and religion, but what was meant by freedom and whether or not the religious outcome – an inadvertent pluralism with a minority official church – was intended, are matters for continuing debate.

There is no doubt that in its early phases opposition to Philip II's policy was led by the magnates. They were concerned about their political role and what the government's reaction ought to be to the growth of heresy. Accordingly Chapter 3 looks in detail at the role of the nobility. In his second contribution, 'The nobles and the revolt', Professor van Nierop begins by distinguishing between the magnates and lesser nobles and goes on to discuss the role of the magnates in opposition to Philip II's policy, in particular with regard to the religious question; how the lesser nobles took the lead in 1566; how eventually most grandees were reconciled in the 1570s but how, although the nobles played a key role in the making of the Dutch Revolt, it also turned out to be their undoing. The outcome was that the grandees had little political influence in the Spanish south and had never had much say in the north where the urban elites triumphed.

If the political role of the nobility had a great deal to do with the outbreak of disaffection then the issue that really brought matters to a head was that of heresy – or rather what to do about a variety of different types of Protestantism. This is the subject of Chapter 4.

In his contribution, 'Religion and the revolt', Andrew Pettegree begins by looking at the abortive early Lutheran and Anabaptist Reformations before going on to look at the new wave of reform in mid-century, the role of the nobles and the events of 1566. Philip II's determination to eliminate heresy and maintain Catholic orthodoxy met with equally determined Calvinist opposition. However, the majority of the population occupied the middle ground in this conflict and favoured some sort of compromise settlement – 'liberty of conscience'. Philip's heresy laws were disliked because they cut across local jurisdictions and were a threat to property and commerce. Equally the iconoclasm of 1566 alienated many moderates. However, the failure of 1566–7 at least resulted in a group of committed exiles and led to the greater prominence of Calvinism in the reformed movement. Moreover, as Professor Pettegree demonstrates, the Calvinist congregations were indispensable for the success of the revolt after it reignited in 1572. But if the Calvinists were essential for the success of the revolt in the north, they were also a major factor in the split with the south which came about after the failure of the short-lived 'unification' of 1576. Their extremism alienated many moderates and all Catholics.

The Netherlands were the most urbanised area of Europe in the early modern period and the towns played a significant role in the revolt. They provided the material and intellectual infrastructure for Calvinism to develop. In addition, there was a tradition of urban revolts and a recent tradition of regional and supraprovincial cooperation, i.e. the rulers of the towns were prepared to look beyond their own interests and be responsible for the common cause. There have been a number of urban studies in recent years on Gouda, Lille, Haarlem and Utrecht; and

Guido Marnef as the author of studies on Mechelen[5] and Antwerp is well placed to summarise the role of the towns as he does in Chapter 5, 'The towns and the revolt'.

Thus far we have concentrated on the revolt from the Dutch perspective; however, that can be deceptive. Geoffrey Parker has long emphasised that the success or failure of the rebels very much depended on the international political situation, in particular Philip II's imperial commitments as well as factional pressures at the Spanish court. Arguably, Philip II caused the rebellion and Philip II could have ended it – either by compromise or by military conquest. In Chapter 6, 'The Grand Strategy of Philip II', based on his latest book, Geoffrey Parker together with Fernando González de León make it clear that although the extirpation of heresy was a primary objective of Spanish foreign policy, geopolitically the Netherlands were of less importance to Spain than the Iberian peninsula, the Indies, Italy and the Mediterranean. Consequently Philip II never applied sufficient means to suppress the revolt as his priorities lay elsewhere. The implication is clear: a concerted, single-minded approach to the suppression or resolution of the revolt could have extinguished it but the failure to do so allowed it to develop and succeed; the longer it went on, the more difficult its resolution became.

One key factor in the success of the revolt, apart from Philip II's global preoccupations, was the strength of Holland, and it has been James Tracy's contribution to the scholarship of the revolt to draw our attention to and explain the financial success of that province. In his earlier books on Holland and finance he has shown that under the constant fiscal pressure to raise revenue for Charles V's wars, the States of Holland had managed to achieve increased control of the fiscal machinery of the province. The States thereby gained considerable experience floating loans on the credit of the province and collecting taxes to support them. Accordingly during Charles's reign the States of Holland were able to increase revenue fourfold. This was achieved largely through the issuing of public bonds, known as *renten*, which proved to be an attractive investment source for many, including the magistrates of the States who issued them.

In Chapter 7, 'Keeping the wheels of war turning', James Tracy attempts to fill a gap in our knowledge by taking the story forward into the period of the revolt. Although records become patchy after 1572, it is clear that payments on bonds (*renten*) ceased as the common revenues were applied to the cost of war; this proved inadequate and in the 1580s a new tax on property – land and houses – met the shortfall. What is also clear is that from the mid-1580s, Holland met about two-thirds of the cost of the rebellion and that after 1594 Holland's credit rating was sufficiently restored for the province to fund its war contribution partly from the resumption of the sale of *renten*. By this stage the northern provinces had arrived at a political solution that entailed becoming a sovereign republic.

And so finally we look at the development of the political ideas which motivated and legitimated resistance to the government of Philip II, and which became the ideological foundations of the Dutch Republic. There was a fundamental difference between Philip II's conception of the Netherlands as his patrimony under his authority and that of the provinces and towns which placed their own laws and privileges first and viewed the power of the prince in a much more confined way. From their point of view, the revolt was essentially conservative in origin – the preservation of traditional practice. Initially opposition was directed against Philip's policies and advisers but eventually the realisation grew that only a complete break could preserve the people's 'liberties'. Accordingly the rebellion embraced republican political theory, a pro-cess that began in the 1570s but was still not complete in 1590.[6] Protest, resistance and eventually abjuration all had to be justified – there were limits to political obedience and there was justice in resistance; but what should replace the exising order? Where did sovereignty lie? How best could the privileges acquired by the cities, guilds, crafts, clergy and nobles be preserved? As we have stated, eventually and haphazardly the United Provinces found their way to sovereignty in a republican format that was designed to preserve liberty, privileges, states and popular sovereignty. Martin van Gelderen has already written at length about these developments elsewhere in *The Political Thought of the Dutch Revolt 1550–1590* (1992) and in the introduction to a collection of documents on the same topic published in 1993. Now in Chapter 8 entitled 'From Domingo de Soto to Hugo Grotius: theories of monarchy and civil power in Spanish and Dutch political thought 1555–1609', he takes his research a stage further and finds some remarkable links between the Dutch legitimation of the revolt and Spanish conceptions of monarchy. In particular he looks at the writings of the Frisian lawyer Aggaeus van Albada whose *Acts of the Cologne Negotiations* were published in 1581, François Vranck's *Short Exposition* (1587) and Hugo Grotius's *Treatise on the Antiquity of the Batavian Republic* (1610) before looking at the close connection between Albada and the Spanish theorists (and counsellors of the king of Spain) Domingo de Soto and Fernando Vázquez de Menchaca; and in particular between Grotius and Vázquez. In the light of the findings it would appear to be too simplistic to contrast Spanish and Dutch political theory in terms of 'Spanish tyranny' and 'Dutch liberty'; it seems Spanish and Dutch political theorists were very much part of a common intellectual tradition. However, 'eighty years' of warfare led to a profound political rupture.

The evolution of the Dutch Revolt and the emergence of an independent sovereign republic were a unique series of events. It was the first and only revolt in the early modern period to lead to the formation of a new political entity. Moreover the outcome was not the intention of the rebels and for a long time they had to pretend they were not rebels at all. From their point of view it was the inflexibility of Philip II that forced them to invent a new identity while at the same time claiming they were defending traditional liberties and ancient customs. So it was that the peoples of the United Provinces, in an attempt to return to the old ways, became radical revolutionaries and in the name of tradition spawned something very new, something very different – an independent, secular, decentralised, bourgeois republic.

Notes

1   Of course contemporaries before 1609 did not refer to what occurred as the 'Dutch Revolt'; they tended to speak of the 'Troubles' or, less often, the civil wars.

2   The metaphor of 'journey' suggests an intended destination, but of course the Netherlanders stumbled only semi-consciously into political independence. They had never expected to achieve it. Initially they resisted Philip in an attempt to renegotiate their relationship with the king. Even the abjuration of 1581 was not seen by all those who accepted it as definitive. For years thereafter a *modus vivendi* with the Habsburgs seemed the most likely outcome. A cartographic tradition that persisted until the mid-seventeenth century treated the 'seventeen provinces' as a political unit; this notion survived among foreigners who therefore looked on the creation of the United Kingdom of the Netherlands in 1815 as a natural development.

3   Alva can be spelt with a 'v' or a 'b'; the pronunciation is the same in Spanish. The reader will come across both spellings in the book. The duke himself often used 'v' for his name and 'b' for his estate. See note 5.

4   It was published as 'De troon van Alva. Over de interpretatie van de Nederlandse Opstand', *Bijdragen en mededelingen betreffende de Geschiedenis der Nederlanden*, 110 (1995), pp. 205–23.

5   The Netherlands is troubled to an inordinate degree by problems of orthography. Mechelen is a good example, being Mechelen in Dutch, Mechlin in English and Malines in French. For this reason it has not been possible to achieve consistency across the various contributions.

6   Historians of political theory place the adoption of avowed republicanism as late as the early 1660s.

1 Narrative of events

Graham Darby

Valois Burgundy

The Netherlands – from the Dutch for 'Low Countries' – refers to the counties, duchies and principalities around the mouth of the River Rhine on the North Sea coast and corresponds roughly to what is today Holland, Belgium, Luxemburg and a small part of northern France (Artois). It is a geographical rather than political term, since until 1548 it did not form a political unit – nor indeed a cultural or ethnic unit. However, in the late medieval period a number of these territories came to be grouped together (but were not in any way united) by sharing a single ruler, the Valois duke of Burgundy.

During the course of the Hundred Years War, King John II of France assigned the duchy of Burgundy as an apanage to his fourth son, Philip the Bold. Through Philip's marriage to Margaret the heiress of the count of Flanders, he gained possession, after the death of his father-in-law in 1384, of the counties of Flanders, Walloon Flanders, Artois and Rethel, the towns of Antwerp and Mechelen, and also the county of Nevers and the free county of Burgundy (Franche-Comté). However, far from representing an extension of French influence into this area, the dukes of Burgundy proved to be interested in building up their own political power.

Duke John the Fearless succeeded to all his father's lands in 1404 and under his son Philip the Good (ruled 1419–67) there was a considerable expansion of territory – through inheritance, war and purchase. The counties of Namur, Holland, Zeeland and Hainault, as well as the duchies of Brabant, Limburg and Luxemburg were all added. Duke Charles (1467–77) temporarily added Gelderland.

In the 1430s Duke Philip attempted to give the territories a degree of institutional centralisation by creating the States General, an assembly of representatives from the various provincial States, a central Chamber of Accounts and the Order of the Golden Fleece (a distinction designed

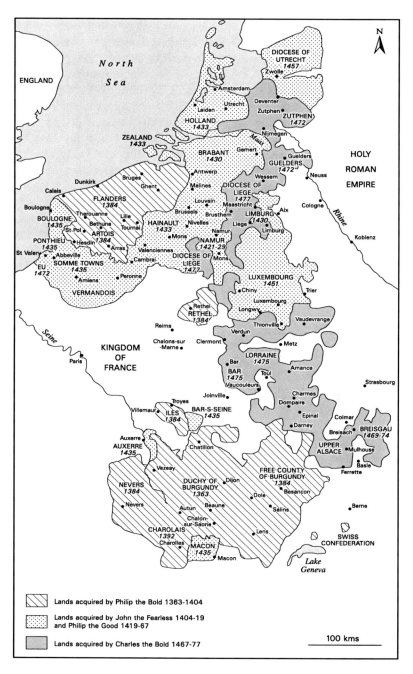

Map 1 Valois Burgundy.

to bind the various magnates to the court), all of which came to be centred in Brussels. Under Philip the Good, some territories were placed under the duke's lord lieutenant or 'stadholder' as provincial governors were called. Despite these developments, the component parts of the Burgundian Netherlands retained considerable autonomy.

The expansion of the Burgundian Netherlands came to a sudden end in 1477 with the death of Duke Charles at the battle of Nancy. The original duchy of Burgundy and some other territories reverted by feudal law to King Louis XI of France, leaving the remainder to Charles's widow Margaret of York, whose step-daughter Mary married Maximilian of Habsburg. Margaret and Mary were faced with revolt everywhere and had to concede the Great Privilege, a charter which confirmed that the provinces' 'liberties', separate customs and laws, would be guaranteed and gave the States General of the Burgundian Netherlands the right to gather on their own initiative whenever they saw fit, as well as drastically curbing the power of the ruler in fiscal and military matters. Holland and Zeeland obtained their own separate Great Privilege. The Valois dukes of Burgundy:

Philip the Bold	1363–1404
John the Fearless	1404–1419
Philip the Good	1419–1467
Charles the Bold	1467–1477

The Habsburg Netherlands

Mary died in 1482 and Maximilian ruled as regent for their son Philip. Rule by the Habsburgs to some extent saved the Netherlands from absorption by France but by 1487 the regent was faced with a general revolt which, though crushed, led to the loss of Gelderland. In 1493 Maximilian became the Holy Roman Emperor and his son Philip was proclaimed of age. At his inauguration in 1494 Philip the Fair had the Great Privilege almost entirely abrogated, though its constitutional provisions remained an aspiration for subsequent generations.

The regimes of Philip I (1493–1506) and the subsequent regency of Margaret of Austria (1506–15) were periods of relative stability, though military activity north of the rivers failed to recover Gelderland or extend authority into Groningen and Friesland. Charles Habsburg – known as Charles of Luxemburg at this point – was declared of age as ruler of the Habsburg Netherlands in 1515 but became King Charles I of Spain in 1516 and Emperor Charles V in 1519, so that the Netherlands were now

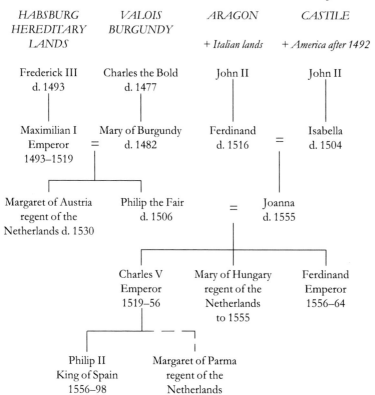

HABSBURG HEREDITARY LANDS	VALOIS BURGUNDY	ARAGON + *Italian lands*	CASTILE + *America after 1492*

Frederick III
d. 1493

Charles the Bold
d. 1477

John II

John II

Maximilian I
Emperor
1493–1519

= Mary of Burgundy
d. 1482

Ferdinand
d. 1516

= Isabella
d. 1504

Margaret of Austria
regent of the
Netherlands d. 1530

Philip the Fair
d. 1506

= Joanna
d. 1555

Charles V
Emperor
1519–56

Mary of Hungary
regent of the
Netherlands
to 1555

Ferdinand
Emperor
1556–64

Philip II
King of Spain
1556–98

Margaret of Parma
regent of the
Netherlands

Figure 1.1 The Habsburg inheritance.

NB: Margaret of Austria, regent of the Netherlands, was in fact two years younger than Philip the Fair and technically should be shown on the right. However, this is a simplified genealogy.

only a small part of a much larger empire. Charles, who had grown up in the Netherlands, was compelled to delegate power first to his aunt Margaret again (regent 1517–30) and then to his sister Mary of Hungary from 1531.

Despite this, territorial expansion continued, largely financed by Holland,[1] with the acquisition of Friesland, Utrecht and Overijssel in the 1520s. In 1531, Charles spent most of the year in Brussels reorganising the government. He set up a Council of State of magnates and jurists, a Privy Council of professional bureaucrats and renewed the Council of Finance. Provinces were grouped together under the same provincial governors or stadholders, though these were not felt necessary for Brabant and Mechelen. Thus Holland, Zeeland and Utrecht (and later Gelderland) were grouped together, as were Flanders, Walloon Flanders and Artois; and later so too were Friesland, Groningen, Drenthe and Overijssel.

Groningen and Drenthe were annexed in 1536 and Gelderland was finally conquered in 1543. In 1548, Charles persuaded the Diet of the Holy Roman Empire in the Treaty of Augsburg[2] to recognise the Habsburg Netherlands as a separate and single entity and laid down that it would pass to the emperor's heirs in perpetuity. This 'Pragmatic Sanction' was then endorsed by all seventeen provinces in 1549. At this juncture the seventeen provinces[3] consisted of Holland, Zeeland, Brabant, Flanders, Walloon Flanders, Artois, Luxemburg, Hainault, Mechelen, Namur, Groningen, Friesland, Gelderland, Limburg, Tournai (which Charles had added in 1521), Utrecht and Overijssel (this included Drenthe). However, a declaration of unity was one thing, reality another, and it is interesting to note that five of the seven provinces which later became the Dutch Republic (i.e. Friesland, Utrecht, Overijssel, Groningen and Gelderland) were quite recent additions. Indeed Habsburg control in Groningen, Overijssel and Gelderland never amounted to much and constituted something of a divide between the north-east and the rest.

Disunited provinces

Thus the process of unification was more apparent than real and this was reflected in the fact that the ruler did not have a single title but many. Thus he was the duke of Brabant, the count of Flanders, the lord of Friesland, etc., designations that emphasised the confederate nature of the Low Countries. In addition, there were physical obstacles to unification.[4] The provinces of Holland, Zeeland, Utrecht and Friesland were practically surrounded by the sea and cut off from the 'heartland provinces' of Hainault, Artois, Flanders and Brabant, by numerous rivers, dikes and lakes. The eastern and north-eastern provinces of Limburg, Luxemburg, Gelderland, Overijssel, Drenthe and Groningen were cut off from the rest by dunes, bogs and heaths and by the independent ecclesiastical principality of Liège. There were linguistic divisions too: the central government and the court used French which was prominent in the south, but the majority to the north spoke varieties of Dutch.[5] There was also something of a divide in terms of religion. Despite initial interest in new religious ideas coming from the German lands, the repressive regime had prevented evangelicals in the towns of

Map 2 The Habsburg Netherlands.

the Low Countries, with the notable exception of the Anabaptists, from developing schismatic congregations. But if the persecution came close to extinguishing the evangelical groups in the 1540s, by forcing suspected dissidents to flee the country, it contributed to the growth of Calvinist churches abroad. These in turn provided leadership for the small Calvinist congregations established in the larger southern towns after 1555. The repressive regime, associated with the Inquisition and mistakenly with its Spanish namesake, was widely resented by the elites because it encroached on privileges intended to provide justice and protect property. In Flanders and Brabant religious passions became most inflamed; further away from this epicentre of confessionalisation the confrontation between Catholics and Calvinists was altogether more muted. In addition to the historical, geographical, linguistic and even in some cases religious differences, there were also marked differences in terms of population and wealth, as a glance at Tables 1.1 and 1.2 will show.

Quite clearly Flanders, Brabant and Holland were more advanced in terms of population, urbanisation and wealth. Half of Holland's population was urban and the even spread of its distribution across Dordrecht, Haarlem, Leiden, Amsterdam, Delft and Gouda reflected a wide dispersal of wealth and had some significance for the subsequent development of Dutch politics and society. Prosperity was derived from the bulk freightage and the herring fishery. By contrast the prosperity of the southern urban economy sprang from the rich trades – textiles, spices, metal and sugar – and of course from the derived finished goods.

The towns valued their political autonomy and guarded their privileges. The government was dominated by a group known as regents – mostly successful financiers and merchants. They were never an oligarchy defined by birth or status but did become a closed political group.[6] In

Table 1.1 Population in 1477 (%)

Flanders	26.0
Brabant	16.0
Holland	10.5
Artois	5.5
Hainault	5.0
Liège	4.5
Gelderland	3.8
Walloon Flanders	2.8
Friesland	2.7
Luxemburg	2.6
Overijssel	2.0

Table 1.2 Tax contributions 1540–8 (the top 12) (%)

Flanders	33.80
Brabant	28.76
Holland	12.69
Artois	5.65
Hainault	5.47
Zeeland	4.37
Lille/Douai	3.29
Gelderland	1.14
Tournai	0.93
Namur	0.90
Friesland	0.59
Overijssel[a]	0.55

[a] Includes Drenthe.

addition there were also about 4000 nobles in the Netherlands. The grandees – consisting perhaps of only about twenty families – were large landowners and had international connections. These magnates tended to reside in the south. The lesser nobility were not so well-off and their lifestyle was sometimes little better than that of a wealthy peasant. What is apparent from all this, then, is the variety and complexity of the Netherlands and the difficult task the Habsburgs had set themselves in trying to weld these lands together into a single political unit.

From the 1540s Emperor Charles V was once again drawn into prolonged warfare with France. As a consequence the provinces were subjected to new heavy burdens of taxation and because of the growing success of the Netherlands economy, the regime was increasingly inclined to rely on this area. However, far from increasing Habsburg control, the regime in effect assigned a larger and larger role to the States in the collection and management of finance. This was to have great significance in the future. In the meantime though, by the 1550s disaffection was beginning to spread, military expenditure doubled and the deficit in 1557 was seven times that of 1544. But by that time the Netherlands had a new ruler.

A new ruler

Prince Philip, son and designated heir of Charles V in the Netherlands, was introduced to his future subjects by means of a royal tour in the spring of 1549. At that time he recognised and confirmed the 'Joyous Entry' a list of constitutional liberties and privileges dating back, in the case of Brabant, to 1356. When Philip inherited the provinces in his own right in 1555 after Charles V's abdication, he inherited territories that had clearly become used to the judicial and financial independence they enjoyed under his father.[7] Moreover, the grandees in the Council of State had also developed an exaggerated idea of the level of participation they had been allowed in the internal administration of the provinces by the successive female regents, Margaret and Mary.

Charles V had appointed the duke of Savoy as regent and determined the composition of the Council of State, but despite becoming king of Spain in 1556 Philip decided to remain in Brussels and exercised power without reference to the Council of State. His colossal tax demands were initially resisted, but the States General finally agreed to them in 1558, by which time the war with France was virtually over and Philip was turning his attention to the problems of Spain and Islam. He left for Spain in 1559 never to return.

The collapse of authority, 1559–1566

Whether or not Philip's departure was a wise decision would depend upon how events unfolded subsequently. The situation in the Netherlands was undoubtedly potentially dangerous. The debt was immense, the States General in a difficult mood, the newly acquired provinces uncooperative, the nobles dissatisfied, the religious situation further complicated by the sudden growth of Calvinism, and the duke of Savoy would not act as regent. Accordingly, Philip appointed his half-sister, Margaret of Parma, as regent. William of Orange was made stadholder of Holland, Zeeland and Utrecht, and the count of Egmont of Flanders and Artois – but power came to reside with Cardinal Granvelle, a fact that was soon resented by the magnates.

This clash of personalities came to a head over the issue of ecclesiastical reorganisation. Originally devised by Charles V, the plan to create fourteen new bishoprics and three archbishoprics (with Granvelle as the primate) was long overdue, but threatened a wide range of vested interests (a career in the church was a traditional avenue for younger sons of nobles without lands of their own) and threatened a new wave of persecution. Following a wave of discontent, the regent petitioned Philip for Granvelle's removal in 1563 and he was withdrawn the following year. Philip also suspended his ecclesiastical reform programme.

This looked like a victory for Orange and the magnates and it seemed to spell the end of the Inquisition. The magnates favoured greater religious freedom because it was felt persecution might lead to civil war, as in France; persecution interfered with established laws and procedures; and they saw no reason why differences of belief should be treated so harshly. However, Philip II was not prepared to compromise any further. In two letters written from his country house in the Segovia Woods and signed on 17 and 20 October 1565 he made his position quite clear. There was to be no amelioration of the heresy laws and no increase in power of the Council of State. It was a clear challenge to the nobles to obey and enforce government policy and it provoked a wave of protests.

A group of lesser nobles led by Hendrik van Brederode took matters into their own hands and formed the League of Compromise in November 1565 to bring about a relaxation of the heresy laws. In April 1566 about 400 of them presented their Petition of Compromise to the regent and Margaret of Parma gave way. These 'beggars' (*les gueux*) as they were called in a pejorative sense, enjoyed the sympathy of the magnates and popularity among the ordinary people. With royal authority breaking down and the Inquisition curbed, there followed a sudden upsurge of Protestant activity – in particular, open-air Calvinist preaching (hedge-preaching as it was known) in Brabant, Flanders, Holland, Friesland and Utrecht. This in turn led to a wave of popular violence against the old church known as the 'iconoclastic fury' in Flanders, Hainault, Brabant, Holland, Zeeland, Utrecht, Gelderland, Friesland and Groningen. The increasing violence and destruction of the iconoclastic fury cast the nobility into mounting disarray as the middle position disintegrated completely. Back in Spain, Philip responded to the situation by accepting the duke of Alva's advice and decided on a military solution. Alva himself was reluctant to go because of his health and because he feared his absence would lead to a loss of influence at court. However, in November 1566 Philip appointed him commander of the army and the following year despatched him together with 10,000 Spanish and Neapolitan troops.

And yet by the spring of 1567 Margaret of Parma had been able to suppress the unrest with the help of some of the magnates (William of Orange had not been one of them; he had sat on the fence and now went into exile). The rebellion seemed dead, but opposition continued through political propaganda which claimed that Alva had violated the privileges and 'freedom' of the Netherlands.

Alva and repression, 1567–1572

The duke of Alva was deeply opposed to Protestantism and determined to take a ruthless approach to the problems in the Netherlands. The regent, Margaret, resigned in protest and eventually he replaced her as governor general. He immediately arrested two leading nobles, Egmont and Hornes. The execution of these two nobles in 1568 and subsequent executions (over 1000) by the 'Council of Troubles' shocked and appalled the populace, as did the billeting of Spanish troops.[8] Following the death of Brederode, William of Orange now became the leader of the opposition. His reputation was not high at this stage but the confiscation of his property and the kidnapping of his eldest son (whom he never saw again) left him with little choice; however, his military campaigns of 1568 all ended in disaster. Orange was no match for Alva on the battlefield.

Alva now completed the episcopal reforms and stepped up the fiscal pressure. In 1569 he convened the States General and demanded three new taxes: the 'hundredth penny' (a one-off 1 per cent tax on wealth), the 'twentieth penny' (a 5 per cent tax on land sales) and the infamous 'tenth penny' (a 10 per cent tax levy on all other sales). The States in effect rejected these last two schemes and as a stopgap Alva accepted temporary subsidies; however, in 1571 he renewed his demands and imposed them unilaterally by decree. His coercive methods of tax collection created universal loathing and the whole issue of the tenth penny seriously undermined the position of the crown and played into Orange's hands by creating widespread popular discontent. The president of the Council of Troubles epitomised this approach when he stated: '*non curamus privilegios vostros*' (we are not concerned with your privileges) – and it was this attitude, this lack of concern for the sensitivities of all sections of society, that more than anything aroused opposition. The scene was set for a further wave of rebellion.

The second revolt, 1572–1576

William of Orange planned another invasion in 1572 but matters were taken out of his hands by the Sea Beggars, a motley band of privateers, exiled nobles and Calvinists who sailed under Orange's flag. Their capture of Brill in April 1572 had a cascade effect. Brill itself was not important but the rebels were soon able to ride a wave of discontent and spread the revolt in the north throughout much of Holland and Zeeland.[9] Orange himself was less successful; he was unable to obtain any official English support and there was little response to his call to arms in the southern provinces. After the St Bartholomew's Day massacre of Huguenots in France had deprived the prince of planned French help, Alva was able to move his troops north and push the rebels back. Alva's policy of ruthless brutality and massacre was successful in bringing about submission in the south and east, but it only led to greater resistance in the north where no possibility of negotiating terms left the towns no choice but to fight. So the revolt came to be focused on the north where most people were behind it, and where there was no strong Catholicism (unlike in the south). That the revolt survived was not only due to northern resistance but had a lot to do with geography as well. Wide rivers and flooded areas hampered Spanish progress. Alva had failed to suppress the revolt and he was succeeded by Don Luis de Requesens in 1573.

The tenth penny, that symbol of Alva's tyranny, was suspended in 1573 but this only served to increase the financial weakness of the Spanish army – another key factor in the survival of the rebellion. Requesens decided to negotiate but the discussions in 1575 just served to highlight the gap between the two sides. Both the matter of heresy and the form of government proved to be stumbling blocks. Philip II would never permit formal freedom of Protestant worship and he did not wish to share in government in a limited monarchy.

The Spanish bankruptcy of 1575 produced a prolonged crisis and the position deteriorated dramatically in 1576. Requesens died suddenly in March and by the summer mutinies in Spain's unpaid army, which had been occurring on and off for several years, now reached serious proportions as loyal provinces such as Brabant and Flanders were subjected to violence and plundering. This had the effect of uniting practically all the provinces against the Spanish presence. In 1576 the various provinces took steps to defend themselves and, led by the duke of Aerschot, most provinces met in the States General to create an armistice with Holland and Zeeland, put aside their differences and combine to expel the Spanish. The two sides signed the Pacification of Ghent in November just after one of the worst examples of mutinous behaviour, the 'Spanish fury' in Antwerp. The latter may have been exaggerated but it was a godsend to Orange's propagandists.

Two Netherlands, 1576–1579

However, this unity was really only skin-deep and soon divisions began to appear. Already in the Pacification, Protestantism (and William of Orange) was only recognised in Holland and Zeeland and not in Utrecht or elsewhere. The Catholic southern provinces of Luxemburg and Limburg were in fact not party to the agreement and most of the magnates were Catholic and still loyal to the Habsburgs. Moreover, moderate Catholics and many of the grandees did not trust Orange. Accordingly when Philip appointed his brother Don Juan as governor, the States General soon reached an agreement with him in early 1577 on the understanding that Spanish troops were withdrawn and the Pacification was adhered to. Holland and Zeeland would not recognise Don Juan as governor (they were increasingly going their own way) and William of Orange was opposed to the deal as well. Later Don Juan went back on his word (in compliance with Philip II's orders) and recalled the Spanish troops; his treachery confirmed that Orange (and Holland and Zeeland) had been right all along. The States General now turned to him and William entered Brussels in triumph in September. However, the grandees, the duke of Aerschot in particular, were not happy with Orange's pre-eminence which now included the stadholderate of Utrecht and the governorship of Brabant. Accordingly in the autumn of 1577 the States General was persuaded to call upon the Archduke Matthias, a Habsburg prince, to replace Don Juan. Orange, who became deputy governor, outwitted the grandees by hedging Matthias in with all sorts of restrictions.

Orange worked hard to place the revolt in the south on a viable basis and he saw Brabant as the key to its future success. However, with the advance of radical Calvinism, rifts were in fact becoming even wider. Ghent, Bruges and Brussels were now not only radically Calvinist but more interested in civic sovereignty than interprovincial cooperation. Brabant was in fact in disarray whereas Holland and Zeeland were much more cohesive and purposeful. Throughout 1578 Protestants made progress in the north; in Amsterdam and Haarlem which had been the last Catholic strongholds in Holland, Catholic services were halted and the churches taken over by Calvinists.

The year 1578 was further complicated by foreign intervention. At the behest of those Catholics opposed to Spain, the brother of the king of France, the duke of Anjou, was invited to give aid and was recognised in August by the States General as 'Defender of the Liberties of the Low Countries'. Queen Elizabeth of England was not happy about French intervention and she, together with Orange, encouraged John Casimir of the Rhine Palatinate to intervene. However, he was more concerned with furthering Calvinism than fighting Spain. William of Orange still tried to accommodate both Catholics and Protestants with his Religious Peace in the autumn of 1578 but this was becoming increasingly difficult. Moreover, in October 1578 fighting broke out between Catholics and Protestants in Flanders. Under these pressures the Pacification was clearly breaking down.

Already in 1578 plans had been drawn up in the north for a defensive structure. This came to fruition in January 1579 as the Union of Utrecht. Initally signed by Holland, Zeeland, Utrecht and part of Groningen, it was later signed by parts of Gelderland, Friesland and Drenthe, as well as Ghent and Antwerp.[10] These provinces became known as the United Provinces. However, Overijssel was too divided, the city of Groningen hostile and the states of Brabant and Flanders opposed. At the same time Hainault and Artois seceded from the States General and concluded the Union of Arras. They were soon joined by Walloon Flanders. Namur, Luxemburg and Limburg were already controlled by Spain and the last two had not been party to the Pacification. By May this Union of Arras was reconciled to Philip II and Orange was forced reluctantly to become a party to the Union of Utrecht: his efforts to build a common north–south revolt accommodating Catholic as well as Protestant worship had failed. There were now two Netherlands – or rather three since Brabant and Flanders (and other areas) were party to neither union. However, the middle ground was rapidly disappearing – the choice seemed to be either king or Calvinism. The revival of Spanish fortunes by Alexander Farnese (he inherited the title duke of Parma in 1586) would drive many to the Spanish side.

Reconquista, 1579–1585

Don Juan had died of the plague in October 1578 and he was replaced as governor by Alexander Farnese. Farnese soon displayed outstanding diplomatic and military skills, to such an extent that the Dutch Revolt was all but extinguished. Using native troops he took Maastricht and 's Hertogenbosch in 1579, Courtrai in 1580 and Breda in 1581. As well as penetrating Brabant he sent troops north to Groningen, taking advantage of the defection of the governor, the count of Rennenberg, to advance from there. In the south his strategy was to occupy the Flemish coast, blockade Antwerp and thereby undermine the economies of Flanders and Brabant.

In March 1580, Philip II had finally outlawed William of Orange creating an open breach. William replied in his *Apology*, extolling toleration and freedom and condemning the tyranny of Spanish rule. The fiction of loyalty to Philip II was at an end, but who should replace the king? For Orange, Anjou seemed the only alternative and a deal was struck with him in September 1580 (Matthias left the following year). Anjou became Prince and Lord of the Netherlands in January 1581 but his powers were heavily circumscribed. Flanders and Brabant accepted the deal, Holland and Zeeland gave only perfunctory acknowledgment and Overijssel, Gelderland and Utrecht did not recognise it at all. In July 1581 the States General finally passed the Act of Abjuration which solemnly deposed Philip II. This was endorsed by delegates principally from Brabant, Gelderland, Flanders, Holland, Zeeland, Utrecht, Friesland, Tournai and

Mechelen. This was a momentous step and a difficult one for many, though Holland and Zeeland had contemplated a full break as early as 1575 and had ceased to refer to Philip in their oaths since 1578.[11]

The duke of Anjou was not a success; admittedly he was kept short of money but he was neither capable nor liked. After a failed coup in 1583 he finally left. Orange reopened negotiations with him in 1584 but Anjou died in June to be followed by Orange himself in July. The victim of an assassin's bullet, Orange died with his life's work in ruins: the Netherlands were divided and the Spanish reconquest was seemingly unstoppable.

Farnese brought the Spanish troops back into the fray in 1582. He took Dunkirk and Nieuwpoort in 1583, Bruges and Ghent in 1584 and Brussels and Antwerp in 1585. Thus he controlled practically all of Flanders and Brabant and had nearly doubled the area of obedient provinces in three years. There remained only one main power centre to reduce – Holland. The situation for the rebels now looked desperate and in the aftermath of Orange's assassination, sovereignty was offered to both the king of France and the queen of England. Both declined; yet Elizabeth did agree to intervene on behalf of the rebels and signed a deal later in 1585. However, her main aim was to restore a military and political stalemate so that a negotiated settlement could be arranged with Philip II. She did not want to force an open breach with Spain; her policy was in fact quite cautious: the objective was to block any future French control while at the same time preventing complete Spanish control – a return to the status quo of the time of Charles V. However, the rebels were not looking for a deal with Spain at this stage.

The English interlude, 1585–1587

The earl of Leicester was now despatched with about 7000 troops and in February 1586 the States General appointed him as their governor general with powers that far exceeded what Elizabeth had in mind. He immediately tried to centralise authority in his person but everywhere came up against the opposition of Holland and Zeeland (particularly over a trade embargo with Spain). Holland was determined to limit the influence of both Leicester and the other provinces. The Holland regents believed they embodied the goals of the revolt, but Calvinists (swollen in number by refugees from the south) looked to Leicester, as did the nobility and all others in the north who resented Holland's dominance. Thus Leicester in effect became the leader of the anti-Holland faction (Utrecht became Calvinist with his connivance) and was therefore quite unable to achieve unity of purpose.

Base for Parma's conquests:
- Luxembourg *(never acceded to States-General)*;
- Walloon provinces *(peace of Arras 1579)*;
- Groningen and Drenthe *(defection of Rennenberg, 1580)*.

Area under States-General in 1589.

Area conquered by Parma and his lieutenants 1578–1589;
Cambrai was in French hands from 1580 to 1594.

N

North

Sea

FRIESLAND

Delfzyl
1580

Groningen
1580

Steenwyk
1582

Koevorden
1580

OVERIJSSEL

Ootmarsum
1581

Enschede
1581

Deventer
1587

Zutphen
1583

GELDERLAND

HOLLAND

UTRECHT

Nymwegen
1585

ZEALAND

Den
Bosch

Grave
1586

Geertruidenberg 1579
1585

Venlo
1586

BRABANT

Eindhoven
1583

Sluis
1587

1604
Ostend

Antwerp
1585

Roermond
1578

Nieuwpoort

Bruges
1584

Ghent
1584

Mechlin
1585

Dunkirk
1583

1583

FLANDERS

Gravelingen

Ypres
1584

Audenhove
1582   1583
Oudenaarde

Leuven
1578

Maastricht
1579

Brussels
1585

Lille

Tournai
1581

Nivelles
1578

ARTOIS
1579

HAINAULT
1579

WALLOON
FLANDERS
1579

NAMUR
1579

Arras

Cambrai
1594

LUXEMBOURG

100 kms

Map 3 The conquests of Parma.

Farnese's reconquest now slowed; he had reached the rebellion's last natural line of defence and was confronted on all sides by water. Still he took Grave and Venlo in 1586 and Deventer and Sluys in 1587. However, Deventer (and the fort at Zutphen) were betrayed by mutinous English soldiery in Leicester's absence and further mutinies and defections generated even greater hostility to the English and strengthened Holland's position. Despite further attempts in 1587, Leicester was unable to bring Holland to heel and eventually he returned home a disappointed man. Short though his intervention was, it did have some considerable significance. It did lead to an open breach between England and Spain (and of course the despatch of the Armada); and it finally convinced many Dutch that they had no need of any foreign princes, so leaving the way open for the ascendancy of the mercantile oligarchs of Holland.

A sovereign republic, 1588–1590

The survival of the northern provinces was due to a combination of both favourable external factors and crucial internal developments. Philip II's decision to launch the Armada against England had a number of important consequences. For one thing it diverted resources from the duke of Parma, as Farnese was known from 1586. Not only was Parma forced to suspend operations in a futile attempt to liaise with the Armada force in 1588 but from 1589 financial shortages led to a succession of damaging mutinies (at a time when the Dutch economy was going from strength to strength). Of even greater significance perhaps was Philip's decision to intervene in France and divert Parma to that theatre in 1590. Parma was opposed to these policy changes, advocated negotiations with the northern provinces, refused to campaign in France in 1591 and was probably only saved from some form of punishment by his death from wounding in 1592. He was, however, an enormous loss to the Spanish war effort since none of his successors were as able.

Another consequence of the Armada was that prior to its arrival in April 1588 Elizabeth withdrew her support for the anti-Holland factions and instructed her commanders to cooperate with Holland in the persons of Maurice of Nassau, stadholder of Holland since 1585, and Johan van Oldenbarnevelt, advocate of Holland since 1586. Indeed it was the lessening of opposition to Holland that led to a greater measure of cohesion among the rebels and made a republican outcome most likely. To some extent this was the achievement of Oldenbarnevelt whose skilful statecraft enabled Utrecht to be recovered for the moderates, and who was largely responsible in late 1589 for the appointment of Maurice of Nassau as stadholder in Utrecht, Gelderland and Overijssel (he was already stadholder of Holland and Zeeland). By these means Holland came to dominate policy-making (Holland was in any event providing two-thirds of rebel revenue) and was largely responsible for the religious and political outcome – religious pluralism within a sovereign republic.

The Dutch had not set out to overthrow Philip II and form an independent state and for a long time they had to pretend they were not rebels at all. Still the issue of who should have sovereignty had come under discussion in 1575 and was a matter for resolution from 1581. However, the experience of Matthias, Anjou and Leicester persuaded many of the rebels that they did not need a foreign ruler. Sovereignty itself then became the issue and from 1586 the rebels developed the doctrine of provincial sovereignty. Accordingly on 25 July 1590 the States General was declared 'the sovereign institution of this country . . . [which] has no overlord except the deputies of the Provincial Estates themselves' – that is to say it was a union of separate provinces. Thus the United Provinces finally became the Dutch Republic after what had been a long and arduous journey.

After 1590 the republic's fortunes improved dramatically. The Spanish war effort faltered, Maurice of Nassau, a general of some ability, made considerable territorial gains (as Map 4 overleaf shows), and the Dutch economy really took off – to such an extent that by 1609 when the republic signed a Twelve-Year Truce with King Philip III of Spain, implicit in the agreement was an acknowledgement that the seven northern provinces (Holland, Zeeland, Utrecht, Gelderland, Overijssel, Groningen and Friesland) were now in fact independent, though official recognition would not come until 1648.

Conclusion

When all is said and done the Dutch Republic does appear to be a largely artificial creation, the product of war and geography. Until 1572 the focus of resistance had been in the south; however, the loss of Flanders and Brabant was largely due to military factors – they could not be defended – whereas the great rivers offered natural protection to the provinces in the north.[12] In addition the diversion of Spanish efforts to other military theatres was a crucial factor in the success of the revolt. However, we should not underestimate the strength of Holland. Holland was able to take the lead so effectively because both its political cohesion and its fiscal system had developed considerably in the decades prior to the revolt, as indeed had its economy. In short, it

N

Emden

Delfzijl
1591

Groningen
1580

FRIESLAND

Steenwyk
1592

Coevorden
1592

OVERIJSSEL

Lingen
1597

North

Sea

Zuider
Zee

IJssel

HOLLAND

Amsterdam

Deventer
1591

The Hague

UTRECHT

Zutphen
1591

Grol
1597

Rhine

Nijmegen
1591

ZEALAND

Geertruidenberg
1593

Grave
1602

Breda
1590

Sluis
1604

Ostend
lost in 1604

Antwerp

FLANDERS

Bruges

Scheldt

Bishopric
of
Liège

Cologne

Rhine

BRABANT

Lys

Brussels

LUXEMBOURG

Luxembourg

100 kms

Map 4 The conquests of Maurice of Nassau, 1590–1604.

provided a sound basis for independent political action (it also came to possess half the population and half the wealth of the new republic).

However, the seven provinces that came to form this republic had no history of cooperation – five of them had been recent additions to Habsburg rule and even within the provinces the preservation of the privileges of individual groups and towns hindered consensus. Religious divisions also caused friction, but the outcome – an official reformed church with a minority following and the toleration of a wide variety of (mainly Protestant) religious practice for the majority – proved lasting.

When the kingdom of Italy was proclaimed in 1861 Massimo D'Azeglio, the Italian writer and politician, is alleged to have said to King Victor Emmanuel: 'Sire, we have made Italy, now we must make Italians', a sentiment that was surely presaged by the makers of the Dutch Republic. A Dutch state had been created but it was an artificial creation and it would take some time for Dutch identity and Dutch national feeling to develop – but develop it did and in the seventeenth century the republic was to enjoy a 'golden age' with a booming economy and a flourishing cultural life. By the end of that century everyone had a much clearer idea of what it meant to be Dutch.

Notes

1 Holland made 'important contributions to these successful campaigns' according to J. Tracy in *Holland under Habsburg Rule* (Berkeley: University of California Press, 1990), pp. 75–6. This should be seen in the context of ongoing conflict with Gelderland. Holland was of course concerned to defend itself against attacks from the east and therefore had a special interest in these conflicts.

2 The Treaty of Augsburg (26 June 1548) put seventeen provinces together in a single Circle (previously they had been divided between the Burgundian and Westphalian Circles) and gave them a unique status within the empire: the Reichskammergericht (the imperial cameral court) had no jurisdiction over members of this Circle which, however, had protection (against France) for a contribution equivalent to that paid by two electors. The Pragmatic Sanction (4 November 1549) was negotiated with the States General in order to ensure the 'pays de pardeçà' remained forever under one and the same prince.

3 Though the Low Countries went by the name of the 'seventeen provinces' from *c.* 1550, contemporaries were unclear whether the 'seventeen' referred to the number of provinces, representative bodies or feudal titles.

4 Historians are divided over whether or not geography represented a serious obstacle to unification. In *Belgium Nostrum* (Antwerp: De orde van den prince, 1987), Hugo de Schepper argues that Brabant, Flanders, Holland and Zeeland were core provinces: they shared similar socio-economic characteristics as well as political and cultural traditions; de Schepper also argues that these core provinces greatly influenced Friesland, Artois and

Utrecht. In *The Dutch Republic* (Oxford: Oxford University Press, 1995), Jonathan Israel, on the other hand, claims that Holland succeeded in going it alone in the revolt because it had distinctive and separate economic interests from those of Brabant – its social structure was different (no court nobility) and it had found little support in its struggle with Gelderland from the southern provinces. Both arguments have their merits, but it would be misleading to suggest that either one has won the argument.

5   French was used in Artois, Hainault, Namur, Tournai and Walloon Flanders. According to a recent study there were as many as twenty-eight Dutch dialects! Those used in the eastern parts shaded into Low German.

6   The term 'regents' was usually reserved for the families in control of Dutch towns in the seventeenth century. That they became a closed group was in no small part due to the efforts of Brussels which removed wherever possible the influence of the guilds, believing a closed oligarchy would be easier to control.

7   This statement is perhaps a little too simplistic. It would appear that two contradictory tendencies were at work at the same time: on the one hand the States of Holland enjoyed greater independence because of their superior ability to raise taxes; on the other hand, centralisation had made much headway under Charles V, especially in the application of the law.

8   The soldiers had been told that all Netherlanders were heretics and they treated all the local inhabitants disdainfully as 'luteranos'.

9   The rebels in Holland and Zeeland were assisted by the withdrawal of most government troops from the provinces as these were deployed to meet the greater military threat in the south.

10 Discrepancies arise between historical works over which provinces signed the Union of Utrecht because some signed at different times and in some cases only parts of provinces signed. It is confused and confusing.

11 The Act of Abjuration (Dismissal) was a logical consequence of the acceptance of Anjou as prince: the title had to be vacant in order to be granted to him.

12 Brabant again became the centre of Orange's attentions from 1577 until the military successes of Farnese forced him to return to Holland in 1583. However, it could be argued that the loss of Flanders and Brabant was due as much to the divisions between the factions as to geography; by contrast the Holland towns were far less riven by religious conflicts.

2 *Alva's Throne* – making sense of the revolt of the Netherlands

Henk van Nierop

What was the revolt of the Netherlands all about?[1] For the anonymous artist who devised the engraving *Alva's Throne* (see frontispiece) it was quite clear. The centre of the picture is taken up by the duke of Alva. He is seated on a huge throne, the symbol of princely power which he has appropriated for himself. On the canopy above the head of the tyrant various instruments of torture are depicted: a rod, birch, handcuffs, an executioner's sword and a garrotte. At his feet lie several torn charters to indicate the laws and privileges of the Netherlands which have been violated. Before the throne seventeen maidens kneel humbly bearing the arms of the Netherlands provinces and bound to the throne by ropes about their necks. Behind them one can make out a group of figures here described as the *oberkeit* (magistrates). In any event the poor ladies can expect little help from them. Their legs have metamorphosed into pillars and they keep their lips tightly sealed. In the centre of the print two scaffolds have been erected on which the counts of Egmont and Hornes and two other men are being beheaded. From a pool into which the victims' blood flows, an obscure figure fishes for confiscated property. In the background still more people are tortured, hanged and burnt. Without any doubt what is represented here is the *political* oppression of the Netherlands.

But whoever looks more carefully will see that more is afoot. Beside the throne there stands a prelate with a cardinal's hat who must surely represent Granvelle (although he does not resemble him). He blows into the ducal ear with a bellows: he is a malicious adviser, a scandalmonger or an agitator. Behind both figures stands Satan, who holds a papal tiara above the cardinal's head and an imperial crown above the duke's head, the symbols of spiritual and worldly power. The character who is scooping up the confiscated property of the nobles ('the duke of Alva's confiscator') is an ecclesiastic. One of the oppressed provinces holds a book with the legend 'God's Word'. Whoever has still not got the message can read the captions. The 'evangelicals', the supporters of the evangelical reform movement are the victims of Alva's reign of terror and behind the Iron Duke stand the demonic powers of the church of Rome.

The print is also remarkable for what it omits. In addition to 'Freedom' and 'Religion' contemporaries sometimes gave a third reason for the resistance. We might call this the materialist or socio-economic motive. Wouter Jacobsz, for example, the Augustine prior who fled in 1572 from Gouda to royalist Amsterdam, wrote in his diary that his compatriots had abandoned the Catholic faith for material motives, 'for outward advantage such as trade'.[2] This motive is, however, only advanced by the opponents of the rebels and the maker of this print cannot be reckoned to be one of them.

The revolt in the historiography

The same three motives of freedom, religion and commerce dominated the older historiography until about 1960. In the nineteenth century Guillaume Groen van Prinsterer (1801–76), the anti-revolutionary politician, archivist and editor of sources looked on the revolt as a divinely led struggle against popery. If that view has now lost much of its popularity, the notion of the revolt as a struggle for liberty has survived somewhat better. Liberal historians like Johannes van Vloten (1818–83) and Robert Fruin (1823–99) interpreted that freedom as national independence, the freedom of the nation of the northern Netherlands from Spanish oppression. Fruin's successor as professor in Leiden, Petrus Johannes Blok (1855–1929), popularised this national and consensual view of the revolt. In Belgium Blok found a counterpart in Henri Pirenne (1862–1935), who in his magisterial survey *Histoire de Belgique* endeavoured to demonstrate the continuity of the Belgian nation since the Middle Ages.

During the inter-war years serious objections were lodged against this whiggish interpretation, among others from Pieter Geyl (1887–1966) and H. A. Enno van Gelder (1889–1973). The first emphasised that the existence of two separate national entities in the north and the south had not been the revolt's point of departure, but rather the outcome, and one which he deplored. The second showed that the revolt, at that time usually called the Eighty Years War, had the character not of a war between states, but that of a civil war similar to that then raging in France. That the nationalist interpretation of the revolt has survived for so long, not least in the classroom, may be ascribed to the shock of the Second World War. Evidently there existed in both the Netherlands and

Belgium (both divided and politically and socially fragmented nations) a need for a unifying myth. The nationalist interpretation of the revolt served that function.

Pirenne likewise emphasised economic and social factors. Inspired by the German sociologist Max Weber (1864–1920) he drew a connection between the early capitalist relationships in the Flemish textile industry and the Reformation and the revolt. It was, in his opinion, no mere coincidence that the revolt forcefully made itself felt precisely in the industrialised part of Flanders. It was not long before the Marxist historian Erich Kuttner (1887–1942) brought this interpretation to its logical conclusion. He viewed the revolt as a classic example of a bourgeois revolution against a feudal regime in which the proletariat did the dirty work. Apart from a brief period in the 1970s, the Marxist interpretation has never found much favour.

In the 1960s the character of Dutch historiography changed and with it changed the image of the revolt. Until then the historiography had been to a large degree whiggish, that is to say that it was implicitly assumed that the course of history was necessarily directed towards a particular goal, in this case towards the formation of two independent nation-states, the one preponderantly Protestant in the north and the other in the south Catholic. The conflict between the rebels and the royalists (and in that connection between the Protestants and Catholics) appeared in hindsight to be self-evident. Juliaan Woltjer, however, emphasised in *Friesland in hervormingstijd* ('Friesland in the Age of the Reformation') the malleable and open character of the religious and political situation during the early years of the revolt. He pointed out that the revolt could only be understood when one investigated the motivation of the majority who strove for reconciliation. The extremists on the left and right (the Calvinists and the supporters of Philip II's Counter-Reformation policies) followed in a certain sense a fixed course; but the centre could decisively affect the course of events by giving or withholding its support to one or other of the extremist wings.[3]

The older historiography had described the revolt from within a national framework which was taken as self-evident. That too changed in the 1960s. Woltjer and many others deliberately chose to describe the Reformation and the revolt in a single province or town. This approach was adopted not only on the grounds that thorough archival research could only be undertaken on a relatively small scale, but also from the conviction that the Burgundian state of Philip II was far from being a unity. In this way the national picture of the revolt was, as it were, undermined from within.[4]

At the same time that national interpretation was also subverted as the realisation dawned that the Dutch Revolt only formed part of a much larger international conflict. Geoffrey Parker in particular has emphasised that the success or failure of the rebels did not depend in the first instance on their own perseverance but on the international situation. Philip II had time and again to decide whether to employ his limited resources against the advancing Ottoman Empire in the Mediterranean or against the rebels in the north. The international political situation, Philip's imperial priorities and factional struggles at the Spanish court exercised a decisive influence on the outcome of the struggle of the Dutch rebels.[5]

The most recent contribution to the discussion on the nature of the revolt is from Jonathan Israel, who in his sweeping overview *The Dutch Republic: Its Rise, Greatness, and Fall 1477–1806* reverted to the older point of view that there were after all fundamental differences between the southern and the northern provinces and that these were instrumental in unleashing the Revolt. Since Pieter Geyl most historians had been accustomed to regarding the seventeen provinces of Charles V as an increasingly coherent polity. Before the revolt, they argued, no meaningful distinction between north and south existed. The outcome of the revolt, two separate and culturally distinct communities, was largely accidental, due to geographical and military factors. Against this widely accepted view Israel argued that the seven provinces north of the rivers Rhine and Meuse did in fact have a distinct identity of their own, as did the ten southern provinces. The seven northern provinces, according to Israel, constituted a separate political arena, had a well-defined common economic orientation and shared a number of cultural characteristics (though not, of course, a common 'national' awareness, as Fruin and Blok had believed). Seen from this perspective, the revolt of 1572 and the ensuing separation between north and south were the inescapable outcome of a duality that had existed for centuries.

As long ago as 1939 Jan Romein (1893–1962) delivered a lecture in which he emphasised that as a result of the continuing tendency for historical research to become more scholarly and specialised the image of the revolt had become ever more complicated to the point where it had disintegrated into 'a fog-cloud of interpretations'.[6] This development was necessary but at the same time Romein lamented it because it was difficult to retain a well-defined and inspirational interpretation. The revolt was neither a religious struggle, as it had appeared to Groen van Prinsterer, nor a national war of independence as it had seemed to Fruin, nor a class struggle as Pirenne and Kuttner had thought (and also incidentally Romein, who considered himself a Marxist), but a highly complex process in which different groups strove for different goals;

moreover in the different phases of that process, these goals also shifted. As the problems differed from one region to another, the conflict did not take the same form in any two places. Gone were the black-and-white conflicts between Protestants and Catholics, between pro-Spaniards and patriots; in their stead emerged a broad spectrum of overlapping interpretations. To complete the misery, the outcome of the conflict was not decided on the walls of Alkmaar or Leiden, but on the battlefields of the Mediterranean and in the council rooms of the Escorial.

It is not, however, necessary to lament that the revolt was 'an extremely complicated process' in which 'many factors' played a role. With a little perseverance it is possible to discern a pattern in what at first sight must seem like a tangle of facts.

The question of the constitution

Around the middle of the sixteenth century the whole of Europe, and therefore also the Low Countries, was beset by two major problems to which there were no easy solutions. The first problem concerned the nature of the state, that is the relationship between the prince and his subjects. The second problem was posed by the new phenomenon of religious division caused by the Protestant Reformation. Both problems were in essence political.[7]

Let us begin by first examining the constitutional problem. When we use the term 'constitutional' we are not of course thinking of a modern written constitution. By 'constitution' I mean the amalgam of unwritten custom law, privileges granted by the prince, local law and princely edicts and orders which together determined how public authority was exercised.[8]

With respect to this 'constitution' there existed two different, indeed mutually contradictory, interpretations. Philip II and his ministers saw the Netherlands provinces as a political entity under the authority of the prince, although princely absolutism should be tempered by custom and equity. In this scheme the inferior powers such as the nobility and the town corporations had a part to play, but their authority derived from the prince's power. The prince was the supreme legislator and judge and the sole source of law, honour and patronage.

Against this 'absolutist' view of the state the opposition in the 1560s set the traditional medieval model of a communal, federal and consti-tutional state. From this perspective the state consisted of a loose federation of autonomous communities. The role of the prince was confined to guaranteeing the internal peace and protection of the whole against external attack. The central government should be exercised in a sort of triangle composed of the prince or his regent, the high nobility and the States General.

Such different interpretations about the character of one and the same polity could exist at the same time because the nature of the state itself was deeply ambivalent. On the one hand, the Low Countries were indeed a federation of seventeen technically independent entities, each with its own institutions, laws and privileges. Each province recognised the prince in a separate inauguration and under a separate title (e.g. duke of Brabant, count of Flanders, lord of Friesland, etc.). But on the other hand the Burgundian and Habsburg princes had succeeded in the century preceding the revolt in converting this heterogeneous collection of autonomous states into a 'modern' state. It is a familiar story: the territory was more or less rounded off by 1543; the Burgundian heredit- ary lands were recognised in 1548 as constituting a separate entity ('the Burgundian Circle') within the Holy Roman Empire, from which they were, however, in practice separated. A few central institutions were called into being, such as a permanently resident regent, a central court of appeal and the three 'collateral' government councils. The central government in Brussels issued ordinances ('placards') which were valid in all the provinces; and it even made an attempt to bring some order to the confusion of local custom laws by codifying and ratifying these, but little came of this ambitious project.

One could look on 'the Netherlands', emphasising its plurality, as a personal union and confederation or as a principality and a federal state: arguments in favour of either of these views could properly be advanced. The prince in the Low Countries had rather less power than the Valois in France or the Tudors in England, but he had far more power than the emperor in the Holy Roman Empire. This ambivalent situation was, however, unstable and there was an undeniable tendency which favoured the modern more centralised monarchy.

The state-building process did not, however, take place evenly through- out the Netherlands. The central government made its presence most felt in the dynamic, urbanised west which depended on commerce and industry, in other words in Brabant, Flanders and Holland–Zeeland. The further one moved away from this core region, the less one noticed the influence of the central government in Brussels. The Walloon pro- vinces (Hainault, Artois, Namur) made a relatively modest contribution to the economy, but they constituted the heartland of the numerous nobility, who provided one of the pillars of the Burgundian state and the ties binding these provinces to the centre. The north-eastern provinces,

from Utrecht to Groningen, had only recently been added by Charles V
to the hereditary lands. They therefore laid claim to separate status and
to a far-reaching autonomy within the commonwealth. Finally, the
south-eastern duchies of Luxemburg and Limburg, which were sparsely
populated, undeveloped and still semi-feudal, hardly played any role in
the new state. For the sake of completeness, we should also mention the
province of Franche-Comté, i.e. the county of Burgundy that was part
of the empire. Geographically it did not of course form part of the real
'low' countries, but in a political sense it certainly did form part of the
Burgundian state. In modern European parlance, one might say that the
Netherlands constituted a two (or more) speed state.

The more modern centralised state had not exclusively been imposed
from above and against the wishes of the subjects. In many respects it
satisfied the needs of the subjects. Most of the lawsuits brought before
the central court of appeal, the *Grote Raad* (Great Council) of Mechelen,
were, for example, initiated by the parties who supposed that the closer
their litigation came to the prince, the greater would be their legal
security. Again, most of the ordinances issued by the Privy Council
flowed from petitions and requests from individuals or organisations;
they were not taken on the initiative of the prince's government. It was
above all the merchants and entrepreneurs (but also many noblemen) in
the western core regions who required uniformity in legislation, justice
and administration.[9]

Paradoxically enough the state-building process did not only lead to a
reinforcement of the central authority, but also to the decentralisation
of certain competencies. In contrast to France, the prince in the Netherlands could not impose taxation without the consent of his subjects,
who were for that purpose convoked as estates to the provincial
assemblies. The virtually incessant and extremely expensive wars with
France obliged Charles V and Philip II to call on the provinces to a far
greater degree than had previously been the case. The provincial States
used their prince's need for money as a lever to extend their own
powers. In exchange for granting financial support they negotiated far-
reaching control over the collection, administration and expenditure of
the tax revenues. In addition, they also discussed all manner of business
apart from fiscal matters and they demanded the right to meet as they
wanted. In this way the States evolved from being instruments of the
prince to become self-conscious representative bodies which could take
responsibility for the public administration. Once again Brabant,
Flanders and especially Holland, which together bore 80 per cent of the
tax burden, took the lead in this development.[10]

The question of religion

The second problem over which Philip II and many of his subjects in the Netherlands differed was presented by the Reformation. The question was not whether the church should remain Catholic or become Protestant, but rather what attitude the authorities should adopt in the face of the phenomenon of religious disunity. In this controversy the king upheld the traditional standpoint that the monopoly of the Catholic church should be maintained, if necessary with the use of force. Many people, however, believed that this policy could not be enforced in a country which had such a large minority sympathetic to reform. They pointed out that the Netherlands was surrounded by countries in which the Protestant Church was either the only one permitted (as was the case in many German principalities and imperial cities and England since 1558) or it was more or less tolerated (as had been the case in France since 1562/3). The uncompromising retention of the existing anti-heretical legislation would lead to violent disorders and jeopardise the country's prosperity.

Many from the politically articulate classes, such as the nobility, the town magistrates and the jurists attached to the provincial courts of justice, subscribed to this moderate standpoint. They had no desire to leave the Catholic church themselves, but an amalgam of humanitarian motives and pragmatic and political considerations persuaded them that it was undesirable to enforce every jot and tittle of the existing rigorous anti-heresy legislation.

Consequently many local magistrates were lax in implementing the 'placards', to the point of actually sabotaging them.[11] In Friesland, for example, the provincial court applied the anti-heresy legislation very loosely until 1559 and not at all thereafter. In remote Groningen edicts of the central government which did not find favour with the town government were simply not published, including the infamous 'blood placard' of 1550; occasionally people were banished for their faith, less because the magistrates thought this was necessary than in order to satisfy the authorities in Brussels. In Amsterdam no one was executed for their religious beliefs between 1553 and 1567 while the provincial court of Holland passed no death sentences between 1545 and 1558. By contrast, in Flanders the zealous inquisitor Titelmans handed over many religious dissidents to the secular arm for execution. But here too his conduct provoked a growing distaste among the town magistrates and other educated laymen.

Between 1555 and 1565 therefore there existed a fundamental difference of opinion, between the king and his government on the one hand

and many subaltern magistrates on the other, about how the ecclesiastical question should be treated. As a result the royal legislation was no longer executed in large parts of the Low Countries. Clearly such a situation could not continue unchanged forever. In the long run either the king would have to accommodate himself to the practices which had grown up, or the magistrates would have to enforce the law. In other words, to solve the ecclesiastical problem, the constitutional problem first had to be taken in hand. That was precisely what happened in the the period between Philip's departure to Spain (1559) and 1566, when royal authority in the Low Countries collapsed.

The opposition to Philip II

In the 1560s an opposition movement crystallised around the two demands for a constitutional government based on the 'privileges' and a moderate and humane solution to the religious question. The opposition's programme was far from clear. Initially it concentrated its attention on the constitutional question. Instead of entering into a debate on the principles, they pressed the case for the withdrawal of Cardinal Granvelle, Philip's strong man in the Low Countries who had been charged with the task of ensuring that royal policy was implemented fully. The campaign took place under the banner of restoring political relations to what they had been under Charles V. This was misleading, for in reality the power of the central state *vis-à-vis* the nobility and the lower authorities had increased sharply under Charles's rule. During the powerful administration of Mary of Hungary (1531–55), for example, the provincial governors had lost much of their freedom of movement, while the high nobility in the Council of State found themselves increasingly overtaken by professional jurists.[12] Following Granvelle's departure in March 1564 the high nobility in the Council of State saw their political aims temporarily realised. They dominated the councils of the central government and the weak regent Margaret of Parma. Now they had their hands free in order to concentrate on the second issue, namely the religious question.

The opposition movement was a coalition made up of very different elements. At first it was led by a small coterie of high nobles headed by Orange, Egmont and Hornes who had come together in the so-called League against Granvelle (on the role of the nobles, see below, Chapter 3). However, these aristocrats gained support from a larger body of lesser nobles who towards the end of 1565 formed the Compromise, a covenant after the French model, also with the purpose of enforcing a moderate religious policy. The noble opposition movement, whose members were known after April 1566 as the *gueux* or *geuzen* ('beggars'), enjoyed widespread popularity in the towns, and therefore also in the provincial assemblies. The Beggars' movement neatly made capital out of the unpopularity of the scheme launched in 1559 for a new diocesan structure and out of the anxiety felt in many quarters about the introduction of the 'Spanish' Inquisition. For this reason too it gained great sympathy among the urban middle classes.[13]

Ordinarily the merchants and artisans in the towns exercised little influence on the urban magistracies. But in a time of crisis public opinion was crucially important. In the eyes of the townspeople the magistrates acquired their legitimacy from the fact that they stood as guarantors for the town's liberty and autonomy. Pressure was exerted on the town governments from two directions. The central government required them to implement strictly the unpopular heresy edicts and furthermore to cooperate with the measures intended to place limits on the autonomy of the towns. The townspeople looked to their magistrates to defend the urban privileges and to leave some space for heterodox currents. The magistrates dared not disregard the voice of the burghers. In most towns there was no garrison and the governors therefore depended for the defence of the town and the maintenance of tranquillity and order on their own armed burghers. During the crisis of 1566 the civic militiamen or *schutters* in many towns refused to act against their own burghers who had been guilty of iconoclasm. As a result the authority of the town government completely collapsed and the consequent vacuum was filled by representatives from the militias. The armed urban burghers also played a decisive role during the revolt in Holland and Zeeland (1572–76) and in the Calvinist 'republics' that were established in Flemish and Brabant towns in 1577.

This heterogeneous opposition movement twice succeeded in achieving its programme. The first occasion occurred during the *Wonderjaar* (Wonderyear) in 1566. In April of that year, after the Compromise of the nobles had handed over the Petition, the persecutions of heretics were suspended. The Calvinists came out from their hiding places and began to hold religious services in public. A few months later, in the aftermath of the iconoclastic riots, Calvinist services were permitted on certain conditions. In the interest of public order the provincial governors like Orange in Holland, Zeeland and Utrecht, Egmont in Flanders and Megen in Guelders allowed the new measures to be applied far more flexibly than Margaret of Parma had intended. In her views the concessions were only temporary until the king had issued a definitive ruling. But few doubted that the solution would be in line with the tolerant programme of the nobility. In the event this first period of religious freedom lasted only briefly and came to an end in the spring of 1567.

The Pacification of Ghent (1576) marked the second success of the opposition. In reality, authority in the Netherlands was now exercised by the States General. These concluded a peace with the rebellious provinces of Holland and Zeeland without the king's consent. A small group of high nobility in the Council of State, led by the duke of Aerschot, even appointed a new regent, the Austrian Archduke Matthias, in place of Don Juan whom the king had sent. In so doing they certainly gave a very broad interpretation to what people still chose to represent as government in accordance with the ancient privileges of the country.

On both occasions, in 1566 and 1576–79, the opposition failed to realise its ambition for the same two reasons: the inflexible attitude of Philip II on the religious question and the extremism of the Calvinists. The king was, if necessary, prepared (temporarily) to grant a greater measure of participation to the high nobility and the States, but he refused on principle to permit 'heresy' in whatsoever form in his lands. On the other hand, the Calvinists were not prepared to make do with the status of a tolerated minority. They wanted to reform both the church and society in their spirit.

In 1566 this Calvinist agenda came to light during the iconoclasm, as a result of which the moderate centre withdrew from the opposition and showed itself prepared to accept the repressive regime of, first, Margaret of Parma and, subsequently, Alva. In the period after the Pacification the moderates were once again detached from the revolt by the fanatical activities of the Calvinists. In the towns governed by the radical Committees of Eighteen, for example at Ghent and Mechelen and in Holland in towns such as Haarlem and Amsterdam, Catholic services were once again forbidden, as they had been in 1566.

In 1578 it became clear that the opposition programme would bring not peace but a resumption of the war. Many moderate Catholics reached the conclusion that reconciliation with the king and the maintenance of the monopoly of the Catholic church were preferable to revolt. That was true not only for the Catholic nobility and the prelates in the Walloon provinces who concluded the Union of Arras in 1579 and became reconciled to Parma and the king, but also for many in the north-eastern provinces which had never felt comfortable in the Union of Utrecht.

The programme of the opposition movements of 1561–6 and 1576–9 had failed. In the two new states which came into being during the following years the ideals of nobility of the anti-Granvelle League and of the loyal Catholic opposition around Aerschot were not realised. In the southern or 'Spanish' Netherlands the king persisted with his absolutist policy and the Catholic church retained its monopoly. The persecutions, however, did come to an end, as the Protestants were allowed to emigrate to the northern Netherlands, while a vigorous Counter-Reformation church successfully recaptured the hearts and minds of those who stayed behind.

In the northern or 'united' provinces the 'privileges' under the leadership of the provincial States, the traditional protectors of the constitutional political standpoint, came indeed to occupy an important place. To that extent the programme of the aristocratic opposition of the 1560s was achieved. Ironically there was hardly any high nobility in the northern provinces to take advantage of the new constitutional situation. But the solution to the ecclesiastical question which was devised here differed substantially from the ideals which the opposition cherished in the 1560s and 1570s. The Calvinist minority now formed the established church and Protestant dissidents were officially tolerated. Catholicism was outlawed, but in most places the authorities turned a blind eye to the the activities of Catholics.[14]

The economy as a factor?

Did what Brother Wouter Jacobsz called 'trade' play a part in the outbreak and the course of the revolt? That depends on what this is taken to mean. One can interpret 'trade' literally, just as contemporaries did, as the search for material gain, the hope of personal profit; one can also consider the economic state of affairs and, finally, the economic structure in a broader sense, i.e. the manner in which the economy as a whole functions, in which case one should also include data about the size of the population and urbanisation.

As for the first case, it is unlikely that the search for material gain played any part in the outbreak and the subsequent course of the revolt. Some did indeed profit from the political changes, but others, among them Orange, were reduced to beggary. It is also difficult to predict what the economic consequences of a particular choice are likely to be. To take one obvious example, Antwerp as a result of the revolt lost its economic hegemony, but Amsterdam, which in 1572 had been one of the few towns in Holland to stay loyal to the king, was able to assume Antwerp's position, also as a result of the revolt. In any case one cannot demonstrate that political or religious choices were determined by the expectation of material gain.

Second, the economic situation. The Marxist model of Erich Kuttner has been sufficiently refuted. In a well-known article Herman van der

Wee tried to establish a link between the data about prices, wages and the standard of living and the outbreak of the revolt.[15] The spectacular growth of the Netherlands economy in the first half of the sixteenth century led, according to Van der Wee, to a 'spiritual emancipation' of substantial groups of the population. A temporary downturn in growth in the 1560s posed a threat to the recently acquired prosperity. Anxiety about impoverishment caused the resistance which suddenly flared up after Granvelle's departure in 1564. In the power vacuum which then developed both the urban middle classes and the workers were receptive to the reformist message. According to Van der Wee economic development may not have been the sole, but it was certainly an important factor when it comes to explaining the revolt.

Several arguments can be advanced against this interpretation. The connection between economic growth and 'spiritual emancipation' is vague and difficult to demonstrate. It is difficult to understand why increasing prosperity should have automatically led to a choice in favour of Calvinism. The model only concerns the commercially and industrially 'advanced' west, not the more traditional agrarian regions. In this respect the term 'southern Netherlands' in Van der Wee's title is misleading. And finally the collapse of the economic situation in the mid-1560s was far from unique. Each decade saw one or more of such crises, often on a larger scale. Why did these not lead to revolt?

The economy in the broader sense of the economic structure certainly was important for the revolt, but not in the way that Pirenne and Kuttner supposed. Rather than class differences I would stress a geographical distinction between the highly developed west and the more traditional agrarian provinces which stretched in a gentle arc from Groningen via Luxemburg to Artois. Flanders, Brabant and Holland–Zeeland were set apart from the rest on account of their dense populations (two of the three million inhabitants) and, closely related to this, their advanced state of urbanisation (almost half the population lived in towns and thirteen of the fifteen largest towns were to be found in Flanders, Brabant and Holland). They also had a highly developed commercial and industrial sector.

It is no coincidence that the highly developed western Netherlands played a disproportionately important part in the outbreak and subsequent course of the revolt. The Reformation here found its greatest support; the iconoclasm broke out in the south-western industrial region and wrought most destruction in the west; in 1572 the revolt broke out afresh in Holland and Zeeland; and the general revolt of the States General had its basis in Brabant and Flanders.

The Union of Utrecht, the 'closer' alliance within the Pacification of

Ghent, is often regarded as an alliance of 'northern' provinces against the south. This misleading impression comes about because that Union later served as a sort of constitution for the 'United' Netherlands. In reality the Union was signed by Holland, Zeeland, Friesland, Utrecht, Guelders and most towns of Flanders and Brabant, while the largest part of the north-east (Groningen, Drenthe and Overijssel) kept aloof. In other words, it was once more the western core that wanted to continue the struggle while the traditional, rural and aristocratic south and east looked for a reconciliation with the king. The relationships crystallised even more sharply in 1581 when the States General abjured Philip II. The Walloon provinces (with the exception of Tournai-Tournaisis) and Groningen were reconciled with the king; Flanders, Brabant, Zeeland, Holland and Friesland declared that he had forfeited his authority; Guelders, Overijssel and Utrecht declined to make a decision. What element in the western core provinces persuaded these to opt for the revolt?

The role of the towns

The dominant position of the towns was more important than purely economic factors. The military aspect played in this respect a subordinate role. In the sixteenth and seventeenth century wars were waged by laying siege to fortresses. A well-fortified town could withstand a siege for a considerable period of time, but this factor was not decisive. Certainly Alkmaar and Leiden withstood sieges by the Spanish, but Haarlem and Zierikzee were captured, albeit with great difficulty, by the Spaniards. The well-fortified towns of Flanders and Brabant were captured, one by one, by Parma between 1580 and 1585. Given sufficient money and resources and much patience, a skilful military leader could evidently capture virtually any town. The amount of money available was determined in Spain and depended on external factors.

It was more important that Calvinism could develop in an urban environment (and therefore above all in the western core regions). This was not because economic attitudes predisposed either the entrepreneurs or the workers (or both groups) to the evangelical movement, but because the towns alone furnished the material and intellectual infrastructure in which the reform movement could thrive: schools and therefore literacy; printers, a book trade and a literary culture; chambers of rhetoric where the new ideas could be discussed; a widespread humanist culture; good communications with other towns and abroad, so that books, pamphlets, news and ideas spread quickly. The Reformation was, to employ the much abused expression of A. G. Dickens, 'an urban affair', as much in the Netherlands as in the rest of Europe.

The second contribution which the urbanised society of the west made to the revolt sprang from the tradition of urban revolts. Wim Blockmans has drawn attention to the 'great' tradition of rebelliousness in Flanders and Brabant.[16] As a result of their traditional resistance to the political and fiscal centralising policies of the princes, the towns developed in the course of the struggle practical and institutional alternatives to princely centralisation. That 'great' tradition was complemented by a 'small' tradition of urban resistance by craftsmen and workers against the oligarchical governments within the towns. Both types of protest were often closely connected. For example, in Ghent in 1539 the radical rebels first seized control of the town government, after which the town dared to defy the authority of Charles V. Both these traditions revived in the revolt. One need only recall the defection of the towns in Holland and Zeeland in 1572 to the revolt and the establishment of the radical regimes of the Committees of Eighteen in the towns of Brabant and Flanders in 1577 and 1578.

The third and final contribution which the urbanised provinces made to the revolt lies in the tradition of regional and supraprovincial co-operation which came into being in the decades before the revolt. James Tracy has described how during the government of Charles V the provincial States assembly of Holland learned to take responsibility for important affairs which affected the entire province.[17] The towns consulted with the high nobility about the defence of the province, despatched on their own initiative embassies to foreign powers and collected taxes and administered the revenues. They issued bonds and guaranteed to pay both the interest and the principal; they assembled on their own initiative and formulated their own political agenda. This fairly recent development enabled the States of Holland to exercise the sovereign power effectively after 1572, and the States General (under the leadership of the towns of Brabant and Flanders) to do likewise after 1576. The revolt was possible because the rulers in the towns were used to looking beyond the immediate interests of their town and to carrying the responsibility for the common cause.

A revolt of the core region?

There existed, therefore, a certain connection between urbanisation and rebelliousness. But this connection is not invariable, for not all the towns rebelled. Lille, a large town with some 30,000 inhabitants and economically integrated into the western industrial region, remained quiet, while the neighbouring towns of Tournai and Valenciennes became veritable hotbeds of the reformed movement. In rebel Holland

and Zeeland only Flushing and Enkhuizen more or less spontaneously adopted the side of the rebels. Other towns, for example Haarlem, joined only after the *schutterijen* had carried out a military coup. Amsterdam (which had been at the heart of the movement for religious renewal in 1566) and Middelburg stayed loyal to the king in 1572. Nor did the peripheral regions remain universally loyal to the royalist government. Relations between Protestants and Catholics were less polarised in distant Friesland which as a non-patrimonial province preserved a greater measure of autonomy from Brussels. Nevertheless the Reformation there found a fairly favourable breeding ground and Friesland joined the Union of Utrecht. Groningen had a comparable relationship with the centre, but became reconciled with the king in 1580. In this case attitudes were determined by the traditionally strained relations between the town of Groningen and the surrounding country-side, the Ommelanden.

Second, rebelliousness was not the monopoly of the towns. The nobility, which had its power base in the peripheral provinces, played an essential role at the outbreak of the revolt (see below, Chapter 3). Most of the nobles enjoyed a far better economic and social position than was once supposed. The high nobility provided one of the pillars of princely authority. Their position of power had, however, been eroded because the prince increasingly appointed to positions of confidence non-noble officials who had undergone a legal training. Until Alva's arrival the brunt of the opposition movement was borne by a group of high nobles and supported by the lesser nobles united in the Compromise (for that matter by no means all nobles took the side of the opposition). What made the situation in 1566 so dangerous for the government was the merging of the movements of political resistance among the magnates and of religious reform.

Nor can the revolt of 1576 be understood unless one pays attention to the role of the high nobility around Aerschot. These nobles were for the most part from the rural Walloon provinces. It is no accident that these magnates were deterred by the violence in the turbulent Flemish and Brabant towns and that it was those Walloon provinces where the nobles and prelates were in the ascendancy that became reconciled with the king. Orange alone of the high nobles realised that the urbanised provinces had the best chance of maintaining the revolt.

Finally, the urban maritime region did not constitute a unity. It had its own dynamics which were determined by differences in the speed of development in the various parts. The religious reform movement first put down roots in the south-west part of the core region (the Flemish textile region and the towns of Walloon Flanders) while the northern part (Holland and Zeeland) remained for a long time comparatively peaceful. Consequently the 'new religion' in the south acquired a relatively more sharply defined and dogmatic character, while in Holland the ecclesiastical contrasts remained in a state of flux for longer. The disturbances of 1566 were in consequence fiercer in the south than in the north. As a result of the difference in the speed of development between the northern and southern core areas, the moderates in the south were more prepared than their counterparts in the north to submit to the central government's repressive regime under Alva. In the south people knew how dangerous it was to give concessions to the Calvinists. In the north, by contrast, Alva's remedies seemed worse than the disease. For that reason the revolt of 1572 enjoyed more success in Holland and Zeeland, while towns such as Antwerp and Ghent, which had been restive in 1566, now kept aloof.[18]

Conclusion

What was the revolt all about? Evidently the anonymous creator of the print which is known as *Alva's Throne* got it right. The revolt was indeed a struggle for both freedom and for religion. The content given to these concepts can, however, differ greatly.

'Freedom' certainly did not signify national freedom from 'Spanish' oppression, although for reasons of propaganda it was sometimes so presented in the pamphlets and satirical prints which the rebels distributed. By 'freedom' people understood an interpretation of the constitution according to which sovereignty was spread across different component parts of the state, while the prince respected the privileges and other rights which his subjects had acquired.

In practice this notion was interpreted in different ways. The nobles in the opposition in 1561–6 and 1576–9 interpreted it very differently from the radical craftsmen in Brussels, Ghent or Amsterdam. It is not then surprising that a movement of opposition which united such different groups on the basis of such vague slogans was doomed to failure.

And what of religion? The Calvinists interpreted the struggle for religion as one in which the monopoly of the Catholic church would be replaced by that of the reformed church. The Calvinists, however, were a minority. Most Netherlanders initially wanted to go no further than to permit a certain degree of freedom to that minority because they regarded the repression as inhumane as well as being impractical. Later, when experience seemed to prove that it was utopian to suppose different religions could co-exist peacefully, many chose a 'reformed' church, broadly defined, within which many tendencies could feel at ease. That was, however, not the sort of church for which the principled Calvinists had fought. The conflict was only decided in favour of the latter at the synod of Dordrecht (1618–19).

In order to understand the revolt we need to keep the socio-economic map of the Netherlands in mind. In the urbanised and commercial west the revolt found more support than in the traditional, rural and aristocratic south and east. The southern part of the core region, that is Flanders and Brabant, were recovered for the king of Spain by force of arms. The north-east was in the following period in like manner (albeit with a measure of support from within) captured by the stadholders Maurice and William Louis of Nassau and brought over to the rebel side. In this way the present border between the north and the south, which stood at right angles to the economic, social and cultural reality, came into being.

Notes

1 Translated from the Dutch by Alastair Duke. For a more fully annotated version of this chapter see H. F. K. van Nierop, 'De troon van Alva. Over de interpretatie van de Nederlandse Opstand', *Bijdragen en mededelingen betreffende de geschiedenis der Nederlanden*, 110 (2), 1995, pp. 205–23.
2 I. H. van Eeghen (ed.), *Dagboek van Broeder Wouter Jacobs (Gualtherus Jacobi Masius) Prior van Stein. Amsterdam 1572–1578 en Montfoort 1578–1579* (2 vols, Groningen: Wolters, 1959–60), vol. I, p. 3.
3 J. J. Woltjer, *Friesland in hervormingstijd* (Leiden: Universitaire Pers., 1962) and 'Political Moderates and Religious Moderates in the Revolt of the Netherlands', in P. Benedict, G. Marnef, H. van Nierop and M. Venard (eds), *Reformation, Revolt and Civil War in France and the Netherlands, 1555–1585* (Amsterdam: Koninklijke Nederlandse Akademie van Weten-schappen, 1999), pp. 185–200.
4 See R. S. DuPlessis, *Lille and the Dutch Revolt: Urban Stability in an Era of Revolution 1500–1582* (Cambridge: Cambridge University Press, 1991); C. C. Hibben, *Gouda in Revolt: Particularism and Pacifism in the Revolt of the Netherlands* (Utrecht: HES Publishers, 1983); G. Marnef, *Antwerp in the Age of Reformation: Underground Protestantism in a Commercial Metropolis 1550–1577* (Baltimore and London: Johns Hopkins University Press, 1996); and C. R. Steen, *A Chronicle of Conflict: Tournai, 1559–1567* (Utrecht: HES Publishers, 1985).
5 G. Parker, *The Dutch Revolt* (London: Allen Lane, 1977), and *The Grand Strategy of Philip II* (New Haven and London: Yale University Press, 1998).
6 'Het vergruisde beeld. Over het onderzoek naar de oorzaken van onze Opstand', in J. Romein, *Historische lijnen en patronen. Een keuze uit de essays* (Amsterdam: Querido, 1971), pp. 147–62.
7 J. J. Woltjer, *Tussen vrijheidstrijd en burgeroorlog. Over de Nederlandse Opstand 1555–1580* (Amsterdam: Balans, 1994).
8 See M. van Gelderen, *The Political Thought of the Dutch Revolt 1555–1590* (Cambridge: Cambridge University Press, 1992); H. G. Koenigsberger,

'*Dominium regale* or *Dominium Politicum et Regale*: Monarchies and Parliaments in Early Modern Europe', in H. G. Koenigsberger, *Politicians and Virtuosi: Essays in Early Modern History* (London and Ronceverte, PA: Hambledon Press, 1986), pp. 1–25; Q. Skinner, *The Foundations of Modern Political Thought* (2 vols, Cambridge: Cambridge University Press, 1978); and J. J. Woltjer, 'Dutch Privileges, Real and Imaginary', in J. S. Bromley and E. H. Kossmann (eds), *Britain and the Netherlands*, vol. V: *Some Political Mythologies: Papers Delivered to the Fifth Anglo-Dutch Historical Conference* (The Hague: Martinus Nijhoff, 1975), pp. 19–35.

9 H. de Schepper, *Belgium Nostrum 1500–1650. Over integratie en desintegratie van het Nederland* (Antwerp: De orde van den prince, 1987).

10 J. D. Tracy, *Holland under Habsburg Rule, 1506–1566: The Formation of a Body Politic* (Berkeley: University of California Press, 1990).

11 A. Duke, *Reformation and Revolt in the Low Countries* (London and Ronceverte, PA: Hambledon Press, 1990), pp. 152–74.

12 P. Rosenfeld, 'The Provincial Governors from the Minority of Charles V to the Revolt', *Anciens pays et assemblées d'états/Standen en landen*, 17 (1959), pp. 1–63.

13 H. F. K. van Nierop, 'A Beggars' Banquet: The Compromise of the Nobility and the Politics of Inversion', *European History Quarterly*, 21 (1991), pp. 419–43.

14 Duke, *Reformation*, pp. 269–93.

15 H. van der Wee, 'De economie als factor bij het begin van de Opstand in de Zuidelijke Nederlanden', *Bijdragen en mededelingen betreffende de geschiedenis der Nederlanden*, 83 (1968), pp. 15–32.

16 W. P. Blockmans, 'Alternatives to Monarchical Centralization: The Great Tradition of Revolt in Flanders and Brabant', in H. G. Koenigsberger (ed.), *Republiken und Republikanismus im Europa der frühen Neuzeit* (Munich: Oldenbourg, 1988), pp. 145–54. M. Boone and M. Prak, 'Rulers, Patricians and Burghers: The Great and Little Traditions of Urban Revolt in the Low Countries', in K. Davids and J. Lucassen (eds), *A Miracle Mirrored: The Dutch Republic in European Perspective* (Cambridge: Cambridge University Press, 1995), pp. 99–134.

17 Tracy, *Holland*.

18 J. J. Woltjer, *Tussen vrijheidstrijd en burgeroorlog. Over de Nederlandse Opstand 1555–1580* (Amsterdam: Balans, 1994), pp. 131–44.

3   The nobles and the revolt

Henk van Nierop

According to contemporary observers, the nobility played a crucial role in the outbreak of the Dutch Revolt.[1] The nobles were responsible for the conflict, so thought all Philip II's advisers for the affairs of the Low Countries, and the king himself endorsed their opinion. According to Cardinal Granvelle:

> the nobles wished to be adorned like kings and lived beyond their means. They sank into debt as a result and were no longer able to support themselves in the style to which they had become accustomed; they found their resources eaten up by the interest which they owed to merchants. They could see no better way out of their situation than to change the government.[2]

Granvelle had little reason to be generous towards the nobles who had brought about his downfall, but his sceptical view was not restricted to the party of the king of Spain. Dutch humanist historians of the seventeenth century like Pieter Corneliszoon Hooft and Hugo Grotius described the position of the nobility in very much the same terms. It took until the nineteenth century before this interpretation came to be challenged. Liberal historians, who regarded themselves as the true spiritual heirs of the revolt, proclaimed that it was not the nobles but the heroic middle classes of the booming commercial towns of Holland and Zeeland which had played the leading part in the birth of the Dutch Republic. But like earlier observers they continued to stress the 'decline' of the nobility, a degeneration that was at the same time economic, political and moral.

The connection between aristocratic economic decline and rebelliousness was not restricted to the Low Countries. In France in particular historians have argued that the nobility underwent disastrous economic and social decline in the sixteenth and early seventeenth centuries, and they have identified this process as one of the causes of the French civil wars. Similarly in other countries (including England) a decline and even a 'crisis' of the nobility were believed to be among the causes of civil wars. But numerous and detailed studies of the economic fortunes of the nobility in many regions of Europe have revealed that as a class they were not at all impoverished. Nor was their opposition to the modern state universal. Many nobles successfully adopted new roles and found wealth, power and status for themselves and their families in the service of absolutist monarchs.[3]

The economic interpretation of the role of the Low Countries' nobility can no longer be accepted. The Low Countries were of course notable for their highly urbanised character, particularly in the western core provinces of Flanders, Brabant, Holland and Zeeland, with their mercantile economies, their booming towns and their self-confident and politically mature merchant oligarchies. Nevertheless it was still the nobility from which the social, political and military elite of the Habsburg Netherlands was recruited.[4]

Magnates and lesser nobles

What did the Low Countries' nobility look like? A fundamental difference existed between a small group of 'great' nobles or *grands seigneurs* and a numerous class of 'petty' or lesser nobles or mere *gentilshommes*. The former were richer and more powerful than the latter, but differences in wealth and status were ultimately based on a different relationship to the ruling dynasty. Only the grandees had direct access to the patronage of the monarch. Charles V and Philip II, like other sixteenth-century princes, depended to a large extent on the services rendered by a group of men recruited from a limited number of noble lineages. The great nobles performed several key functions for the prince. They served in his private household or in the household of his regent, as both Charles and Philip with their sprawling empires spent little time in the Netherlands. A great nobleman might have a military commission, for example as captain of a mounted company (*bande d'ordonnance*). Aristocrats served as governors or stadholders in one or more provinces and they sat in the Council of State, where they advised the regent on weighty policy matters. Many of them were also members of the highly prestigious Order of the Golden Fleece. A nobleman did not have to perform all these functions to be regarded as a member of the aristocracy, but most grandees combined several of them.[5]

The sixteenth century saw a rising number and an increasing influence of legally trained professional civil servants. But the monarch could not dispense with the services of the nobility, for only a great nobleman would command respect and obeisance among the lesser provincial nobles and in the towns. The nobles were richly rewarded for their services. The monarch presented them with annuities, pensions, landed estates and manors. He transformed their unobtrusive *seigneuries* into counties, principalities or duchies and so enhanced the status of their owners with an honorific title. For their younger sons he often found a fitting (and lucrative) clerical dignity.

Thus a handful of noble lineages (in 1557 the Venetian envoy discerned only twenty-two *grands seigneurs*) monopolised a large number of influential, honourable and profitable functions. More than half of all provincial governorships, for example, between 1503 and 1572 were held by members of only seven noble families: Croy, Nassau-Orange, Egmont, Lalaing, Berghes, Lannoy and Montmorency.

One of the astonishing accomplishments of the Habsburg dynasty was the loyalty it commanded from the Netherlands' nobility. This had not always been the case. Overmighty subjects such as Philip of Cleves during the revolts that broke out after the death in 1477 of Charles the Bold, duke of Burgundy, turned to France for support. But the loyalty of the aristocracy was not at stake in the long series of wars that Habsburg and Valois fought between 1494 and 1559. An explanation for the devotion of the nobles may be that many of them with fiefs on both sides of the border between France and the Netherlands had craftily divided their patrimony between different sons. They thereby established French and Netherlandish branches of the same lineage, one loyal to the Valois, the other equally devoted to the Habsburgs. Charles V's sister Mary of Hungary, during her long and energetic reign as regent (1531–55), high-handedly curtailed the powers of the provincial governors. This inevitably gave rise to conflicts, but on the whole the magnates realised that they owed their exalted position to their cooperation with the monarchy.

A strong *esprit de corps* among the scions of aristocratic families gave rise to numerous in-group marriages. The result was that noble estates came to be spread over many provinces. Hence a great nobleman like Lamoral, count of Egmont, whose ancestral estates were in Holland, drew more than half his annual income from seigniorial properties in Flanders, Lille, Artois and Brabant. Similarly, the prince of Orange owned estates and fiefs scattered over Brabant, Holland, Flanders, Luxemburg and the Franche Comté.

The properties belonging to the *grands seigneurs* were spread unevenly over the Netherlands, with the centre of noble power firmly in the southern provinces, particularly in Hainault, Artois, Brabant and

Flanders. Only a few magnates hailed from the provinces north of the rivers Rhine and Meuse that were eventually to form the Republic of the United Provinces. In the west, in the counties of Holland and Zeeland, most of the lineages that had made up the aristocracy during the fifteenth century had become extinct. The eastern provinces Utrecht, Guelders and Overijssel had a more numerous nobility but these areas had been added to Charles V's Burgundian patrimony only recently, in 1528 and 1543 respectively. These *pays de nouvelle conqueste*, newly conquered lands as they were called, were not yet sufficiently integrated into the fabric of the Habsburg state for their nobility to play a significant role. In the remote northern provinces of Friesland and Groningen feudalism was unknown, nor was the nobility represented in the provincial States assemblies.

Historians have often explained the insignificant role of the aristocracy (apart from the house of Orange) in the Dutch Republic as a consequence of the revolt. But the uneven division of noble families over the Low Countries preceded the revolt and the split between north and south. As we shall see, the preponderance of the high nobility in the southern provinces was to have a significant impact on both the course of the conflict and its outcome.

The petty nobility or mere *gentilshommes* played a far less prominent part in the government of the Burgundian–Habsburg state.[6] They were, as owners of manors or *seigneuries*, responsible for jurisdiction, administration and legislation in the countryside. Most of them were entitled to sit in the provincial States, but not all nobles made use of that prerogative. A fair sprinkling of minor nobles held government offices at the local level, for example as sheriffs or bailiffs in a town or a country district. Others served as judges in the provincial courts of justice, where they rubbed shoulders with the relatively new class of legal officials of bourgeois origin. Office-holding, however, did not at this time elevate the latter to noble status. The number of lesser nobles holding office declined from the mid-sixteenth century, for reasons that are not yet well understood. But even if a few lesser noblemen continued to play significant roles at the local or provincial levels, their voices carried little weight with the government councils and the regent in Brussels.

Great *seigneurs* and petty *gentilshommes* did not, however, inhabit entirely different worlds, different as their political responsibilities might be. Multifold ties of kinship, friendship, fidelity, patronage and interest, as well as a common outlook, a certain aristocratic *mentalité*, connected high and low. Bastard children of the aristocracy married into lesser noble families, thus creating durable alliances. A minor nobleman might enter into the service of a great lord, as a *gentilhomme domestique* in his household, a castellan or steward of one of his estates, or a man of arms in his cavalry company. Thus the magnates disposed of a clientage of their own: men recruited from the regional nobility who wore the livery of their master.

The association between higher and lesser nobles posed a potential threat to the Habsburg rulers. Ideally, the grandees served as power-brokers, passing on the prince's patronage to his lesser subjects. But in situations of conflict the great nobles might as easily mobilise their clients against the prince. It is not sufficiently clear to what extent aristocratic patrons did use their clientages for faction-building. The aristocrats who formed the League against Granvelle decided in December 1563 to dress their household nobles in uniform liveries. They thereby made their opposition visible, underlined their mutual solidarity, and at the same time secured the support of their clients for their cause. The leaders of the Compromise of the Nobility of 1566 made extensive use of existing patronage and family networks when canvassing for support. This partly explains why backing for the Compromise was much more substantial in some provinces than in others.

The vicissitudes of the lesser nobles in the service of William of Orange may serve as an example of how aristocrats mobilised their clients for their cause, but also as a warning not to exaggerate the impact of patronage. A considerable number of lesser nobles in Orange's service supported the Compromise, signed the Petition of the Nobility, followed their patron into exile and served him as military commanders or in some other capacity. But their fidelity was never unconditional. Many of Orange's clients in 1567 in fact did *not* follow their master into political limbo, and many of them ended up in the service of the king of Spain, fighting their erstwhile patron. Noble affinity would last, it appears, only as long as a patron was able to deliver.

The nobles and the question of the constitution

The nobility's key position in the Burgundian–Habsburg state made it inevitable that they played a major part in the making of the revolt. I have argued that one of the issues at stake in the revolt was the interpretation of the 'constitution' of the Netherlands (see Chapter 2 above). These fundamental laws (partly customary, partly a mishmash of treaties and charters regulating the relationship between the prince and the various towns and provinces, and collectively referred to as 'privileges') were basically ambiguous. Philip II and his ministers regarded the Netherlands as a top-down type of polity. The nobility did play an important role in this governance, but not an independent one.

It was the task of the nobility to serve as courtiers, soldiers, governors and councillors. The prince was expected to reward them lavishly for services rendered. If for the nobles serving the prince was honourable, the latter augmented his own reputation by being the sole fount of honour and patronage.

The aristocratic opposition of the early 1560s challenged the king's 'absolutist' interpretation of the state. Rather they regarded the Netherlands as a loose federation of largely autonomous communities. The chief task of the prince was to guarantee internal peace and to defend the country against external threats. Government ought to be carried out jointly by the prince or his deputy, the *grands seigneurs* and the States General as the representatives of the people. It is evident that this model provided the nobility with much greater opportunity for power, wealth and prestige than the absolutist model. The great nobles, as the natural leaders in the provinces and commanding respect from both the lesser nobles and the towns, did not only counsel the prince, but actually shared responsibility for government with him.

The conflicts of the 1560s reveal something about the political imagination of the nobles, high and low. They regarded themselves foremost as the king's vassals, not his subjects. At the time of the acceptance of their fiefs they had sworn an oath of loyalty to Philip, pledging counsel and aid to their overlord. Yet their loyalty was not unconditional. As vassals they shared responsibility with the prince for the common welfare of the country. A vassal could of course help his liege lord impose his will on his subjects, but a better way to serve would be to help him to promote the common good. If he believed that the policies of the prince were detrimental to that purpose, his duty was to point this out by way of a remonstrance. In such situations the vassals invariably blamed not the prince, but his inept or malignant councillors.

This was exactly what happened between 1561 and 1566, a period of mounting tensions between Philip II in Spain and the discontented Netherlandish aristocracy. William of Orange and other members of the Council of State repeatedly expressed their grievances in letters to Philip. They even threatened to resign if the king did not pay heed to their advice. Several high-ranking noblemen went to Spain, first to argue in person with the king for the dismissal of Granvelle, then for a moderation of the anti-heresy 'placards'. When all efforts by the great nobles had failed, the lesser nobility presented a petition to the regent in which they emphatically presented themselves as vassals:

> Madame! It is common knowledge that throughout Christendom the people of these provinces have always been praised for the great

fidelity of their seigniors and natural princes . . . and that the nobles have always been prominent in this respect, since they have spared neither life nor property to conserve and increase the greatness of their rulers. And we, very humble vassals of His Majesty, wish to do the same and even more, so that night and day we are ready to render him most humble service with life and property.[7]

The loyalty that the nobles were obliged to render to their liege lord by no means precluded a critical attitude. The 'Joyous Entry' of Brabant (the oath sworn by the Burgundian and Habsburg rulers when they became dukes of that province) stated explicitly that if the prince persisted in any harmful policies, vassals were allowed temporarily to suspend their obedience, without, however, ending their loyalty on which that obedience was founded.[8]

The specific and restricted character of feudal faith became evident when the government in January 1567 demanded that all vassals and nobles swear a new oath of allegiance to serve the king 'towards and against all . . . without limitation or restriction'. The new oath reflected the new mood of self-confidence of the royal government after it had regained authority following the horrors of the 'Wonderyear', but such unconditional loyalty was very different from anything the nobles had previously sworn. In the end most of the oppositional grandees grudgingly agreed to swear the new vow, but Orange and a few lesser nobles refused. Orange pointed out that the obedience demanded was formulated in such unconditional terms that it could not be ruled out that the king might ask a service that was contrary to Orange's conscience, or harmful for king and country, or not in accordance with Orange's earlier oath as a liege man. None the less, he still regarded himself as a faithful vassal of the king by his previous oath.

The nobles and the religious question

The other issue that tore the Netherlands apart in the 1560s was religion (cf. Chapter 4). Contrary to what was the case in the constitutional question, the nobility's social position did not predicate them to embrace either position, i.e. adopt the new, reformed religion or stick with the old church. But it would be misleading to consider the religious problem as one pertaining only to the private consciences of individual nobles. Religion in the sixteenth century was essentially a political issue, if only because the state had to formulate a policy towards religious dissent. The nobles, in their capacity as councillors of state, provincial governors and local *seigneurs*, were directly involved with the implementation of the

anti-heresy placards. They were also extremely sensitive to the consequences of a religious policy that was highly unpopular with the
population. Strict enforcement of the anti-heresy placards, so argued the
members of the Compromise, would cause rebellion and the economic
ruin of the Low Countries:

> We have carefully pondered all these matters and duly considered
> the duty to which we are all bound as faithful vassals of His Majesty
> and particularly as nobles, that is, as His Majesty's helpers whose
> function it is to maintain His authority and greatness by providing
> for the prosperity and safety of the country through our prompt
> and willing service. We have come to the conclusion that we cannot
> perform our duty but by obviating those disastrous consequences
> and by trying at the same time to provide for our personal safety and
> that of our possessions so that we may not fall a prey to those who
> would wish to enrich themselves at the cost of our lives and goods
> under the pretext of religion.[9]

Many nobles thus felt compelled by the rising tensions of the 1560s to
criticise the king's religious policies. Yet this does not imply that they
converted to the new religion or even felt much sympathy for the
Calvinist movement. The great nobles in particular remained aloof.
William of Orange, who was to join the Calvinists only in 1573, in 1566
professed his loyalty to the Catholic church. The counts of Egmont and
Hornes, who died on the scaffold for their attitude in 1568, were deeply
pious Catholics. Floris van Pallandt, count of Culemborg and Hendrik,
lord of Brederode were greater nobles who did sympathise with the
Reformation movement, but neither of them held significant government positions. Since many high-ranking nobles in their capacity as
provincial governors were actively involved in the persecution of
religious dissidents, they shared the *political* point of view that Philip's
religious policy was damaging to public order and the welfare of the
country. On top of that a number of great nobles, among them Hornes,
Brederode and not least William of Orange, had German-born
Lutheran spouses. They therefore took a keen personal and dynastic
interest in a more tolerant religious policy.

A number of lesser nobles, however, did convert to reformed
Protestantism. They were a minority amongst the nobility, but they
played a key role in the dissemination of the new creed as they were
prepared to introduce evangelical preaching in their manors, support
the reformed ministers and put the fledgling consistories under their
protection.

It is not possible to make a reliable quantitative assessment of noble support for the Calvinist movement in 1566. The only sources that could be used for this purpose are the various documents listing the names of nobles who supported the Compromise of the Nobility, roughly 400 individuals. But it would be misleading to regard all supporters of the Compromise and the Petition as Protestants. About half of those professing their support did so because they opposed the 'Inquisition' for political reasons, but at the same time they remained faithful Catholics. The other half were Protestants of some sort, but certainly not all adherents of Calvinism.

It is tempting, but impossible, to put these figures in relation to the total number of nobles in the Netherlands. If H. A. Enno van Gelder's (unsupported) claim that there were approximately 4000 (male, adult) nobles in the Netherlands is anything near reliable, roughly 10 per cent of the Netherlands' nobles would have signed the Compromise, and perhaps 5 per cent would have been Protestants.[10] But support for the Reformation was uneven in the different provinces. Roughly half of the fifty-four nobles who signed in the county of Holland alone can be identified as Protestants. This would imply that in Holland in 1566 one out of eight nobles may have sympathised with the new religion.[11]

These figures are far from reliable, but it is evident that Calvinism counted far fewer adherents among the nobility in the Netherlands than was the case in France during the same period. Here allegiance might be as high as 40 per cent in some regions.[12] One may only guess at the reasons why Calvinism was more popular in France. The Calvinist movement in France had an earlier start and thus more time to win converts, both among the population at large and among the nobility. By the mid-1550s great nobles such as Condé and Coligny had been won for the new movement. In the Low Countries, by contrast, none of the great nobles converted, and hence there was no pressure on their clients to follow their example. If in France the clientage system was one of the main mechanisms through which Calvinism was diffused, the lack of enthusiasm among the Low Countries' grandees must have prevented its spread among the lesser nobility. Another element may have been the absence of nobles among the Protestant ministry. A significant number of pastors who were sent from Geneva to France were of noble origin, but the Low Countries' nobility did not bring forth one single Protestant minister. And finally repression of dissidents was far more severe in the Netherlands than in France. More than 1300 individuals were executed on heresy charges in the Netherlands between 1523 and 1566, considerably more than the nearly 500 known victims in France.[13] The difference is even more striking if one realises that the Netherlands had approximately two million inhabitants, against eighteen million in France. One can easily imagine that under these circumstances many nobles were eager to protest against the 'Inquisition' but far more reluctant actively to join the evangelical movement.

In spite of these obstacles, a number of nobles did join the reformed movement. As was the case among the French nobility, women played a crucial role in their conversion.[14] A fair number of nobles had married into the Lutheran nobility of the German Rhineland. Antoine de Lalaing, count of Hoogstraten, was married to Elizabeth von Manderscheidt, a devout Lutheran who brought her own minister with her. Hoogstraten remained a staunch Catholic, but their son Floris van Pallandt, count of Culemborg, became a Calvinist. Hendrik van Brederode, the leader of the Compromise, was married to the Lutheran Amalia von Neuenahr; Philip of Montmorency, count of Hornes, had married Walburgis, another Neuenahr. Hornes remained a good Catholic, but in his absence Walburgis connived with the image-breaking in his *seigneurie* of Weert. Otto van den Boetzelaer, who introduced the new religion in Langerak, was married to Odilia von Flodorp; Karel van Bronkhorst and Batenburg was married to another lady of Flodorp, who favoured the evangelical movement in her manor near Roermond. But a noble lady did not have to be German to be a Protestant. Marie of Hornes, the wife of Philip of Egmont, was 'reputed as a heretic'; Charles of Croy alleged that his wife Mary of Brimeu had seduced him to Calvinism; Catharina van Ghiselin, Otto van den Boetzelaer's wife, brought Calvinist ministers, including Hermannus Moded, to her husband's manor.

Family networks were of paramount importance for the propagation of the new faith, although the decision to join the Calvinist church was ultimately an individual one. As was the case in France, whole families converted lock, stock and barrel. As these families frequently intermarried, the Protestant nobility of the Netherlands can almost be regarded as one huge family.[15]

The Van Boetzelaer family of Asperen in Holland may serve as an example. The *pater familias* Wessel van den Boetzelaer signed the Compromise, smashed with his own hands the images in the parish church of Asperen and was exiled along with his six sons and a further bastard son. Wessel had been married to Françoise van Praet van Moerkerken, who had died in 1562; her sister Petronella was married to Herman van Bronckhorst and Batenburg in Guelders, whose three sons were also Protestants and signed the Compromise. Another Praet sister was married to Robert de Bailleul, a great champion of Calvinism in south-west Flanders, where he had already organised Protestant conventicles by 1559. All three families, the Praets, the Bronckhorsts and the Bailleuls, were fervent supporters of Protestantism, and it is evident that the Praet sisters played an important part in the dissemination of the new creed. According to the Council of Troubles, however, it was not Wessel's deceased wife Françoise who had led him astray, but his *concubine ou femme putaine* (mistress or whore-wife) Judith van Helmond. Wessel van den Boetzelaer's son Rutger was married to Agnes de Bailleul, another son was married to Elizabeth van Bronckhorst and Batenburg. Thus the four Protestant families of Boetzelaer, Bronckhorst, Praet and Bailleul were tightly interconnected, forming a clan that went over to Protestantism almost in its entirety.

The attitudes of the nobility were thus shaped in various ways. In the *constitutional* conflict the nobles were predicated to sympathise with the opposition movement. That did not imply, however, that they agreed on what means were necessary for realising their demands. As the revolt in due course became more radical, many nobles felt that safeguarding their position within the constitutional framework of the state was less important than loyalty to the dynasty to which they owed their exalted social position. In the *religious* conflict many nobles favoured freedom of conscience or even freedom of worship, but sympathy for the Calvinists was uneven. Particularly after the image-breaking of 1566 and again after the establishment of radical Calvinist regimes in Brussels, Ghent and elsewhere in 1577–8, many nobles reluctantly conceded that the king and the conservatives might have been right all along. It became increasingly clear that tolerating religious dissidents inevitably led to sedition, anarchy and loss of authority for the nobles themselves.

From opposition to revolt, 1559–1572

It is likely that the Habsburg rulers of the Netherlands and their nobility had felt differently about the problems of polity and religion for a long time, but it was only after 1559 that their differences came into the open. What had changed? First of all, the peace concluded between Philip II and Henry II at Cateau-Cambrésis allowed Philip to leave the Netherlands and settle in Spain – never to return, as it turned out. All major policy decisions regarding the Netherlands were from now on to be taken by Spaniards. This soon became evident, even if Philip had made sure to appoint a number of high-ranking noblemen as provincial governors and members of the Council of State. The peace must also have interrupted the military career opportunities of many noblemen serving in the *bandes d'ordonnance*, as was the case in France. There is, however, no evidence that in the Low Countries loss of employment disposed the nobles to either Calvinism or revolt.

The king's departure also marked a turning point on the religious front. The peace freed the hands of both Philip II and Henry II for a concerted drive against heresy. Philip launched his long-prepared plan for a reform of the bishoprics in the Low Countries. The reorganisation would render the struggle against heresy more effective and increase the king's influence in the affairs of the church. The twin developments of the hispanisation of government and the tightening of religious control seemed inseparable to the inhabitants of the Low Countries. They were summarised (erroneously, but from the point of view of political propaganda quite effectively) as the introduction of the 'Spanish Inquisition'.

Between 1561 and 1566 the largely instinctive notions the great nobility held about the nature of the constitution developed into a rudimentary political agenda. They advocated more substantial influence for noble councillors in the Council of State and regular consultation of the States General in all matters of importance. With the new regent, Philip's half-sister Margaret of Parma, displaying far less character and stamina than her predecessor Mary of Hungary, the nobles saw an opening for enhancing their political influence.

The obstacle they found in their way was the newly appointed archbishop of Mechelen, the astute Antoine Perrenot, Cardinal Granvelle. It was Granvelle's task to ensure that the king's policies were implemented in the Low Countries. The nobles, if they were to realise their goals at all, first had to neutralise the cardinal. A number of aristocrats banded together in a League against Granvelle. The League cleverly exploited the broad popular opposition against the planned reform of the bishoprics and forced the king to withdraw his minister in March 1564. With Granvelle gone, the grandees made a bid for power. They monopolised the Council of State, subsumed the other government councils under it and made Margaret of Parma dance to their tune.

The magnates thus created a political platform from which to tackle the religious problem. William of Orange made a speech in the Council of State on 31 December 1564 in which he criticised the persecutions and advocated a policy of religious toleration. This heralded a period of feverish activity aimed at putting an end to the persecutions of religious dissidents. But the efforts of the nobles ended in failure with Philip's notorious 'Segovia' letters (October–November 1565), in which the king stated in no uncertain terms that he would stick to his uncompromising religious policy. Philip's rebuttal made it clear that the Leaguers had reached the limits of what was possible.

At this point the appearance of the lesser nobility on the political stage saved the day for the aristocratic opposition movement. Several nobles organised a 'Compromise', a covenant or pressure group dedicated to putting an end to the persecution of Protestants.[16] The core members of the Compromise, such as Nicolas de Hames, Orange's brother Louis of Nassau, Culemborg and the quick-tempered Hendrik van Brederode were sympathetic to the Calvinist cause, but the objectives of the Compromise were deliberately formulated in broad terms. They thus enabled moderate Catholic noblemen to join. More than 400 nobles signed up. They hailed from all provinces except Zeeland, Groningen, Limburg and Tournai-Tournaisis. The leadership of the Compromise closely cooperated with the League of the great nobility. Several of its leaders such as Brederode and Culemborg were members of both organisations. The continuity between the League and the Compromise was not lost on contemporaries. 'The first league has generated the second one', wrote Granvelle to the king in May 1566.[17] Although some of the more radical members of the Compromise were prepared to take up arms, the great nobles in the League convinced them to present a petition to Margaret of Parma.

The event took place in Brussels on 5 April 1566. The long and awesome procession of some 200 noblemen marching through the streets of Brussels was enough to convince the regent that the use of violence and indeed the danger of civil war was no longer merely theoretical. The example of France loomed large in this respect. A Frenchman had already warned the Netherlands' government in 1562 to take heed of what was going on between the Huguenots and the Catholics, 'for, at the sound of the flute of France, you will have to dance here'.[18] Granvelle foresaw that granting freedom of conscience would have the same disastrous effects as in France and worse, for there were not only 'Huguenots' in the Low Countries but also Lutherans and even more Anabaptists; and the latter 'have various very different sects among themselves, some of which favour community of goods and even of women, and you may imagine the sort of household we shall have if this sect were permitted to multiply'.[19]

The action undertaken by the Compromise resulted in the suspension of religious persecutions. The hitherto clandestine 'churches under the Cross' surfaced and organised open-air meetings ('hedge-preaching'). At a meeting at St Trond in the independent bishopric of Liège the Calvinist consistories discussed the possibilities for armed resistance with the leaders of the Compromise. The increased confidence of the Calvinists led to image-breaking in August 1566. Faced with mass violence in many big cities, the regent was forced to legalise reformed Protestant gatherings.

Politically, the Compromise had saved the day for the aristocratic League. The aristocrats with their programme of religious toleration realised they were at the peak of their power. It was the *grands seigneurs* who in August 1566 on behalf of the regent concluded an agreement with the Compromise which allowed Calvinist services to be conducted where they had been held so far – a concession that went far beyond a mere suspension of the anti-heresy placards, which in itself would have been completely unacceptable to Philip. To prevent further unrest in Holland, Zeeland and Utrecht, Orange allowed the new rules to be interpreted far more liberally than had been Margaret's intention. The Calvinists in several towns, with the approval of Orange, were given churches for organising services, including the celebration of the Lord's Supper.

Such far-reaching concessions for the Calvinists would have been unthinkable without the religious riots of August 1566. Nevertheless, the image-breaking also signalled a turning point in the fortunes of the opposition movement. The government, in return for allowing Calvinist preaching, required that the Compromise be disbanded. Moderate Catholic nobles, appalled by the religious violence that their own initiative had unleashed, withdrew their support. But a number of radical nobles, most of them converted to the reformed religion, were prepared to take up arms and defend the newly won religious liberty. Money collected by the consistories in a vain attempt to buy religious toleration from Philip II was employed to pay for mercenary troops under the command of Brederode, and a number of towns were occupied (Valenciennes, 's Hertogenbosch). But the armed revolt ended in disaster. An attempt by Jean de Marnix, lord of Toulouse to seize the strategic island of Walcheren in the Scheldt estuary failed, and his motley band of troops was routed under the walls of Antwerp. The government recaptured Valenciennes, and Brederode's attempts to secure Utrecht and Amsterdam to establish a stronghold in the north came to nothing.

By May 1567 the 'Wonderyear' was over. With the regent firmly in power, Calvinist preaching was forbidden. Orange, Brederode and the other nobles implicated in the opposition movement hastily sought safety across the German border.

For the nobility, the significance of the tempestuous events of 1566 was twofold. On the one hand, it was clear that the short-lived freedom for the Calvinists was to a considerable extent due to the initiative and the sustained support of the nobility. On the other hand, Calvinist violence had revealed a deep rift within the nobility. While a few nobles were prepared to take up arms against the government, the majority kept aloof while the government defeated the rebels. Several nobles actively supported the authorities in crushing the rebels, such as the counts of Aremberg and Megen, who served as Margaret's military commanders against the insurgents.

After the arrival of the duke of Alva in August 1567 those nobles who had not fled the country remained loyal to the new regime. They realised that their programme for constitutional and religious reform had failed. The trial and execution of the counts of Egmont and Hornes made a devastating impression. Both men had been good Catholics, but in the interest of public order they had pushed for liberty of conscience. According to their understanding of the constitution they had loyally served the king, but Philip had dealt with them like common criminals and traitors. Many people believed that the verdict was illegal. As Knights of the Golden Fleece they were entitled to a trial by their peers. But Philip and Alva deemed the privileges of the Order null and void in cases of lese-majesty (treason). The two opinions reflect a different interpretation of the fundamental laws of the Low Countries.

The Council of Troubles, Alva's newly instituted tribunal for punishing the culprits of 1566, pronounced the death sentence on several nobles they had managed to lay their hands on. But the majority of those involved with the Compromise and the Petition, the image-breaking and the development of the reformed church, escaped. The Council of Troubles condemned them *in absentia* to eternal exile and confiscated their property. Many exiles now chose to support Orange's armed struggle. One in four captains in Orange's Sea Beggars' fleet, for example, was of noble birth. There was little else they could do, for unlike merchants or craftsmen who took their capital and skills with them into exile, the nobles could not continue their accustomed way of life once they were cut off from their estates. Thus Alva's policy of repression caused many originally moderate nobles to take a more radical stand. Many nobles in exile who had not already done so joined the Calvinist church.

From rebellion to pacification to renewal of the war, 1572–1580

The revolt that broke out in Holland and Zeeland in 1572 caused new divisions among the nobility. Those nobles who had been exiled by Alva and the Council of Troubles returned to the seditious provinces. Many of them received military commissions in the insurgents' infantry companies or served as military governors in the cities. Native nobles of Holland and Zeeland who returned from exile regained their confiscated properties. On the other hand, Catholic nobles from Holland and Zeeland who had served under Alva or who disagreed with the new regime now left. The revolutionary States of Holland and Zeeland sequestered their manors and estates.

The war lasted for more than four years. Only in November 1576 did the Pacification of Ghent bring an end to the hostilities. It created a new situation for the nobility. Catholic and royalist nobles who had fled from Holland and Zeeland in 1572 were now allowed to return. Similarly, nobles who had been exiled by the Council of Troubles were permitted to come back to the other provinces that had stayed loyal to the king of Spain. In all provinces confiscation of property was lifted. Thus in all parts of the Netherlands the status quo that had existed before the arrival of the duke of Alva was restored.

The years between the Pacification of Ghent and the Unions of Utrecht and Arras (1579) witnessed a repeat of the conflicts about the constitution and the religious problem that had divided the country in the 1560s. A group of Catholic magnates, mostly from the rural and quasi-feudal southern provinces of Artois and Hainault, and known as the Malcontents, revived the programme of the League against Granvelle. They strove for noble control of the Council of State, a significant role for the States General and a moderate solution for the religious problem. They also opposed too much power for William of Orange.

The programme of the Malcontents failed due to the same obstacles it had met in 1566, that is on the one hand the fanaticism of the Calvinists and on the other hand Philip II's unwillingness to compromise about religion. The Calvinists, far from being satisfied with a tolerated minority position, wished to reform church and society according to the Genevan model, while the king stubbornly refused to make a deal with heretics. By 1578 polarisation had progressed to such an extent that it became apparent that the programme of the opposition would lead to a renewal of the war. This time war would pitch Orange and Protestant Holland and Zeeland against the new regent Don Juan and Philip II. Most of the towns of Flanders and Brabant, dominated by radical Calvinist 'Committees of Eighteen', were prepared to conduct such a war. The Malcontent nobles, however, gradually came to the conclusion that if war could not be avoided, they would rather wage it on the side of their lawful prince against Orange and the Calvinist riff-raff.

The background for what has been termed a 'psychological recon-version' of the nobility was twofold.[20] The nobles had remained loyal to the Catholic church and they distrusted the radical movements in the towns of Flanders and Brabant. The duke of Aerschot, governor of Flanders, had never forgiven the revolutionary burghers of Ghent for arresting him in 1577. It is therefore not coincidental that it was the States assemblies of the rural, semi-feudal southern (Walloon) pro-vinces, dominated by the nobility and the first estate, that concluded the

Treaty of Arras and came to terms with Philip II. Their reconciliation was possible because Philip had authorised his new regent, Alexander Farnese, prince (later duke) of Parma, to grant far-reaching concessions to the nobility. Among these concessions were the restitution of their confiscated property, amnesty for their role in the revolt (and even payment for offices held from the revolutionary States General) and the promise of key positions in a future government.

It thus seemed that the Walloon grandees in 1579 largely realised the constitutional demands of the aristocratic opposition of the mid-1560s. It was not difficult for the nobles to fulfil Parma's only condition that they drop their demands concerning religious policy: the king was unflinching on this point, and it had become abundantly clear that the Calvinists could not be trusted.

In the north-eastern provinces, too, where enthusiasm for the Union of Utrecht was limited, many nobles opted for reconciliation with the king. Among them were the governor of Groningen, Friesland and Drenthe, the count of Rennenberg (a member of the Lalaing family), and the governor of Guelders, Orange's brother-in-law count van den Bergh. Dutch historiography has anachronistically dismissed their attitude as 'betrayal'. But from the point of view of the nobility in the 1580s, after all attempts for peace had failed, reconciliation was preferable to rebellion and continuation of the war.

William of Orange was once again almost the only one among the *grands seigneurs* who opted for carrying on the revolt. One reason for his attitude was that he could not drop the religious issue, another that he mistrusted Philip's sincerity. History proved him right: after the States assemblies of the southern provinces had agreed to the return of the Spanish army, the terms of the Treaty of Arras were consigned to oblivion.

Thus the development towards a more centralised monarchical state continued in the southern or 'royal' Netherlands, with a concomitant decline of the political significance of the nobility. By the middle of the seventeenth century the nobility of the south had been replaced by a new class of legally trained officials of bourgeois descent. The king of Spain granted them patents of nobility, thus creating a new nobility of the robe alongside the ancient feudal nobility.

If the nobles had played a key role in the making of the Dutch Revolt, the revolt also turned out to be their undoing, both in north and south. In the 'royal' or Spanish Netherlands the tendency towards absolutism continued, transforming the nobles from a power elite to an elite of wealth and honour. The Dutch Republic, where the *grands seigneurs* had never been particularly numerous or influential, became an early example of a polity where the urban elites were predominant.

Notes

1 For a more fully annotated version of this chapter see H. F. K. van Nierop, 'The Nobility and the Revolt of the Netherlands: Between Church and King, and Protestantism and Privileges', in P. Benedict, G. Marnef, H. van Nierop and M. Venard (eds), *Reformation, Revolt and Civil War in France and the Netherlands, 1555–1585* (Amsterdam: Koninklijke Nederlandse Akademie van Wetenschappen, 1999), pp. 83–98.

2 H. H. Rowen (ed.), *The Low Countries in Early Modern Times: A Documentary History* (New York: Harper and Row, 1972), p. 27.

3 J. Dewald, *The European Nobility, 1400–1800* (Cambridge: Cambridge University Press, 1996).

4 S. Marshall, *The Dutch Gentry, 1500–1650: Family, Faith and Fortune* (New York: Greenwood Press, 1997); H. F. K. van Nierop, *The Nobility of Holland: From Knights to Regents, 1500–1650* (Cambridge: Cambridge University Press, 1993).

5 P. Rosenfeld, 'The Provincial Governors from the Minority of Charles V to the Revolt', *Anciens pays et assemblées d'états/Standen en landen*, 17 (1959), pp. 1–63.

6 Ibid., note 4.

7 E. H. Kossmann and A. F. Mellink (eds), *Texts Concerning the Revolt of the Netherlands* (Cambridge: Cambridge University Press, 1974), p. 62.

8 Rowen, *The Low Countries*, pp. 12–16.

9 Kossmann and Mellink, *Texts*, p. 60.

10 H. A. Enno van Gelder, *Van beeldenstorm tot pacificatie. Acht opstellen over de Nederlandse revolutie der zestiende eeuw* (Amsterdam and Brussels: Agon Elzevier, 1964), p. 55.

11 G. Bonnevie-Noël, 'Les tendances religieuses des signataires du Compromis des Nobles', *Vereniging voor de geschiedenis van het Belgisch Protestantisme* 6 (1974), pp. 8–22, 46–56; Van Nierop, *The Nobility*, pp. 185–91.

12 J. M. Constant in Benedict *et al.* (eds) *Reformation*, p. 70.

13 A. Duke, *Reformation and Revolt in the Low Countries* (London and Ronceverte, PA: Hambledon Press, 1990), p. 71; W. Monter, 'Heresy Executions in Reformation Europe, 1520–1565', in O. Grell and B. Scribner (eds), *Tolerance and Intolerance in the European Reformation* (Cambridge: Cambridge University Press, 1996), pp. 48–64.

14 S. Marshall Wyntjes, 'Women and Religious Choices in the Sixteenth Century Netherlands', *Archiv für Reformationsgeschichte* 75 (1984), pp. 276–89.

15 S. Marshall Wyntjes, 'Family Allegiance and Religious Persuasion: The Lesser Nobility and the Revolt of the Netherlands', *Sixteenth Century Journal* 12 (1981), pp. 43–60.

16 H. F. K. van Nierop, 'A Beggars' Banquet: The Compromise of the Nobility and the Politics of Inversion', *European History Quarterly* 21 (1991), pp. 419–43.

17 E. Poullet and C. Piot (eds), *Correspondance du cardinal de Granvelle (1565–1586)* (12 vols, Brussels, 1877–96), vol. I, p. 269.

18 Ibid., vol. I, p. 11.

19 Ibid., vol. I, pp. 207, 240.

20 H. de Schepper, 'De mentale rekonversie van de Zuidnederlandse hoge adel na de Pacificatie van Gent', *Tijdschrift voor geschiedenis* 89 (3), (1976), pp. 420–8. *See also* H. F. K. van Nierop,'Willem van Oranje als hoog edelman: patronage in de Habsburgse Nederlanden?', *Bijdragen en mededelingen betreffende de geschiedenis der Nederlanden* 99 (4), (1984), pp. 651–76.

4 Religion and the revolt

Andrew Pettegree

The outbreak of the Dutch Revolt in 1566 was for those who lived through it an astonishing and awe-inspiring event. For a few brief months in the summer of this year political authority seemed to have dissolved. The provinces of Flanders and Brabant were among the most prosperous and populous regions of Europe, but they now witnessed a rush of organised dissent of a type unprecedented in the Netherlands. First, there was the so-called hedge-preaching, where thousands gathered in orderly and disciplined crowds in the open air to sing and listen to sermons. Then, in a savage and appalling contrast, these same sober congregations turned in fury on their Catholic churches, which were swiftly and ruthlessly desecrated. In the space of a few weeks some of the richest churches in Europe were stripped of the art work and ornamentation accumulated over centuries of pious giving.

Contemporaries were aware that they had witnessed something truly astonishing. 'We have had this night past a marvellous stir', wrote the English financial agent, Richard Clough, from Antwerp in 21 August; 'all the churches, chapels and houses of religion utterly defaced, and no kind of thing left whole within them, but broken and utterly destroyed'.[1] And what was most truly astonishing was the total absence of any attempt by the authorities to prevent the destruction. It was as if government was afflicted by a sudden but totally debilitating paralysis: so much so that even in places where the numbers of active church-breakers were small they went about their work totally undisturbed.

Viewed from a historical perspective the unfolding of these events was puzzling for two reasons: first, because the state apparatus in the Netherlands was both advanced and well organised; there certainly existed instruments of government that might have protected the churches. Second, this was a regime which had set its face more determinedly against the spread of heresy than any other in Europe. From the beginnings of Luther's movement the spread of Protestantism in the

Netherlands had been resisted with every weapon at the state's disposal, and with considerable success: executions for heresy had begun in the Netherlands in the 1520s, and continued up until almost the eve of the outbreak of the revolt. To understand why it then was that this retarded and persecuted Reformation movement was able to erupt with such force and fury in 1566 requires some explanation; and for this one must look back some forty years to the very beginnings of Dutch Protestantism.

It is now recognised that there were considerable obstacles to the successful exportation of Luther's movement out of his native Germany.[2] But in fact Luther's initial call for reform found a strong resonance in the provinces of the Low Countries. Like Germany, this was a highly urbanised region, with proud and prosperous urban communities eager to sponsor a renovation of religious life. Their articulate, highly literate populations received with approval the printed literature of the Reformation, both local editions of Luther's own writings (quickly translated into Dutch in quantities not equalled in any other European language) and the Bible in their own language. Between 1520 and 1540 there were some eighty editions of Luther's works published in Dutch in the Netherlands (the comparative figure for England is three). But for many the greatest impact of the new religious climate would have been seen in the proliferation of new editions of the vernacular Bible: a total of over sixty New Testaments and complete Bibles in the equivalent period, many of them lavishly illustrated.[3] There was also much to criticise in the local church, including a governmental structure not altered since the high Middle Ages, and woefully inadequate to meet the needs of a population which had grown rapidly since those days. For the whole seventeen provinces, with a population of over two million, there were only four bishops. So those who raised their voices in support of Luther's calls for reform found a ready response. By the mid-1520s Erasmus and other local commentators were reporting a flight from the monasteries, and the growth of a real popular following for those who styled themselves Lutheran or evangelical.

Left to itself, there is little doubt that this groundswell of support, particularly among the educated and opinion-formers in the towns, might have made of the Netherlands a second stronghold of the Reformation movement. But the Netherlands was not Germany: in particular the Dutch towns were not free to follow their own independent political course. Specifically, the ruler of the Dutch provinces, the very same Charles V who had laboured so unsuccessfully to thwart Luther in the empire, was determined not to see his own Dutch patrimony fall victim to the German heresies. Almost from the beginning, in fact even before Luther was formally condemned in the empire, Charles began to marshal the agencies of repression against the new beliefs. A decree of 1520 forbade the publication, sale or dissemination on any unauthorised religious works. By 1529 infringement of the proclamations (placards) on matters of religion was made punishable by death. In 1523 Charles underlined the seriousness of his purpose by ordering the execution of two prominent supporters of the evangelical doctrines. These were the first executions of Luther's supporters anywhere in Europe, and initiated a campaign of repression unrivalled for its sustained ferocity: in the next forty years 1200 men and women would be put to death in the Netherlands for their religious beliefs, and many more forced into exile.[4]

This persecution served its purpose. By 1530 the leadership of the first generation of Netherlands evangelism had been effectively destroyed, most of its leading figures having been forced either to recant their views or take flight to Germany. The rise of Anabaptism in the following decade (which at its height, at the time of the Anabaptist kingdom of Münster, found many adherents in the Netherlands) only seemed in retrospect to have completed the social exclusion and marginalisation of Dutch Protestantism. The discovery of small evangelical cells in several cities in the 1540s led to a new wave of executions and exile. At the time of Charles V's abdication in 1555, he could justly pride himself that he had preserved his northern kingdom for Catholicism, albeit at a considerable human cost.

But as events would prove, Dutch evangelism was not completely dead. The repressive measures undertaken by Charles may have retarded its development by a full generation, but the social conditions which had encouraged the first growth of Lutheranism were not fundamentally changed. In particular there had been no renovation of the Netherlandish church which might have equipped it to repulse a new movement of reform.[5]

In the middle years of the sixteenth century events conspired to make such an outcome possible. In effect, this change came about by a largely fortuitous coincidence of three developments: the growing influence of the new force of Calvinism in northern Europe; the accession of Elizabeth in England; and the outbreak of religious warfare in France.

Dutch Calvinism, ironically, was very largely a creation of the ruthless repression of Charles V's later years. Among those forced to flee abroad as a result of the persecutions of the 1540s were a number of educated men who had professed little more than a mild evangelism. Left to themselves they would probably have been little threat; but once settled abroad they had little choice but to band together with more determined opponents of the regime who now huddled together in small refugee communities. These exile churches soon fell into the intellectual orbit of Calvin and his new church at Geneva. Calvin, it should be recalled, had started his career as a minister to such a refugee congregation (at Strasbourg) and his Genevan church order offered a clear and appropriate model of church organisation for such groups. Calvinism, with its strong sense of discipline and providential destiny, proved an ideal creed for groups existing in hazardous and difficult conditions. Within a few years the local authorities in the Netherlands found themselves faced with an embryonic Calvinist church in their own territories, small secret communities which were sustained and abetted by the exile congregations.[6]

All of this might have come to very little but for the marked shift in the geopolitical balance of northern Europe which followed the accession of Elizabeth I to the throne of England in November 1558. The death of the devout and unswervingly Catholic Mary meant that Philip II lost far more than a wife. With Mary's death England was transformed from a reliable Catholic client into a major irritant and, increasingly, a hostile adversary.[7] One of the first intimations of the new cold climate in Anglo-Spanish relations was the easy welcome afforded by the Elizabethan regime to religious refugees from the Low Countries. Not only were they permitted to settle in England, they were also allowed to re-establish the foreign churches in London (which Mary had closed), and a number of new satellite churches in Norfolk, Essex and Kent, principally at Norwich, Colchester, Sandwich and Canterbury. These became convenient bases for increasingly violent raids upon their homeland. Repeated representations on the part of successive Spanish ambassadors failed to persuade Elizabeth's ministers to restrict the exiles' freedom of movement, and the issue became a major cause of the final rupture between the two countries. For the exiles, the safe haven in England was a vital base of operations in the half-decade before the outbreak of the revolt.

This was troublesome enough, but a difficult strategic situation rapidly became yet more treacherous with the outbreak of the French Wars of Religion. In the years after 1559 the French monarchy was going through its own crisis of authority. Following the death of Henry II in a freak jousting accident, the authority of his young sons Francis II and Charles IX (who succeeded his brother in 1560 at the age of nine) came under sustained attack. As in the Netherlands, the issue was partly constitutional – who should take the lead in government in the absence of a mature adult king – but antipathies among the leading counsellors were dramatically sharpened by differences over policy towards Protestant heresy.

After 1559 French Calvinism embarked on a period of buoyant and apparently uncontrollable growth. Fuelled by a sense of the vacuum at the centre of political power, and directly encouraged by the leadership of the French Calvinist movement in Geneva, the new religious movement was making converts at a remarkable rate. By 1561 there were over 1000 separate churches in France, and in some towns (always the centre of the movement) the new church had won the support of over 25 per cent of the population.[8] The following year, 1562, the strains of containing the mounting antagonisms between the religious confessions proved too much, and France toppled into civil war.

In terms of scale, Netherlandish Calvinism was at this stage no more than a pale shadow of its French counterpart. As against 1000 or more churches at the beginning of the 1560s, there were scarcely more than a handful in the Low Countries, and of these only the important Antwerp church seems to have enjoyed a near continuous existence. Other urban congregations in places like Bruges and Ghent, and in the Walloon (French-speaking) provinces at Valenciennes and Lille, scattered and re-formed as opportunity arose or persecution dictated. Dutch evangelicals could still only wonder at the freedoms enjoyed by their French counterparts.

Nevertheless, the turbulence in France had a profound impact in the Netherlands for several reasons. In the sixteenth century all borders were much more porous and open than they would subsequently become in the modern era. The concept of a border as a clearly demarcated line is essentially an invention of the eighteenth century: before that it was more often an ill-defined zone, in which political authority was often uncertain or contested. This was particularly so of France's northern border with the provinces of the Netherlands, because this lowland area possessed no geographical feature to define or divide, in a region which in any case shared a common language. In consequence there was little to restrict the free movement of people, goods or ideas. The eruptions in France thus inevitably caused reverberations in the provinces in the Netherlands, particularly in the Walloon provinces which were directly adjacent to the French domain. Here Calvin's works could be read in their French original, and the government in Brussels could do little to prevent the circulation of huge quantities of such illicit literature. But the growth of French Calvinism also had a profound impact on the nascent congregations in the Dutch-speaking areas. The leaders of Dutch Calvinism followed with close attention the stages in the growth of a national church in France. In 1561 one of their ministers, Guido de Brès, presented a draft of a national Confession of Faith, based wholly on the recently published

French confession. Shortly thereafter the Netherlandish churches began to create a structure of church government, again based on the model of the French national synods.

Most of all the apparently providential success of the French churches gave evangelicals in the Netherlands courage: courage to show the same defiance to official persecution that had brought such dividends in the French kingdom. One of the most remarkable features of Calvinism in these years was its irrepressible self-confidence, often in defiance of any realistic expectations of success. And why not? In this period of almost unbelievable progress for Calvinism in northern Europe, when a tiny group of enthusiasts had converted Scotland to a Calvinist nation, and when God had obligingly carried off persecuting monarchs in both France and England, why should Netherlandish Calvinists not hope for a similar providential deliverance? In the years following the outbreak of fighting in France, Dutch Calvinists therefore began to imitate the provocative and confrontational behaviour that had brought French evangelicals such success. For the first time Dutch Calvinists shrugged off the secrecy which had previously clothed their activities, and staged defiant open services; sometimes, to make the provocation more extreme, they preached in the churchyards of Catholic churches. In 1562, in a further ominous development, for the first time the minister preaching at one such service was protected by armed guards.[9] When these dangerous activities resulted in the arrest of participants, evangelicals on occasions staged raids to free their condemned colleagues from prison.

Faced with this increased evidence of religious anarchy the authorities in the Netherlands could not but be concerned. But the rebirth of domestic heresy was not only a problem of order for the Dutch political classes: it also represented something of an opportunity. For the last, and by no means the most insignificant, impact of French events in the Netherlands was that it also gave the Dutch nobility an example of how political crisis could be turned to their own advantage. In this respect some close attention to these parallel French events is instructive.

Until the death of Henry II in 1559, Calvinism had made only limited progress in securing the support of members of France's leading noble families. Some members of the clans of Montmorency and the princely house of Navarre/Condé had shown some interest, and a few among their womenfolk a more definite commitment, but there was as yet little to suggest that Calvin's energetic pursuit of the leading grandees would bring tangible rewards. The bedrock of support for evangelism remained, as it had been since the first generation of reform, in the towns. This changed very rapidly with Henry's death. The attempt by the Guise family to monopolise power during the brief reign of their nephew, the young Francis II, brought a realignment of power loyalties which for the first time embraced the growing religious divisions. Specifically, those who wished to challenge the Guise hegemony saw increasing merit in opposing their policy of uncompromising opposition to religious dissent. By doing so they could not only advance their own claims to influence; they could also tap the growing strength of the Calvinist communities and thereby create a new network of allegiance to challenge the power which accrued to the Guise by their monopoly of patronage.

In the years after 1559 first Anthony of Navarre and then, with greater conviction, his brother Henry of Condé, became increasingly identified as champions of the new religion. Their example was soon followed by large numbers among the lesser nobility, many of whom contemplated an uncertain and impecunious future since the ending of the Franco-Habsburg war in 1559 had taken away their livelihoods. The religious controversies thus became a vehicle for wider social and political discontents. By the time that war broke out in 1562, it is estimated that as many as half of France's nobles had defected to the new faith.

There are striking parallels with the situation in the Netherlands in the years before the outbreak of the Dutch Revolt. Here too one can discern a discontented and alienated nobility, consumed with the issue of their own apparent exclusion from power, and anxious to find a means to demonstrate to the government, led by Margaret of Parma, regent for the absent Philip II, their own indispensability. They were bound to be influenced by the conduct of the French nobility, to whom in many cases they were linked by ties of kinship and marriage. In the course of the years after 1562 noble leaders of Netherlandish society, both within and outside the Council of State, began to associate themselves with calls for a relaxation of the laws against heresy.

One must not, however, assume that the motives of the nobles who took up the call for reform were entirely cynical. As governors of the various towns and provinces of the Low Countries, the Netherlands grandees had direct responsibility for the maintenance of public order, and could not but be alarmed at the evidence of an growing climate of disaffection. By 1563 and 1564, there was clear evidence of a crisis at hand in the management of heresy in the Netherlands. Emboldened by open insurrection in France, Dutch Calvinist communities were increasingly willing to force the issue by provocative gestures. There was a steady growth in reported attacks on the objects of Catholic veneration and even incidents of public preaching.

Most ominously, it was clear that the urban authorities, which inevitably bore the major burdens in the struggle against religious dissidence, had lost the stomach for salutary justice. In 1564 the Antwerp authorities attempted to put to death by burning a Calvinist minister who had fallen into their hands. The crowd gathered to witness the execution rioted in support of the condemned man, and an attempt to rescue him from the stake (and lynch the executioner) was only barely averted. Such a challenge to authority would have shaken the will of any urban government in the sixteenth century, for in an age before standing police forces any law required the implicit consent of the governed for the social values which underpinned justice.[10] In the case of execution of respectable fellow citizens for differences on matters of conscience, this was manifestly no longer present. Hereafter the Antwerp authorities simply chose not to notice the evidence of the growing evangelical congregations in their midst. Elsewhere in the most populous parts of the Netherlands it was a similar story. Most Holland towns had abandoned executions for heresy (often after similar incidents) as early as 1559, and by 1563 the three major towns of Flanders had embarked on legal action to prevent the provincial inquisitor, the industrious Titelmans, from operating within their jurisdiction.

So there was considerable justification for the claim made by the grandees on the Netherlands Council of State that the present policy against heresy could not be sustained. In 1564 the leading nobles dispatched the greatest of their number, Count Egmont, to Spain to make the point to Philip II in person. Egmont was received with fair words, and on his return to the Netherlands he gave an encouraging account of his negotiations. So when, in November 1565, Philip made clear that his views had not been changed, and ordered that the heresy laws should continue to be enforced in all their severity, the leading Netherlandish nobles could justly feel that they had been betrayed.[11] They took their revenge by ostentatiously withdrawing their support from the embattled regime of Margaret of Parma; there was even, in the case of one of their number, William, prince of Orange, discreet contact with the growing number of the lesser nobility who had now associated themselves with the call for reform. It was these allies in the lesser nobility who now took up the initiative, gathering together a petition demanding an end to persecution; but the signal given by the grandees when they formally withdrew from the Council of State in January 1566 was also crucial. When in April 1566 the noble Confederates defied the regent's authority by appearing armed in her presence to present their demands, her powerlessness to resist was obvious.

Thus politics certainly played its part in the collapse of authority which usehred in the first Dutch Revolt in 1566. Against this, nothing but the religious fervour that had been gradually building during these years of political persecution explains the *intensity* of the reaction to these events in 1566. The scale of the demonstrations of support for change clearly took both the regent and her noble opponents by surprise; the noble conspirators quickly discovered that they had called into existence a force that it was beyond their power to control. In this respect the events of 1566 were crucial to the future evolution of Dutch Calvinism. At an early stage, and in crucial contrast to the movement in France, the Dutch Calvinist communities emancipated themselves from reliance on their noble patrons.

When, in May 1566, and under the severest duress, Margaret of Parma ordered a temporary suspension of the heresy laws, this was widely interpreted, both in the Netherlands and elsewhere, as ushering in a permanent change in policy. Dutch Calvinists in exile hurried back to their homeland to take advantage of the new freedoms. Existing congregations began to meet with greater openness and others were swiftly formed. The summer of the hedge-preaching seemed a glorious celebration of the new freedoms: part religious service, part demonstration against a regime whose authority was swiftly ebbing away. Then in August came the iconoclasm. To contemporaries the apparently wanton destruction of church property was an enormous shock. For many of the Calvinists' allies in the nobility this was the final encouragement to abandon an alliance in which many of them had been frankly uneasy, and had now led to such dreadful consequences.

The iconoclasm was a traumatic and shocking event, but viewed in its contemporary context should not have been entirely unexpected. Throughout the Reformation century, occasions where Protestants seized the reins of power against the wishes of the local authorities tended to be accompanied by episodes of this nature. Numerous examples could be cited from Germany and Switzerland in the first generation of reform, such as the famous 'Bilderstreit' that established Protestant dominance in Basle in 1528, or even the violence and destruction in Wittenberg orchestrated by Karlstadt in Luther's absence at Christmas 1521. Equally, during the recently unfolding events in France, the Huguenot advance had been accompanied by widespread desecration of churches.[12] Iconoclasm might take different forms, and serve subtly different purposes. In the first generation it had frequently been orchestrated as a polemical means of making a theological point: demonstrating the powerlessness of previously revered sacred objects as they were cast down and humiliated.[13] In the cities of France it also undoubtedly served to force the hand of town governments reluctant to act to authorise reformed worship without higher authority. This seems to have been the primary motive in the Netherlands, though examples of desecration rituals could also be cited.[14]

In the short term the violence certainly achieved its objectives. In the days and weeks following the iconoclasm a badly shaken government conceded all the churches at this point desired: a new decree of September granted freedom of worship in places where Protestant congregations already in practice existed. In a series of local settlements with respective town councils and governors this was translated into permission to occupy suitable places of worship, or, where this would have proved too provocative (as in Antwerp), to erect their own church buildings. The exultant congregations set about their work with a will, gathering funds for their new churches and erecting the structures of congregational government which were the hallmark of a full Calvinist system. Each church now elected elders to assist the ministers in the government of the community and the maintenance of congregational discipline. Deacons were appointed to supervise the provision of poor relief. By Christmas most cities in the Netherlands had a fully organised Calvinist church, and in cities such as Ghent and Antwerp the newly erected church buildings added a new and distinctive profile to the city skyline.[15] The speed with which these churches were thrown up was an ostentatious demonstration that those who adhered to the new congregations included many from among the cities' financial elites.

But even as the Calvinists celebrated their good fortune, the political tide was beginning to turn against them. In retrospect it appears that the iconoclasm, while achieving the immediate objectives of forcing the regent's hand, had dealt a fatal blow to the loose opposition coalition which bound together the reformed and their allies in the nobility. Many among the uncommitted had been appalled by the destructive force that accompanied the assault on the churches. To the nobility it was a powerful signal that the forces that they had unleashed posed a real threat to the established political order. So the regent, struggling to re-establish her authority in the autumn of 1566, found some surprising friends among former critics of the regime. By the end of the year she was ready to take the offensive, and the Calvinists were faced with the difficult choice of capitulation or outright military defiance; if they chose the latter, they would remove any last shred of credibility from their claim to be loyal subjects of the king. In the event the Calvinist leadership fell uncomfortably between the two. In December 1566 Tournai, the most recalcitrant of the Walloon towns, was forced to open its gates to the regent's troops. The following March Valenciennes surrendered and a motley force of irregulars raised by the Calvinist congregations was put to flight outside Antwerp, while members of the city's church watched impotently from the walls. With that, resistance was effectively ended, and in the spring of 1567 most who had

tplace.

ch Revolt [Paperback] [2001] Darby, Mr Graham;

mall business.

de feedback for the seller please visit
to Your Orders in Your Account. Click the seller's
ler Information" section, click "Contact the Seller".

Order ID: 026-3450685-6556360

Thank you for buying from spindlewood on Amaz◄

Quantity	Product Details
1	**The Origins and Development of th◄** **Darby, Graham** **SKU:** GG-M59M-GTE2 **ASIN:** 0415253799 **Listing ID:** 1101O47QJMQ **Order Item ID:** 46642028870499 **Condition:** Used - Good **Comments:** Dispatched promptly from rel◄

compromised themselves through membership of the churches took flight.

The collapse of the revolt in 1567 and the subsequent retribution was obviously a dark hour for those who had greeted the events of the 'Wonderyear' with such optimism. Notwithstanding Margaret of Parma's eventual success in restoring order, Philip in Spain lost no time in dispatching his most feared general the duke of Alva to stamp out the last embers of opposition. His arrival in Brussels in August 1567 was swiftly followed by the establishment of the notorious Council of Troubles. In a four-year period the Council of Troubles condemned over 10,000 to death, concentrating especially on those known to have been involved in the iconoclasm, or those who had held office in the churches as elders or deacons. Although former leaders of the congregations writing from exile now tried to distance themselves from responsibility for the church-breaking, blaming the fickle crowds or (more implausibly still) Catholic priests, the tribunals had a very clear sense of where responsibility lay.[16]

Yet for Dutch Calvinism these were not altogether years of darkness and despair. The moment of religious freedom during the Wonderyear may have been fleeting but it had achieved a great deal of real importance for the future. The fact that of the 10,000 who received the death sentence from the Council of Troubles, 90 per cent were tried *in absentia*, tells its own story: those who were most implicated in the events of 1566 had succeeded in taking themselves off to safety abroad. Most importantly, the brief period of optimism in the summer and autumn of 1566 had caused many who had previously held aloof to join the churches, and these were now compromised beyond return. In the face of Alva's relentless pursuit, they had little choice but to join the exiles, most settling in England or Germany where they brought new vitality to the exile churches.

The huge growth in the numbers adhering to the exile churches in this period was a demonstration of a further critical consequence of the Wonderyear. For it became manifest that even at the cost of apparent defeat the Dutch Calvinist church had emerged as the dominant force among the competing evangelical groups in the Netherlands. Before this a certain diversity among Protestant opponents of the regime had been an inevitable legacy of the generation of persecution. It is quite possible that in simple numerical terms before 1566 Calvinists might have been outnumbered by Mennonites and other Anabaptist groups, particularly in Holland and the north where the Calvinist presence had been negligible. In Antwerp, both groups competed with a substantial Lutheran community, which drew strength from its connections with

Germany. The Wonderyear brought this competition to an end. The clear supremacy manifested by Calvinism during this year, both in terms of its internal organisation and its prominence in the opposition, ensured that henceforth it would play overwhelmingly the dominant role in religious opposition to the regime.

In the enforced period of exile after 1567 Dutch Calvinists set about consolidating this advantage. The speed of events during the Wonderyear had led inevitably to a degree of variation in the practice among the new churches that had sprung up in the Netherlands. The interval of the exile allowed the churches to review this experience and establish the total harmony of church order and liturgical practice to which they aspired. This was achieved at the synod of Emden in 1571, a milestone event for Dutch Calvinism conducted with a spirit of purpose and with a sense of measure not always evident in such gatherings. As well as confirming a common statement of beliefs and church order, the synod also established the putative organisation of the Dutch church, ranging the individual congregations into colloquies and local synods. This organisation structure encompassed both the exile churches and churches back in the Netherlands temporarily in suspension. Given that in 1571 there was no real reason to expect that the opportunity would ever arise to re-establish these churches, the synod's decisions give a valuable insight into the sort of unquenchable optimism that might result from the Calvinist sense of providential destiny.

The synod of Emden was also important for what it revealed of the Calvinist church's relationship with the erstwhile political opposition. In the years following the collapse of the first revolt, Calvinist exiles would forge a new and ultimately decisive alliance with the leading figure among the opposition grandees, William of Orange. This relationship was not without its difficulties. In the immediate aftermath of the Wonderyear, the Calvinist leadership had reason to treat William with great suspicion. His vacillating conduct during the rebellion was not forgotten; in particular they found it difficult to forgive his decision, as governor of Antwerp, to do nothing to prevent the slaughter of the Calvinist forces at Oosterweel. When in 1568 William declared war upon Alva to recover his confiscated lands and offices, the Calvinist churches did little to assist him. The calamitous failure of this expedition taught William that unless he sank his own cause into that of the religious struggle his prospects were hopeless. The year 1569 saw William and his brother in open negotiation with the French Huguenot leadership, and it was at the head of a new expeditionary force sponsored by the French that William would return to the Netherlands in 1572.

Even so, this was an association in which the churches would function as an equal, if not senior, partner. The synod of Emden ostentatiously refused to adopt William's political objectives as a formal part of their protocols, despite his clearly expressed wishes. It was a highly significant gesture. Henceforth the balance of power within the rebel association would always favour the goals of the congregations, rather than William's vision of an open, essentially nationalistic conflict against Spanish rule. Dutch Calvinism had successfully resisted long-term subjugation to the interests of their partners in the nobility which had so decisively shaped French Calvinism: and arguably very much to its disadvantage.

Thus it was that when, in the spring of 1572, the chance seizure of two port towns of Brill and Vlissingen unexpectedly reignited the revolt in Holland, the Calvinist congregations quickly made themselves indispensable to the conduct of the war. In the months and years that followed the renewal of the fighting the exile churches played a vital role as providers of men, munitions and financial support for the military effort. This was a contribution that became all the more important following the swift collapse of William of Orange's ill-supported campaign in the south. William had little choice but to make Holland the new centre of his operations during a period in which he too revealed unknown depths of resilience and determination, as the Spanish armies under their new governor Requesens bent every effort towards the rebels' final subjugation. But in a series of epic sieges the rebels held out. The Dutch Revolt, and with it the Dutch Calvinist church, was saved.

The churches extracted a high price for their renewed commitment to the rebel cause. In the Holland towns that joined the rebellion in the summer of 1572 the Calvinist congregations lost little time in appropriating the principal churches for their worship. Where the municipal authorities proved slow to respond, they again used the time-honoured tactic of iconoclasm to secure their demands.[17] Thus far William was prepared to accommodate his allies, but he balked at their next demand, that the Calvinist faith be the *only* form of worship permitted in the liberated towns. This demand completely cut across William's goal of an inclusive, tolerant autonomous state free of Spanish troops. But in the heated atmosphere of a desperate struggle for survival William had little choice but to give his allies what they demanded. In December 1573 William recognised the inevitable and finally joined the Calvinist church. The following year he did not intervene when the States of Holland formally banned the Catholic mass.

These events set the tone for a period of Calvinist triumphalism which may, ultimately, have done the cause of the revolt as much harm as good. In 1576 Spanish forces suffered their most serious reverse in the entire conflict. Exhausted, unpaid and driven beyond endurance by the apparently endless siege warfare, Spanish troops staged a spectacular mutiny. Descending on Antwerp they took what they felt was their due in three days of looting and mayhem known to history as 'the Spanish fury'. The sack of Antwerp was a traumatic and decisive event, and one that would live in the Dutch consciousness as vividly as the St Bartholomew's Day massacre in the French. Appalled, the previously loyal provinces of the south now rapidly concluded negotiations and made common cause with Holland and Zeeland to rid themselves of the plague of Spanish troops. This agreement, the Pacification of Ghent, fleetingly held out the prospect of a free Netherlandish state encompassing the whole seventeen provinces, with William of Orange as its respected elder statesman.

This vision was as short-lived as it was appealing. Rivalries among the nobility and a new spirit of conciliation on the part of the Spanish administration soon eroded the apparent solidarity between the provinces. But the heaviest blows to hopes of an all-embracing free state were dealt by William's most stalwart allies, the Reformed themselves. Forbidden by the terms of the Pacification of Ghent to disturb the religious peace of the southern provinces, the Calvinists nevertheless pressed eagerly for the renewal of public worship in former urban strongholds such as Ghent and Antwerp. In 1578 they went further, staging a civic coup which overthrew the town government in both cities, and established a new radical Calvinist regime.

For many of the conservative nobility this was the last straw. By the Treaty of Arras in May 1579 the Walloon provinces of the south formally reaffirmed their allegiance to Spanish rule, and readmitted foreign troops. Earlier the northern provinces had responded to the Union of Arras (6 January 1579) with their own treaty, the Union of Utrecht (23 January 1579), and the battle-lines were drawn. From this point on the borders between an independent northern state and a loyal Spanish satellite in the south would be determined by military action.

For Dutch Calvinism it was a matter of great regret that this new northern state would not encompass the major cities of Flanders and Brabant in which the church had first been successfully incubated. One by one the cities of the southern plains fell to the remorselessly advancing armies of the duke of Parma: Brussels in 1583, Ghent in 1584, and Antwerp, the jewel in the Calvinist crown, in 1585. It was physical geography, rather than any innate proclivity, which would make Holland the centre of the new Calvinist republic. By the time that the borders were becoming settled in the 1590s, churches in Holland had enjoyed almost thirty years of uninterrupted existence: sufficient time to put down real roots. The closure of the major southern churches would also bring a new accession of manpower and strength, as Flemish and Walloon Calvinists who had no wish to remain in a re-Catholicised south resigned themselves to a new exile: in this instance mostly in the free north, rather than the exile churches of England and Germany.

It was now, as the threat of reconquest gradually receded, and the northern provinces progressed tentatively towards an independent nationhood, that the distinctive character of Dutch Calvinism began to be fully manifest. Its role in the struggle for freedom had ensured the church a central place in the life of the new state. In towns across the nation, the Reformed congregations now possessed the most prominent (in the case of smaller communities, the only) churches, now appropriately 'cleansed' and reordered in the austere Dutch manner familiar from countless paintings of the Dutch Golden Age. The churches' ministers enjoyed regular and reasonably generous salaries, paid by the state and guaranteed on the incomes of former church lands. Their services were usually well attended, at least in the major centres of population.

And yet, as the years rolled by, many among the Reformed *dominees* could not suppress the ungrateful thought that things might have been so much better. Prominent though their place was in the life of the new nation, there were many among their flocks who proved stubbornly resistant to the full implementation of the ministers' visions of a fully Reformed society. Although a large proportion of the population frequented their services, only a relatively small number became full members of the church, placing themselves under its discipline and attesting their faith through an examination of doctrine. Most painfully of all, in crucial areas where the ministers hoped to establish their influence, the town magistrates frequently withheld their cooperation. Poor relief and schooling, for instance, in a full Reformed system such as that operating in Geneva, very much the province of the church, remained firmly under magisterial control. Nor did the magistrates always live up to the ministers' demanding expectations in their pursuit of drunkenness, immorality or recreation culture, particularly those pastimes disapproved of by the godly, but much beloved of the city elites, such as dancing and the theatre.[18] And while other competing churches were never fully authorised, the magistrates did little to prevent the numerous dissenting groups, notably the Mennonites, from gathering for worship. As the threat from Spain diminished even Catholics (a surprisingly numerous residue, especially in the conquered Generality lands of North Brabant) were permitted to gather together virtually unhindered.[19]

The ministers had not expected that the magistrates would prove such uncooperative partners in the building of a godly society, and on occasions frustration would spill over into bitter recrimination. But from the point of view of the magistrate, their position was understandable enough. Having embarked on a long and bitter struggle to free themselves from one form of Inquisition and intolerance, the magistrates had little intention of subjecting themselves voluntarily to another.[20] And so the ministers were left to thunder their imprecations and warnings of retribution to appreciative, but not always dutiful, congregations.

In this respect the seventeenth-century Dutch Republic would inherit what the Dutch ministers themselves would have recognised as only a very incomplete Reformation. But for all that it was an achievement which posterity would acknowledge as remarkable. Whereas in France the initially much more numerous Huguenot congregations were by now reduced to a stubborn rump in a Catholic state, the Reformed church in the Netherlands would never lose its claim to a central part in the life and cultural identity of the Dutch Republic. This much had been assured by the Calvinist role in the first critical years of the revolt, the resistance to Alva, and the obdurate campaigns with William of Orange. By the convictions and sacrifices of this first generation, Calvinism was firmly embedded in the foundations of the free Dutch state.

Notes

1 Clough to Richard Gresham, printed in J. M. B. C. Kervyn de Lettenhove, *Relations politiques des Pays-Bas et de l'Angleterre sous le règne de Philippe II* (10 vols., Brussels, 1882–1900), vol. 4, pp. 337–8.

2 See the essays collected in Andrew Pettegree (ed.), *The Early Reformation in Europe* (Cambridge: Cambridge University Press, 1992), and more recently Pettegree, *The Reformation World* (London: Routledge, 2000).

3 Bart Rosier, *The Bible in Print. Netherlandish Bible Illustrations in the Sixteenth Century* (2 vols., Leiden, 1997). For evangelical printing in general, Andrew Johnston, 'Printing and the Reformation in the Low Countries', in Jean-François Gilmont (ed.), *The Reformation and the Book* (Aldershot, 1998), pp. 154–83.

4 Alastair Duke, 'Building Hell in Heaven's Despite: the early history of the Reformation in the Towns of the Low Countries', in his *Reformation and Revolt in the Low Countries* (London: Hambledon Press, 1990), pp. 71–100. Comparative figures for other parts of Europe are collected in William Monter, 'Heresy Executions in Reformation Europe', in Ole Peter Grell and Bob Scribner (eds), *Tolerance and Intolerance in the European Reformation* (Cambridge: Cambridge University Press, 1996), pp. 48–64.

5 Ironically, Philip II's attempt to address this deficiency, with his plan to erect a large number of new bishoprics, became a critical element of his growing alienation from the Netherlandish nobility.

6 For a case study, Guido Marnef, *Antwerp in the Age of Reformation* (Baltimore: Johns Hopkins University Press, 1996).

7 Just how hostile is only now becoming apparent from newly published research. See Steven Alford, *The Early Elizabethan Polity. William Cecil and the British Succession Crisis, 1558–1569* (Cambridge: Cambridge University Press, 1998).

8 The best account of this phase in the growth of the French Calvinist movement is to be found in Nicola Sutherland, *The Huguenot Struggle for Recognition* (New Haven: Yale University Press, 1980). Estimates of the total size of the church at this stage can be found in Mark Greengrass, *The French Reformation* (Oxford: Oxford University Press, 1987), pp. 42–3; Mack Holt, *The French Wars of Religion* (Cambridge: Cambridge University Press, 1995), pp. 30–1.

9 Marcel Backhouse, 'The Official Start of Armed Resistance in the Low Countries: Boeschepe, 12 July 1562', *Archiv für Reformationsgeschichte*, 71 (1980), pp. 198–225.

10 David Nicholls, 'The Theatre of Martyrdom in the French Reformation', *Past and Present*, 121 (1988), pp. 49–73.

11 The text of Philip's notorious letter from the Segovia Woods is to be found in English translation together with many other texts in E. H. Kossman and A. F. Mellink, *Texts Concerning the Revolt of the Netherlands* (Cambridge: Cambridge University Press, 1974), pp. 53–6.

12 On France, Olivier Christin, *Une révolution symbolique. L'iconoclasme huguenot et la reconstruction catholique* (Paris, 1991).

13 Carlos Eire, *War against the Idols* (Cambridge: Cambridge University Press, 1986).

14 As, for instance, in Leiden. See my discussion of the iconoclasm in *Emden and the Dutch Revolt. Exile and the Development of Reformed Protestantism* (Oxford: Oxford University Press, 1992), ch. 5.

15 The sketch made by a curious citizen of Ghent of the new Calvinist church is reproduced in Alastair Duke, Gillian Lewis and Andrew Pettegree (eds), *Calvinism in Europe, 1540–1610. A Collection of Documents* (Manchester: Manchester University Press, 1992), p. 154.

16 An example of this spurious attempt to distance themselves from responsibility is provided by the extract from Philip Marnix, *True narrative and apology of what happened in the Netherlands in the year 1566* (1567), in Kossman and Mellink, *Texts Concerning the Revolt*, pp. 78–81.

17 Alastair Duke and Rosemary L. Jones, 'Towards a Reformed Polity in Holland, 1572–1578', in Duke, *Reformation and Revolt*, pp. 199–226.

18 I discuss these protracted disputes in my article, 'Coming to Terms with Victory: The Upbuilding of a Calvinist Church in Holland, 1572–1590', in Andrew Pettegree, Alastair Duke and Gillian Lewis (eds), *Calvinism in Europe, 1540–1620* (Cambridge, 1994), pp. 160–80.

19 The best description of the religious complexion of the new state is A. Th. Van Deursen, *Plain Lives in a Golden Age. Popular Culture, Religion and Society in Seventeenth-Century Holland* (Cambridge: Cambridge University Press, 1991).

20 For an acute discussion of the importance of fear of the Inquisition in the opposition to Spain, see Alastair Duke, 'Salvation by Coercion: The Controversy Surrounding the Inquisition in the Low Countries on the Eve of the Revolt', in his *Reformation and Revolt*, pp. 152–74.

5 The towns and the revolt

Guido Marnef

The sixteenth century was marked by princely centralisation. In most European countries, this process of state-building occurred at the expense of urban privileges. In the Netherlands, the process became intertwined with the emergence of the Protestant Reformation and with the outbreak of a revolt against the Spanish authorities. The cities were predestined to play a crucial role in this revolt. Along with northern Italy, the Netherlands represented the most urbanised region in Europe. In the 1560s the Florentine Lodovico Guicciardini wrote that the Low Countries counted no less than 208 enclosed or walled towns. In addition, there existed about 150 open places that could be considered as towns.[1]

Yet, it is important to see that not all Netherlandish provinces were equally urbanised. The three core regions, Flanders, Brabant and Holland, dominated demographically and economically. However, in the long run, the towns in these regions were remarkably different both in their demographic growth and their social evolution.

As we can see from Table 5.1, the Flemish cities – Bruges and Ghent – reached their demographic peak prior to cities in Brabant and Holland which in their turn experienced a rapid increase in population during the sixteenth century. Around 1500, the percentage of people living in towns in Flanders, Brabant and Holland was 33, 29, and 44 per cent respectively. Because of the strong economic expansion of Antwerp, the number of urban dwellers in Brabant had increased to 47 per cent by 1565. The revolt, however, would seriously disturb this process and cause substantial migration from the southern to the northern Netherlands, particularly to the towns in Holland. Yet no town in sixteenth-century Holland could ever claim a position as dominant as Antwerp, Ghent or Bruges before that time. The urban population in Holland was divided much more equally, with five towns counting over 10,000 inhabitants in 1500 and seventeen with more than 2500. However, the

Table 5.1 Demographic evolution of the cities of Flanders, Brabant and Holland, *c.* 1500–*c.* 1600[2]

	c. 1500	*c. 1560*	*c. 1600*
Ghent	40,000	45,000	30,000
Bruges	30,000	35,000	26,000
Antwerp	40,000	100,000	55,000
Brussels	30,000	40,000	45,000
Mechelen	20,000	30,000	12,000
Amsterdam	12,000	27,000	66,000
Haarlem	11,500	14,000	30,000
Leiden	14,000	14,000	26,000
Delft	10,500	14,000	17,500
Dordrecht	11,500	10,500	15,000

presence of this urban network would be of key importance later during the revolt.

The economic structure of the Netherlandish towns varied enormously, although in this area, too, Brabant, Flanders, Holland and Zeeland dominated. In general, the sixteenth century was a period of strong economic expansion culminating in the rise of Antwerp as the commercial metropolis of the west.[3] The absorption of the Netherlands into the Habsburg empire undoubtedly stimulated its integration into the world economy and led to considerable commercial expansion. This commercial expansion stimulated existing Antwerp industries and attracted new ones, such as those in luxury goods. But Antwerp's expansion created a dynamic that reached far beyond its city walls. Because of its function as a hub of the transit trade, the city attracted a great deal of economic activity from far and wide. In the second third of the sixteenth century, the Antwerp market stimulated the southern export industry in particular. Through Antwerp highly specialised and luxury items found their way to the international market.

From 1530–40 onwards, the economy of the northern Netherlands – particularly that of Holland and Zeeland – also profited from the Antwerp expansion.[4] This is true for the primary sector and trade, but not for traditional export industries, such as beer and cloth production, which suffered from southern competition. However, the Holland and Zeeland ports, already important in 1500, should not be seen as mere outports of Antwerp. Amsterdam, as well as Hoorn and Enkhuizen played an increasingly important role in the Baltic trade. When the merchants of Holland and Zeeland succeeded, thanks to their technical creativity in shipbuilding and navigation, in integrating the Baltic trade and their trade with France, Spain and Portugal into one system, they had created a trading network that would in time make an enormous contribution to the economic success of the later republic.[5] Although the northern Netherlandish economy undoubtedly had its own specific orientation,[6] it would be wrong to perceive the economies of the northern and southern Netherlands as two separate entities at this stage. The powerful influence of Antwerp's world market role prevented this from happening. Indeed, the urbanised and economically advanced regions of Flanders, Brabant, Holland and Zeeland had more in common with each other than with the recently incorporated north-eastern periphery or the agrarian Walloon provinces where the nobility and clergy still dominated. The north–south divide that occurred later would be difficult to identify in the middle of the sixteenth century. It is clear though that the southern regions dominated industry as well as commerce. The revenues of the central taxes make this plain: between 1540 and 1548, Flanders and Brabant contributed 63 per cent of the central taxes, whereas Holland and Zeeland only provided 17 per cent.[7]

Changes in social structure in the cities also reflected the strong economic growth of the first half of the sixteenth century. The triumph of commercial capitalism created unprecedented opportunities for a limited number of merchants and bankers. This was especially true for Antwerp, but in other cities and regions with export industries traders and entrepreneurs profited too. In addition, smaller traders, independent artisans, professionals and artists all benefited from this development. Taken together, they belonged to a relatively wealthy but heterogeneous middle class. Because of this heterogeneity, it is probably more correct to refer to them as 'middle classes'. More research is needed to investigate their size and nature, but we are certain that the situation differed considerably from city to city.

Despite the emergence of these middle groups, commercial capitalism was also responsible for social polarisation. The mere fact that a small number of the socio-economic elite accumulated the greater part of urban wealth is one indicator.[8] For most artisans and wage workers, the sixteenth century was anything but a Golden Age. Until the middle of the century, rising grain prices and house rents contrasted with lagging wages. Unfortunately, the level of employment is an unquantifiable factor. Generally speaking, the situation was most favourable in those cities where commercial expansion was the most pronounced. This was especially true for Antwerp. However, in cities with declining industries such as Ghent and Leiden a deterioration in the standard of living was obvious.[9]

Some authors have identified a causal connection between this economic development, the revolt and the Reformation. The Belgian historian Herman van der Wee developed an influential thesis attributing a central role to the emancipated middle classes.[10] In the long run, the economic growth of the sixteenth century allowed the development of an emancipated middle class which was more critical of the church and the establishment. In the short term, a number of crises threatened the prosperity of these middle classes. The Netherlandish–English conflict in 1563–4 hurt the finishing industry and the winter of 1564–5 was exceptionally severe. Furthermore, the closing of the Sont – the gateway to the Baltic world – endangered grain provisioning. Taken together, these factors created an anxiety among the middle classes. This psychological malaise induced mass conversions to Calvinism and stimulated participation in the troubles of the Wonderyear.

There is, however, little evidence to substantiate this short-term explanation. As Van der Wee himself admits, in 1565 the crisis had already passed its peak. If a threat to prosperity had been the crucial factor, the iconoclastic riots and the political resistance by the Calvinists from the summer of 1566 to the spring of 1567 should have taken place one year earlier. It is clear that it was the changed political situation and the ensuing power vacuum in 1566 that allowed for massive conversions to Protestantism. Furthermore, there is no evidence that the desire to improve material conditions was the principal motivation for these conversions.[11] Nevertheless, the urban middle classes played a crucial role during the Wonderyear. To explain this role, Van der Wee's long-term analysis is much more convincing. Indeed, economic growth created a context which stimulated the cultural emancipation of the middle classes. A well-established education system met a real demand among the trading people.[12] Reading and writing, arithmetic, basic accounting and foreign languages were increasingly taught in elementary schools managed by the laity. In some private schools, one could even take classes in Latin, a subject traditionally taught by the clergy. The high degree of literacy and the relatively widespread knowledge of foreign languages struck many foreigners visiting the Netherlands. Another remarkable feature was the explicit importance of girls' schooling. In 1576, Antwerp counted eighty-eight officially registered male and seventy female teachers. Obviously, the school expansion took place first in cities where trade and the export industry dominated. The effects were, however, noticeable in smaller towns too. In the Flemish West Quarter, a solid network of schools existed even in the smallest villages. In many cases, well-trained teachers taught Greek in addition to Latin.[13]

Because of this extensive educational provision, the Netherlands could boast a high, although quantitatively immeasurable degree of literacy compared to the rest of Europe. Increased purchasing power and a better education brought the products of the printing press within the reach of most members of the middle classes.[14] This allowed a greater familiarity with new ideas and a more critical attitude toward the established church and the prevailing customs and practices. The plays by the rhetoric chambers were clearly a reflection of the ideas prevalent among the middle classes. These chambers – rather like amateur theatre companies – were urban in nature and were especially popular in Flanders, Brabant and Holland. Religious issues were a popular topic for their plays. The chambers regularly criticised the traditional church and its classic channels of mediation and reaffirmed the importance of faith and the Bible as sources of salvation.[15]

This evidence unambiguously confirms the Van der Wee thesis of the importance of the long-term cultural emancipation of the urban middle classes. It is thus unsurprising that traditional religious practices faded away too. This can be evidenced by a decline in the number of devotional gifts made in churches in Antwerp, Ghent, Delft and Utrecht from the 1520s onwards.[16] A critical attitude towards the traditional church drove some to join a variety of Reformation movements, while others formed a growing religious middle ground.[17] When in the 1560s politics and religion became intertwined, the Calvinist movement paved the way for revolt. The events of the Wonderyear would demonstrate the crucial role played by the emancipated urban middle classes. This does not, however, mean that the roles of the urban elites and wage workers were unimportant; they also deserve attention in any analysis of the revolt.

At this point we must address another aspect of the important role played by the cities in the development of the revolt. The cities of the Habsburg Netherlands followed two traditions that historians have recently labelled the 'great tradition' and the 'little tradition' of revolt.[18] In the 'great tradition' whole cities were set against the policies of the central government while in the 'little tradition' broader sections of the urban population challenged the position of the urban elites. In this way the character of the revolt could differ from region to region. This development exerted the most force in the provinces where economically powerful cities already constituted an important political force, above all in Flanders. The great cities of Bruges, Ghent and Ypres played such a significant role in their territories that they could completely dominate the surrounding countryside and the small towns, rather like city-states. From the late fourteenth century the state-building of the dukes of Burgundy had clashed with the ambitions of these powerful and autonomous Flemish cities. The revolts of Bruges (1436–8) and

Ghent (1447–53) were, however, suppressed by Philip the Good. Nevertheless, the state-building process did not occur only for the benefit of the ruler. After the death of Charles the Bold in 1477 his daughter, Mary of Burgundy, was forced to grant the 'Great Privilege'. The concessions that were given in this constitutional document applied to the entire Burgundian Netherlands and reinforced the position of representative institutions. A century later, the rebels would refer more than once to the Privilege in their struggle against Spain. Moreover, the slow restoration of previously reduced privileges was reinforced through a series of revolts that broke out in a number of cities in Flanders, Brabant and the northern provinces during the first part of the sixteenth century.

The urban elites who rose in revolt against central authority did so in the name of the entire urban community, for the 'commonwealth'. The concerns of the urban oligarchy, however, were not in step with those of the broader population base, as is evident from the series of revolts associated with the so-called 'little tradition'. In the Flemish cities following the defeat of the French army at Kortrijk (1302), a reaction against the preponderance of French-speaking patriciates led to the guilds gaining an important place in city government. In Brabant and Holland guild members also strove for political and social recognition, but in those provinces the urban patriciate mostly succeeded in maintaining its monopoly of power until late in the fifteenth century. This historical evolution explains why the guilds in Flanders had, in general, a stronger position in town government than was the case in towns in other provinces.

Consequently, these two different strands of development – the 'great and little traditions' – determined in large measure the composition of city government and relations between the city and the central authority. In the first half of the sixteenth century the impact of the central state increased and at the same time an aristocratisation of town government occurred. The establishment of new central and provincial institutions and of an extensive standing army – primarily necessary for the many wars of Charles V – presented a real threat to the cities. The cities saw themselves constantly confronted with an ever-stronger central monarchy and, what is more, this central monarchy with its growing bureaucracy and army imposed a considerable and growing financial burden upon them.

Nevertheless, the cities did not always set themselves against the monarchy. Urban elites and the central government could, out of self-interest, work together to resist the demands of guild members and wage workers. However, increased fiscal pressure on the latter groups led to revolts in a number of cities, such as Deventer (1511), Utrecht (1511–12), Zierikzee (1514), Kampen (1519 and 1529), 's Hertogenbosch (1525), Brussels (1528 and 1532), and Ghent (1539–40). Rebellion erupted especially in cities where the guilds had acquired a significant place in city government and consequently were able to develop a forum where they could voice their displeasure. Charles V tried to reduce the political influence of the guilds. As a result of the punishments handed down after the rebellions, they usually lost their place on the city councils or were forbidden to attend the meetings of the 'Brede Raad' or Great Council. The most spectacular manifestation of this was probably the repression of the old dominant guilds in Ghent and Utrecht which lost their political influence entirely and became once again purely trade organisations. The building of a fortress or 'Spanish Castle' made it clear that both cities were to be under the watchful eye of the central authority in the future. Moreover, the ruler subsequently reserved the right to appoint all of the city magistrates.[19]

The suppression of guild influence led to a further narrowing of the personnel within city government. Although any systematic investigation of this development has yet to be undertaken, there are, nevertheless, indications that in various places a coalition between the monarchy and some urban elites (which mainly consisted of landowners and *rentiers*) began to occur during the reign of Charles V. The emperor tried to tie members of the urban patriciate class to him by endowing them with offices and even by elevating some to the nobility. The way in which members of the city magistracy – usually the burgomasters and aldermen – were chosen and appointed could vary from place to place, but in general there was a trend toward further interference from the central government. In a limited number of cities such as rebellious Ghent and Utrecht, the ruler achieved complete control over the election of magistrates. In other cities he could choose from double lists of nominees submitted by the sitting magistrates. On the other hand, in the more peripheral provinces of Groningen, Overijssel and Gelderland, the ruler had little influence over the election of magistrates. Moreover, in the cities of Holland the town councils (*vroedschappen*), consisting of a large number of individuals from the richest and most notable citizens, filled an important role. Membership was for life and replacement was by a system of internal co-optation. At first they advised only the burgomasters and aldermen, but during the sixteenth century they acquired a more and more dominant political role. In Rotterdam the central government had no hold over the choice of town councillors.

The cities of the Netherlands were based, from an early period, on their autonomy and privileges. Yet, implicit in this situation was an inherent weakness. In defence of their own particular agendas the cities often quarrelled with each other about political and economic interests, and as a result they were weakened as a group in relation to the monarchy. This weakness was significant in a period when the ruler strove for increased authority and territorial expansion; through expansion he could use the resources of more and more provinces against the rebellious cities. Nevertheless, there arose in some periods intercity solidarity that could extend even beyond the borders of the provinces. The Flemish-Brabantine Treaty of 1339, inspired by Jacob van Artevelde, leader of rebellious Ghent, became a cooperative platform between both regions in which the cities played a crucial role.[20] The possibility for permanent interurban collaboration lay in the representative institutions, especially in the meetings of the provincial States and the States General, which had been convoked by the Dukes of Burgundy since 1464. James Tracy has shown how the regular meeting of the States of Holland developed important traditions of cooperation between the towns and nobles represented. It was, in the first place, pressure from external enemies that induced the towns to start collaborating in new ways. The collaboration that grew in this fashion would be extremely important later in the period of the revolt.[21] Yet this urban solidarity should not be overstated. The example of rebellious Ghent – which received no real support from the other Flemish cities in its resistance to the fiscal policies of Charles V – is a salutary reminder of this fact.

During the reign of Philip II the precarious balance between the central authority and the cities came under still further pressure. One element that strongly contributed to this pressure was the religious policy of the Spanish king and his advisers. In the 1550s and 1560s Anabaptism and Calvinism spread widely. Philip II continued to require the strict application of the edicts against heresy. City rulers saw a threat in this development for more than one reason. Among the city magistrates were quite a few who belonged to a group who could be described as political moderates.[22] They were convinced that the execution of ordinary people, who allegedly erred only in their beliefs, went much too far. Some advocated a measure of toleration, while others argued for lighter punishments. At the same time, pragmatic considerations of a political and economic nature played a role. The strict application of the heresy edicts and the appointment of inquisitors always constituted a threat to urban privileges and jurisdiction. Moreover, the public executions of 'innocent' Protestants threatened to disturb the peace. In Haarlem and Rotterdam the planned execution of Anabaptists in 1557–8 led to riots and in Valenciennes (1562) and Antwerp (1564) riots occurred when Calvinists were brought to the scaffold.[23] Finally, the moderate aldermen were afraid of any dislocation of economic life. This was most obvious in the city of Antwerp where the city fathers were apprehensive that a too rigorous repression would drive foreign and other merchants out of the city. The result of this spirit of resistance was that the persecution of heresy in some places either decreased or came to a standstill. In Amsterdam this development manifested itself exceptionally early and after 1553 no more heretics were executed. From the 1560s elsewhere in Holland there was also a strong unwillingness to send heretics to their death. In Antwerp the aldermen tried to spare the well-off as much as possible.

In 1564–5 the opposition of the high and low nobility led to a gradual erosion of the power of the central authority.[24] The power vacuum that began in this manner ensured that the political and religious developments in the cities of the Netherlands escalated during the Wonderyear. The complex interplay of politics, religion, and socio-economic factors demonstrate how developments of the past played a role.[25] The presentation of the Petition (5 April 1566), in which the confederated nobility demanded that the Inquisition be abolished and edicts against heresy suspended, had an immediate effect on the aspirations and affairs of the Protestants. Numerous exiles, including preachers who had fled, returned to their homeland. Mass Calvinist preaching in the open air, the so-called hedge-preaching, started in May 1566 and spread rapidly across the country from Flanders to the northern provinces. This hedge-preaching, held outside the city walls, attracted crowds numbering hundreds and even thousands, and constituted an extremely important vehicle for Protestant mobilisation. That the Protestants – and above all the Calvinists – were able to increase their following in short order was the result of a number of factors. First, the Calvinists could fall back on an already existing, excellent organisation. There were organised congregations with a consistory in the chief towns of the Walloon area, Flanders, Brabant and Zeeland. Moreover, Calvinist hedge-preachers found a large potential public in religious and cultural middle groups. As a result of the new political mood, people could become acquainted with the Protestant message during the spring and summer of 1566 without risking persecution.

The Calvinist upsurge first erupted in iconoclastic fury near Steenvoorde in West Flanders on 10 August 1566 and swept through the Low Countries over the course of the following months. The motivation behind the iconoclastic fury was complex and manifold.[26] It was, in the first place, ideologically inspired, but social motives also played a role, especially in the Flemish West Quarter. The iconoclasm also constituted an *acte de présence* by which the Calvinists claimed their rights within the towns, including places for preaching and worship. The nature of the iconoclasm could differ markedly, varying from random violence to a process of supervised purification; this latter approach occurred through the local authorities in a number of places in the north of the Netherlands. In general, the iconoclasm was a very well-organised undertaking endorsed by a majority of the Calvinist leadership. In Antwerp, seven men who held office in the reformed community were among the organisers and in Valenciennes all the leaders were members of the consistory.

Equally interesting is the question of why iconoclasm succeeded in some towns and failed in others. It is clear that the attitude of the urban authorities often tipped the scales. Where the Calvinists were confronted with the energetic appearance of a Catholic magistracy, iconoclasm never got off the ground. This occurred in cities such as Bruges, Lille, Namur and Dordrecht. The case of Lille – a leading textile and trading centre – underscores the importance of structural elements. There, a united ruling class which was sympathetic to commerce and industry succeeded in maintaining urban stability. The Lille city fathers supported small units of production, preventing the monopolisation of raw material supplies and the employment of low cost labour, and they developed an elaborate welfare system. As a consequence, the ruling class prevented large-scale dissatisfaction among artisans and merchants which might have found an outlet in the Calvinist movement.[27] The city magistrates could, however, only press their will when they could fall back on effective force and in this context the city militias played a crucial role. If the civic militias refused to move against the iconoclasts, the city fathers were powerless to act. In Holland especially the militias often refused to suppress the iconoclasts. In a number of towns they even furthered the cause of Protestantism.[28] In the cities where the iconoclasm succeeded, the Calvinist movement quickly gained an advantage in virtually every instance. Overwhelmed by these developments, Margaret of Parma reluctantly conceded freedom of Protestant worship in all areas where it was already taking place and she asked the grandees to enforce this accord in the areas under their charge. Important in this respect was the accord that William of Orange arrived at on 2 September 1566 in Antwerp with the representatives of the Protestant community. It was later applied in Holland and Utrecht. The Antwerp accord granted the Protestants basic rights, even permitting Calvinists and Lutherans to build churches within the city walls.

Iconoclasm also had negative effects, however. As a result of the violent aspects of Calvinism, many leaders turned away from the reform movement. A number of the high nobility were now resolutely for the party of the central government. As a consequence, the centre of gravity of the resistance against the central government's policies passed to the Calvinists in the cities. They profited greatly from their strong organisation. In imitation of synodal meetings, representatives of the Calvinist church came together – almost always in Antwerp – from all over the Netherlands to discuss political developments. An important role was played by a new institution which was established in a number of cities, the Committee of Deputies, also known as the 'new consistory'.[29] These committees functioned alongside the actual consistories and looked after the political interests of the Calvinist community in relation to the local and supralocal authorities. The Antwerp Committee of Deputies in particular played a central and coordinating role in these developments.

The Calvinist movement also derived additional power through its dynamic social recruitment. The Committees of Deputies were peopled by rich merchants and the social profile of the consistories shows a similar picture. These rich merchants gave the Calvinist movement a strong social foothold, supplying the Calvinist church with prestige and money. Furthermore, it is clear that in a number of rebellious towns the Calvinist movement profited from a split between the political and mercantile elites. Indeed, the narrowness of city government had often created a dichotomy between the administration and those involved in the economy. There are indications that Antwerp's Calvinist deputies hoped, over time, to take political power in their city. In Amsterdam too political and religious dissidents converged during the Wonderyear. An alliance of great merchants and entrepreneurs opposed a small group of zealous Catholics who had dominated the city government since 1538. However, the coalition between political and religious dissidents manifested itself most clearly in the Walloon city of Valenciennes. There wealthy Calvinist merchants took power in 1566 and were resolute in their resistance to the central government.

That the Calvinist church took the lead in the resistance movement became clear during and immediately after the important synod which gathered in Antwerp at the end of November and in early December 1566. Besides the deputies from Antwerp, there were also representatives from the reformed communities in Ghent, Ypres, Valenciennes, Gelderland and from other places we do not know about. The Calvinist leaders present firmly endorsed a policy of armed resistance. Immediately after the meeting, deliberations took place with a number of leading Confederate nobles. As a result, the leadership of the armed resistance was offered to Brederode and not to William of Orange who rejected a resistance movement completely dominated by Calvinists.

Then Antwerp's Calvinist deputies set up a network for the collection of money in the Netherlands. Eventually the clash between the central government and the rebellious Calvinists ended in a disaster for the latter. Deprived of foreign support, sufficient money and adequate military leadership, the badly equipped Calvinist armies were no match for the experienced *bandes d'ordonnance* of the regent. In March 1567, the defeat of Beggar armies at Oosterweel – near Antwerp – and Walcheren, and the capture of Valenciennes by government troops, made it clear that the balance of power had shifted in favour of the regent and her central government. However, the events of the Wonderyear proved that peaceful co-existence between Catholics and Protestants was impossible. That the experiment in a number of cities failed was just as much due to Calvinist intransigence as it was to the campaigns of the regent.

After the suppression of the resistance movement Margaret moved on to the punishment of the rebellious cities. Her main concern was to punish the chief instigators of the troubles of the Wonderyear. At the same time, she left room for reconciliation. A brutal, all-encompassing repression would, according to her, lead to a massive emigration and significant damage to the economy of the territory. Furthermore, she thought it unnecessary for the king to send a punitive expedition since she had suppressed the revolt. Yet the hardliners prevailed at the Spanish court and Philip II sent the duke of Alva with a vast army. Alva chose harsh action and in 1567 established a special tribunal, the Council of Troubles, for the punishment of the offenders of the Wonderyear. This council handed down about 1100 death sentences and convicted another 8000 people by default. A look at the distribution by location gives us some idea of the importance of various cities in the spread of revolt. To the south of the great rivers we see a number of high figures. Tournai was among the highest with 1063 convictions while Valenciennes had 425. In Flanders there were 478 convicted in Ypres, 248 in Ghent and 149 in Bruges. Smaller cities such as Ronse and Oudenaarde had 283 and 207 respectively – taken together a particularly high number. In the cities of the northern provinces the number convicted was generally lower. Amsterdam and Utrecht had the highest number convicted with 242 and 288 respectively.[30] The harsh repression of the duke of Alva, together with his fiscal policies, alienated most people including many moderate Catholics and no doubt increased their susceptibility to resistance as well.

This became clear when in 1572 revolt broke out in Holland and Zeeland.[31] The cities of Holland and Zeeland were initially very reluctant to join the rebellion, but they ultimately would make a crucial contribution to the success of the revolt. The revolt started rather by accident on 1 April 1572 when 600 Sea Beggars under the command of Count Lumey seized the small port of Brill. In the days following, churches were plundered and stripped of images, the clergy were arrested and a few were even killed. Later in April the Zeeland town of Vlissingen – a strategically important harbour – surrendered and Beggar troops entered Veere. In May the north Netherlands fishing port town of Enkhuizen chose to side with the Revolt and in the following two months so did Hoorn, Alkmaar and Haarlem. In southern Holland, Gouda went over to the revolt on 21 June and was the first important city to do so; thereafter Leiden and Dordrecht followed. All of this does not mean that the citizens of Holland and Zeeland spontaneously and heartily threw open their gates to the Beggar army. In fact it really came down to a choice between the lesser of two evils. The militant anti-Catholicism of the Sea Beggars that had already manifested itself in Brill was for most townsmen an anathema and was clearly at odds with the tolerant Protestantism advocated by William of Orange. Nevertheless, the dislike for Alva and his soldiers was even greater. In and after 1572 the 'Iron Duke' paid a heavy price for his harsh and repressive policies.

That a city was prepared to allow the Beggars in was commonly the result of power struggles within that city. In most cases the regents in power refused to choose the side of the revolt and it was rather internal pressure that led to a change. In the rivalry between the pro-Habsburg ruling elite and the business community, the position of the civic militias often played a decisive role. In many cases returned exiles formed an active minority that achieved a political reversal. Also of importance was the discontent of fishermen and seamen whose livelihoods were at risk as a result of the blockades of the Sea Beggars. As Jonathan Israel rightly emphasised, 'it was the seamen, fisherman, and the middling sort who formed the backbone of the Revolt'.[32]

As far as the organisation of the revolt was concerned, on a political and military as well as a financial level, it was of particular importance that the rebels had at their disposal a structure that allowed the cities to make decisions in an overarching institutional context. The strong tradition of provincial States meetings that had grown up in Holland even before the revolt was in this respect particularly important. The first 'free' assembly of all the States of Holland was held in Dordrecht on 19 July 1572. Representatives from the 'large towns', Dordrecht, Haarlem, Leiden and Gouda, and from a number of smaller towns, were present. They acknowledged Orange as stadholder and captain general of Holland, Zeeland and Utrecht. Marnix of St Aldegonde declared that it was Orange's intention 'that there will be freedom of religion for both

Reformed and Catholics'.[33] However, the cooperation within the States did not prevent the continuation of particularism and rivalry between the cities. In 1575 Delft even proposed to burn down The Hague – which was unfortified – alleging that it was a potential base for the Spanish army.[34] The well-documented history of Gouda amply shows how the regents' policies were conditioned by a fierce particularism.[35]

William of Orange's religious ideas, formulated at the first free States assembly, did not reflect what was happening on the ground. Usually the towns of Holland and Zeeland let the Beggars in on condition that they neither harassed the clergy nor damaged churches and cloisters. In practice, however, the terms of the agreements were violated soon after the Beggar troops entered the towns. In the spring of 1573, the parish churches were either closed or already in use by the Calvinists. The position of the Catholics weakened, moreover, because they were seen as potential traitors in the struggle with Alva. As a result the revolt took on the character of a civil war.

In 1572, however, the revolt was not limited just to Holland and Zeeland. William of Orange wanted to attack Alva and his forces on various fronts. Orange's brother Louis of Nassau invaded Hainault from France and captured Mons on 24 May 1572, obliging Alva to keep the bulk of his army in the southern Netherlands. Around the same time, Orange's brother-in-law Count Willem van den Berg attacked from Germany and won Gelderland, Overijssel and parts of Friesland for the revolt. In August 1572 William of Orange finally set out with another army, making for the southern core provinces. Mechelen and a number of smaller cities in Brabant and Flanders chose the side of Orange but, just like Mons, they were recaptured in September and October.

One must ask why Orange enjoyed relatively little success in the south and why the towns in Holland and Zeeland above all persistently pursued the war further. Strategic factors of a politico-military and geographical nature played a crucial role. For instance, Alva placed priority on the relief of Mons and after the St Bartholomew's Day massacre the rebels lost the necessary support of the Huguenots in the south. Furthermore, the Spanish were at a disadvantage against the Sea Beggars in the north because the low-lying provinces of Holland and Zeeland were surrounded by water, a factor that proved decisive for the relief of Leiden in 1574. But there is also another explanation.[36] In the southern core provinces the differences that had occurred during the Wonderyear were not forgotten and the Calvinists were viewed as extremists. The recollection of these earlier events no doubt created a dislike among the well-off citizens for any new experiments advocated by the ordinary people. To the north of the rivers the Protestants had been less extreme. In Dordrecht, Gouda, Rotterdam and Haarlem iconoclasm had never occurred, so the citizens had fewer reasons to fear the actions of the Calvinists. Conversely, Utrecht and Amsterdam, restless in 1566, long remained loyal to the king in the 1570s – until 1577 and 1578 respectively. Moreover, the radical actions of Alva against a few rebellious cities, especially the massacres at Mechelen, Zutphen and Naarden, made the rebels in Holland and Zeeland feel that they had little choice but to carry on.

After the duke of Alva had left the Netherlands, the new regent, Don Luis de Requesens, pursued the war in the north with reasonable success from the end of 1573. His unexpected death in March 1575 robbed the Spanish army of its commander, and the bankruptcy of the Spanish crown in the same year led to the famous mutiny of the unpaid Spanish soldiers. The 'Spanish fury' caused heavy damage and fed anti-Spanish sentiment, particularly in the core provinces of Flanders and Brabant. The Spanish fury in Antwerp, in which at least 2500 people lost their lives, formed the indisputable high point in this development. After the solemn signing of the Pacification of Ghent (8 November 1576) William of Orange saw his influence in the Low Countries increase. In the north he succeeded in bringing cities loyal to the king – such as Amsterdam, Haarlem and Utrecht – under his obedience through treaties of 'satisfaction'. After the new Spanish regent Don Juan made himself master of the citadel of Namur (24 July 1577) and the States army at Gembloux had been beaten (31 January 1578), radical revolutions broke out in Flanders and Brabant.

Developments in the Flemish and Brabantine cities demonstrate how political, religious and social tensions were closely interlinked and how the traditions of the past could play a role. This came to full expression most clearly in the old rebellious city of Ghent. During the night of 28/29 October 1577 a number of Orangists arrested a number of prominent aristocrats and prelates who had come to Ghent for the meeting of the States of Flanders. Those arrested belonged to the group that attempted to go against the influence of Orange after the Pacification of Flanders. A few days later, a Committee of Eighteen was established in Ghent that would wield decisive political influence in the following month. Shortly thereafter, the members of the committee became part of the city government in Ghent. All were convinced supporters of Orange; in the future they would reveal themselves as Calvinists. On 14 January 1578 William of Orange moved on to the replacement of the city magistrates. The great majority of the appointed aldermen were newcomers: 'good patriots' who had the support of the Committee of Eighteen and of Orange.

These political upheavals in Ghent in the winter of 1577–8 led to the demise of the old magistrate class and *homines novi* took power. The new rulers were, moreover, anti-clerical and supported the expansion of the Calvinist church. In social terms the new regime was based, above all, on the urban middle classes, whose political influence had waned after the strict punishment of the city in 1540. They devoted themselves to the restoration of their old political rights and to the spread of Calvinism. The new power-holders pursued, from the outset, the restoration of the old privileges, which they succeeded in getting with the support of Orange. Moreover, from February 1578 just about all the Flemish cities were brought *manu militari* to the side of Ghent. Subsequently the magistracy was placed under the strict control of the radicals in Ghent and in a number of places Committees of Eighteen were installed. In this manner the old dream of a city-state of Ghent dominating all of Flanders seemed close at hand. Another development that harked back to the glorious medieval past was the renewal of the Flemish-Brabant treaty of alliance of 1339. It was precisely the Committees of Eighteen from Ghent and Brussels that formed the driving force behind this renewal.

In the duchy of Brabant parallel developments took place.[37] Here also radical committees were established which resolutely chose for Orange and the revolt. In Brussels a Committee of Eighteen had been functioning since August 1577, chosen from the nine 'nations' which represented the guilds. In Antwerp early in February 1578, on the advice of Orange, the new magistracy appointed eight colonels belonging to the merchant class. Both committees were charged with the security and defence of the city, but in practice exercised a great deal of political influence. The Committee of Eighteen in Brussels consisted in large measure of Catholic patriots, and the Antwerp college of colonels was in the beginning certainly not exclusively made up of Calvinists, and possibly Calvinists did not even make up a majority. In Brabant the watershed was later in 1579–80. In these years various city governments were purged. Catholics had to give up their places to convinced Calvinists. This purification went hand in hand with a social shift. In cities such as Antwerp, Brussels and Mechelen, the old magistracy, originating from the lower nobility and the landed aristocracy, was replaced by *homines novi* with a rebellious and Calvinist past. Moreover, the decision-making bodies in the cities under discussion, just as in Ghent, were regularly assembled 'democratically' in the Great Council. This council, in which the craft guilds had a large representation, not only decided fiscal policy, but also deliberated over political and religious problems which arose during the course of the revolt.

The general politico-religious evolution from 1578 led to a growing polarisation in the cities of the Netherlands. Catholics who initially supported resistance against Don Juan increasingly began to ask more questions about a revolt in which there was a chance that their own religion might be undermined. The events in radical Ghent were good evidence of this. On the other hand, the discovery of a number of plots in which Catholic clergy were repeatedly involved affirmed Catholic unreliability in the eyes of the Calvinist rebels. In this manner there began a mutual process of alienation in which political centrists in the cities were eliminated. The failure of the Cologne Peace Conference (1579–80), precisely because of this religious problem, confirmed and strengthened the process. The result was that the revolt in growing measure took on the character of a civil war in which Catholics and Protestants within the same city came to stand against each other. Similarly the Unions of Arras and Utrecht, formed in January 1579, each quickly took on contrasting Catholic and Calvinist characteristics.

Usually the presence of the right connections determined which party would gain the upper hand. This was especially clear in Brabant, a province that felt particularly threatened since the defeat of the States army at Gembloux. Beginning in June 1579 the Catholic Philip of Egmont – son of Lamoral who was executed in 1568 – tried to make himself master of Brussels. The seven companies that he had encamped in Brussels began a struggle against the companies of the governor of Brussels, Olivier van den Tympel who obtained the support of the Protestant citizens. After a day of intense fighting Egmont and his soldiers were forced to abandon the city. Five new companies, consisting of Protestant Scots, would in the future also act as safeguard for the Protestant and rebel stance taken by the city. In Mechelen, around the same time, an armed confrontation arose between a garrison from Holland, assisted by Calvinist citizens, and Catholic citizens. After the regrouping of the States garrison, power quickly passed over to the advantage of the Catholic royalists who joined with the Walloon reconciliation movement. Just one year later, the city would be brought back into the camp of the revolt through a surprise military attack. In the second half of 1579 a violent internal power struggle raged in 's Hertogenbosch where the radical *Schermers* guild lost the day and the city magistrates ultimately went over to the royalist side. In the northern Netherlands Orange's brother, John of Nassau, played an important role with the help of both garrisons loyal to the States and Calvinist minorities.[38] In the autumn of 1578 he installed States garrisons in the Gelderland towns of Nijmegen, Arnhem and Zutphen and he renewed the term of the sitting city magistracies. In the spring of 1579 he brought the recalcitrant Amersfoort in the province of Utrecht into the camp of the Union of Utrecht by military force and he purged the magistracy in other cities. Through the 'treason' of the stadholder Rennenberg in March 1580 the northern city of Groningen went over to the side of Farnese. Its crossing resulted, however, in an anti-Catholic reaction in the rebellious cities and provinces and strengthened the position of the Calvinists.

For William of Orange it was of crucial importance that the rebellious cities and provinces were ready to cooperate and to put their financial and military resources at the service of the Generality. In the States General, which after the split of the Catholic nobility and prelates was always completely dominated by representatives of the cities, the decision-making process proceeded particularly slowly. Moreover, the delegates allowed themselves, in large measure, to be led by self-interest.[39] Financial resources were often only released when they benefited their own region. This was painfully clear during the siege of Maastricht. The capture of the city by Spanish troops on 29 June 1579 was not only attributable to the military brilliance and perseverance of Alexander Farnese, but to the inability of the rebellious provinces to produce the funds necessary for the support of the States army. William of Orange blamed radical Ghent and Flanders in particular. This region, so rich in cities, was always supposed to come up with around one-third of the financial means of the Generality. But Flanders was not solely to blame; during the siege of Maastricht, Holland and Zeeland had also given priority to the payment of garrisons encamped in their own districts.

This regional and urban particularism and the lack of a strong central authority also played a part during Farnese's *reconquista* in the 1580s.[40] Tournai surrendered at the end of 1581 after the States General had announced that they could send no help. It was, above all, from 1583 that Farnese began a systematic conquest of the Flemish and Brabantine cities. Ypres capitulated in 1583, Bruges and Ghent in 1584 and Brussels, Mechelen and Antwerp – after a long and exhausting siege – in 1585. In both Flanders and Brabant the rebellious city governors complained about the failure of Holland and Zeeland to send adequate help. Moreover, Farnese skilfully played off the internal opposition in the besieged cities. The oppressed Catholics began to be increasingly more confident and these developments generated defeatism in the Protestant ranks. Many were convinced that the capitulation of the cities of Holland and Zeeland was inevitable. That this did not ultimately come to pass can be attributed to a combination of factors. In particular there was the economic strength of Holland and Zeeland; the merchant elites could fall back on extensive financial resources. But the priorities of Spanish foreign policy were equally important. Philip II gave preference to military intervention against England and France, and ordered Farnese to switch to a defensive war against the northern Netherlands.

The year 1585 undoubtedly marked a crucial stage in the history of the revolt. The fall of Antwerp – the most powerful city in the entire Netherlands – was later seen as the beginning of the division between 'north' and 'south'. For contemporaries, however, this was not at all clear. The border between the royal Spanish Netherlands and the Republic of the United Provinces, which was confirmed in 1648 at the Peace of Westphalia, was the unpredictable result of a decades-long political and military struggle.[41] For the cities of both states the consequences of these developments were far-reaching.

The Republic of the United Netherlands exhibited a politically decentralised structure.[42] Sovereignty rested with the provincial States. The composition of the provincial States – which met more often than was the case before the revolt – could vary depending upon the socio-economic structure, but in general it was dominated by the cities. This was certainly the case with Holland, by far the richest province, providing 60 per cent of the funds in the first decade of the republic. Here Amsterdam was particularly prominent. Thus it was, above all, the wealthy merchants of Holland who determined policy, not only locally but also at a national and international level for the republic as a whole. A decentralised power structure could, in a period of war, represent a considerable disadvantage. However, the long struggle against Spain compelled the various cities and provinces to undertake a minimal union and a measure of agreement at a federal level. Domination by one well-defined centre never came about. Urban particularism and intercity rivalries blocked the formation of a centralised national state.[43] The privileged Calvinist church offered no alternative model for central-isation either. There was, it is true, a coordinating structure of *classes* and synods, but the focal point remained the local community.

In the Spanish Netherlands, on the other hand, the cities came out of the conflict weakened. Alexander Farnese had not set out to crush the rebellious cities of Flanders and Brabant completely; he left room for traditional urban privileges. The centre of power, however, lay with the Spanish king and the central government in Brussels. Also during the rule of the 'sovereign archdukes' Albert and Isabella (1598–1621), Madrid continued to take a close interest in the government of the southern Netherlands. The provincial States were left some room for manoeuvre, but it was symptomatic that the States General, with few exceptions, never reassembled.[44]

The results of the revolt for the cities were even clearer in socio-economic terms. On a demographic level, Farnese's campaign of conquest led to wholesale emigration. Every time the Spanish regent compelled a city to capitulate, hundreds or even thousands fled to the rebellious north. The city of Antwerp saw its population shrink by roughly half in only four years, from around 80,000 to 42,000. For the Spanish Netherlands the emigration of numerous merchants, well-trained artisans, intellectuals and artists meant a great loss, but for the cities of the republic it was a pronounced windfall. Because of immigration, the degree of urbanisation grew, from the middle of the 1580s, to an unheard-of level. Above all, a number of the cities of Holland saw their populations increase spectacularly because of this development. Amsterdam, which counted about 30,000 inhabitants in 1585, housed no fewer than 105,000 in 1622. Leiden and Haarlem likewise experienced explosive growth.[45] In economic and cultural respects the exiled south Netherlanders contributed to the Golden Age of the Dutch Republic. With their capital and skills they made a prominent contribution to the success of the struggle against Spain.

Notes

1 L. Guicciardini, *Beschrijvinghe van alle de Nederlanden; anderssins ghenoemt Neder-Duytschlandt* (Amsterdam: Willem Jansz, 1612), p. 6 (first edition published in Italian in 1565).
2 Figures based on J. Israel, *The Dutch Republic. Its Rise, Greatness, and Fall 1477–1806* (Oxford: Oxford University Press, 1995), pp. 114, 328; P. M. M. Klep, 'Het Brabantse stedensysteem en de scheiding der Nederlanden, 1565–1650', *Bijdragen tot de Geschiedenis*, 73 (1990), pp. 102, 128; E. Hélin, 'Demografische ontwikkeling van de Zuidelijke Nederlanden', in D. P. Blok *et al.* (eds), *Algemene Geschiedenis der Nederlanden*, vol. V (Haarlem: Fibula – Van Dishoeck, 1980), pp. 179–80.
3 See the classic work by H. van der Wee, *The Growth of the Antwerp Market and the European Economy (Fourteenth–Sixteenth Centuries)* (3 vols, The Hague: Martinus Nijhoff, 1963).
4 J. L. van Zanden, 'Holland en de Zuidelijke Nederlanden in de periode 1500–1570: divergerende ontwikkelingen of voortgaande economische integratie?', in E. Aerts *et al.* (eds), *Studia historica oeconomica. Liber amicorum Herman van der Wee* (Leuven: Universitaire Pers., 1993), pp. 357–67.
5 J. de Vries and A. van der Woude, *Nederland 1500–1815. De eerste ronde van moderne economische groei* (Amsterdam: Balans, 1995), ch. 9. Cf., for Zeeland, V. Enthoven, *Zeeland en de opkomst van de Republiek. Handel en strijd in de Scheldedelta c. 1550–1621* (Leiden: Luctor et Victor, 1996).
6 Emphasised by Israel, *Dutch Republic*, pp. 116–19.
7 W. P. Blockmans, 'The Formation of Political Union, 1300–1600', in J. C. H. Blom and E. Lamberts (eds), *History of the Low Countries* (New York and Oxford: Berghahn Books, 1999), pp. 117–18.

8　See, for the unequal distribution of wealth in Antwerp, G. Marnef, *Antwerp in the Age of Reformation. Underground Protestantism in a Commercial Metropolis 1550–1577* (Baltimore and London: Johns Hopkins University Press, 1996), pp. 9–12. Cf. for a number of towns in Holland, J. A. van Houtte, 'Maatschappelijke toestanden', in J. A. van Houtte *et al.* (eds) *Algemene Geschiedenis der Nederlanden*, vol. IV (Utrecht: W. de Haan, 1952), pp. 237–8, and J. A. Faber, 'De Noordelijke Nederlanden van 1480 tot 1780. Structuren in beweging', in Blok *et al.*, *Algemene Geschiedenis der Nederlanden*, vol. V, p. 225.

9　H. Soly and A. K. L. Thijs, 'Nijverheid in de Zuidelijke Nederlanden', in D. P. Blok *et al.* (eds) *Algemene Geschiedenis der Nederlanden*, vol. VI (Haarlem: Fibula – Van Dishoeck, 1979), pp. 56–7; H. van der Wee, 'Handel in de Zuidelijke Nederlanden', in ibid., pp. 75–7, 9–93; De Vries and Van der Woude, *Nederland 1500–1815*, ch. 12; Faber, 'Noordelijke Nederlanden', pp. 199–200. It should be noted that H. van der Wee presents a more favourable picture than Soly and Thijs.

10　H. van der Wee, 'The Economy as a Factor in the Revolt in the Southern Netherlands', *Acta Historiae Neerlandicae*, 5 (1971), pp. 52–67, reprinted in his *The Low Countries in the Early Modern World* (Aldershot: Variorum, 1993), pp. 264–78.

11　G. Marnef, 'The Dynamics of Reformed Militancy in the Low Countries: The Wonderyear', in N. Scott Amos, A. Pettegree and H. van Nierop (eds), *The Education of a Christian Society. Humanism and the Reformation in Britain and the Netherlands* (Aldershot: Ashgate, 1999), pp. 193–210; Marnef, *Antwerp in the Age of Reformation*, ch. 6.

12　H. de Ridder-Symoens, 'Education and Literacy in the Burgundian–Habsburg Netherlands', *Canadian Journal of Netherlandic Studies*, 16 (1995), pp. 6–21; Marnef, *Antwerp in the Age*, pp. 33–6; Johan Decavele, 'Het culturele en intellectuele netwerk: middeleeuwen en 16de eeuw', in *Le réseau urbain en Belgique dans une perspective historique (1330–1850). Un approche statistique et dynamique. Actes* (Brussels: Crédit Communal, 1992), pp. 371–81.

13　Decavele, 'Culturele netwerk', pp. 375–6; J. Decavele, *De dageraad van de Reformatie in Vlaanderen (1520–1565)*, vol. I (Brussels: Koninklijke Academie, 1975), pp. 106–7.

14　A. G. Johnston, 'L' imprimerie et la Réforme aux Pays-Bas 1520 – c. 1555', in J.-F. Gilmont (ed.), *La Réforme et le livre. L' Europe de l'imprimé (1517 – v. 1570)* (Paris: Editions du Cerf, 1990), pp. 155–90.

15　G. K. Waite, 'Reformers on Stage: Rhetorician Drama and Reformation Propaganda in the Netherlands of Charles V, 1531–1556', *Archiv für Reformationsgeschichte*, 83 (1992), pp. 209–39; Decavele, *De dageraad*, vol. I, pp. 196–229; Marnef, *Antwerp*, pp. 29–33; F. van Boheemen and Th. van der Heijden, *Met minnen versaemt. De Hollandse rederijkers vanaf de middeleeuwen tot het begin van de achttiende eeuw* (Delft: Eburon, 1999).

16　G. Marnef, 'Instellingen van culturele verandering: de Kerken', in *La ville et la transmission des valeurs culturelles au bas moyen âge et aux temps modernes. Actes* (Brussels: Crédit Communal, 1996), pp. 260–1, and P. Benedict, 'Introduction', in P. Benedict *et al.* (eds), *Reformation, Revolt and Civil War in France and the Netherlands 1555–1585* (Amsterdam: Koninklijke Akademie, 1999), pp. 12–13, with further references.

17 J. J. Woltjer, 'Political Moderates and Religious Moderates in the Revolt of the Netherlands', in Benedict *et al.*, *Reformation, Revolt*, pp. 194–200.

18 M. Boone and M. Prak, 'Rulers, Patricians and Burghers: The Great and the Little Traditions of Urban Revolt in the Low Countries', in K. Davids and J. Lucassen (eds), *A Miracle Mirrored. The Dutch Republic in European Perspective* (Cambridge: Cambridge University Press, 1995), pp. 99–134; W. P. Blockmans, 'The Impact on State Formation: Three Contrasting Territories in the Low Countries, 1300–1500', in P. Blickle (ed.), *Resistance, Representation, and Community* (Oxford: Oxford University Press, 1997), pp. 256–71.

19 J. Dambruyne, 'Stedelijke identiteit en politieke cultuur te Gent', in H. Soly and J. van de Wiele (eds), *Carolus. Keizer Karel V 1500–1558* (Ghent: Snoeck-Ducaju, 1999), pp. 111–21; B. J. Kaplan, *Calvinists and Libertines. Confession and Community in Utrecht 1578–1620* (Oxford: Oxford University Press, 1995), pp. 132–4.

20 Boone and Prak, 'Rulers', pp. 105, 107; P. Avonds, 'Beschouwingen over het ontstaan en de evolutie van het samenhorigheidsbesef in de Nederlanden (14de–19de eeuw)', in *Cultuurgeschiedenis in de Nederlanden van de Renaissance naar de Romantiek. Liber amicorum J. Andriessen s.j. – A. Keersmaekers – P. Lenders* (Leuven and Amersfoort: Acco, 1986), pp. 45–51, who emphasises the influence of the 1339 treaty during the Dutch Revolt.

21 J. D. Tracy, *Holland under Habsburg Rule 1506–1566: The Formation of a Body Politic* (Berkeley: University of California Press, 1990). Yet Jonathan Israel's statement (*Dutch Republic*, p. 170) that Holland 'was the only province in the Habsburg Netherlands with a measure of real institutional cohesion' deserves further research.

22 See, on the concept and development of this middle group, Woltjer, 'Political Moderates', pp. 186–94.

23 Tracy, *Holland under Habsburg Rule*, pp. 200–2; A. Duke, *Reformation and Revolt in the Low Countries* (London and Ronceverte: Hambledon Press, 1990), p. 94; Marnef, *Antwerp in the Age of Reformation*, p. 87.

24 See the contribution by H. van Nierop in this volume.

25 See, for the developments during the Wonderyear, Marnef, 'Dynamics of Reformed Militancy', pp. 193–210, with references to further literature.

26 See, on this issue, A. Duke, 'De calvinisten en de paapse beeldendienst. De denkwereld van de beeldenstormers in 1566', in M. Bruggeman *et al.* (eds) *Mensen van de Nieuwe Tijd. Liber amicorum voor A.Th. van Deursen* (Amsterdam: Bert Bakker, 1996), pp. 29–45.

27 R. S. DuPlessis, *Lille and the Dutch Revolt. Urban Stability in an Era of Revolution 1500–1582* (Cambridge: Cambridge University Press, 1991).

28 J. C. Grayson, 'The Civic Militia in the County of Holland, 1560–81: Politics and Public Order in the Dutch Revolt', *Bijdragen en mededelingen betreffende de Geschiedenis der Nederlanden*, 95 (1981), pp. 35–63.

29 See, on these Committees of Deputies which have been overlooked in the older historiography, Marnef, 'Dynamics of Reformed Militancy', pp. 203–9.

30 Figures based on M. Dierickx, 'De lijst der veroordeelden door de Raad van Beroerten', *Belgisch Tijdschrift voor Filologie en Geschiedenis*, 40 (1962), pp. 415–22. Compare with Israel, *Dutch Republic*, pp. 159–60.

31 G. Parker, *The Dutch Revolt* (Harmondsworth: Penguin, 1990), ch. 3; Israel, *Dutch Republic*, chs. 9–10; J. J. Woltjer, *Tussen vrijheidsstrijd en burgeroorlog: Over*

de Nederlandse Opstand 1555–1580 (Amsterdam: Balans, 1994), ch. 1, who all offer references to further literature.

32 Israel, *Dutch Republic*, p. 182.

33 Quoted in G. Marnef, 'The Dynamics of Reformed Religious Militancy: The Netherlands, 1566–1585', in Benedict *et al.*, *Reformation, Revolt and Civil War*, p. 61.

34 M. 't Hart, 'Intercity Rivalries and the Making of the Dutch State', in C. Tilly and W. P. Blockmans (eds), *Cities and the Rise of States in Europe A.D. 1000 to 1800* (Boulder: Westview Press, 1994), p. 202.

35 C. C. Hibben, *Gouda in Revolt. Particularism and Pacifism in the Revolt of the Netherlands 1572–1588* (Utrecht: Hess, 1983), esp. ch. 3.

36 Cf. Woltjer, *Tussen vrijheidsstrijd*, ch. 1.

37 G. Marnef, 'Brabants calvinisme in opmars: de weg naar de calvinistische republieken te Antwerpen, Brussel en Mechelen, 1577–1580', *Bijdragen tot de Geschiedenis*, 70 (1987), pp. 7–21, with further references.

38 A. J. Tjaden, 'De reconquista mislukt. De opstandige gewesten 1579–1588', in Blok *et al.*, *Algemene Geschiedenis der Nederlanden*, vol. VI, pp. 244–9.

39 See, on the study of particularism during the Dutch Revolt, G. Malengrau, *L'esprit particulariste et la Révolution des Pays-Bas au XVIe siècle (1578–1584)* (Leuven: Presse universitaire, 1936).

40 See, on Farnese's *reconquista*, L. van der Essen, *Alexandre Farnèse, prince de Parme, gouverneur-général des Pays-Bas, 1545–1592* (5 vols., Brussels: Librairie nationale d'art et d'histoire, 1933–7), esp. vols. 3–4.

41 H. de Schepper, *'Belgium Nostrum'. Over integratie en desintegratie van het Nederland* (Antwerp: Orde van den Prince, 1987), pp. 19–24.

42 See, on the institutional framework of the Dutch Republic, Israel, *Dutch Republic*, ch. 13; W. Frijhoff and M. Spies, *1650: Bevochten eendracht* (The Hague: Sdu Uitgevers, 1999), chs. 2–3; M. C. 't Hart, *The Making of a Bourgeois State. War, Politics and Finance During the Dutch Revolt* (Manchester: Manchester University Press, 1993).

43 See also 't Hart, 'Intercity Rivalries'.

44 De Schepper, *'Belgium Nostrum'*, pp. 26–32; G. Parker, *Spain and the Netherlands 1559–1659. Ten Studies* (Glasgow: Fontana Press, 1990), ch. 9.

45 J. Briels, *Zuid-Nederlanders in de Republiek 1572–1630. Een demografische en cultuurhistorische studie* (Sint-Niklaas: Dante, 1985); De Vries and Van der Woude, *Nederland 1500–1815*, pp. 84–9, 104.

6 The grand strategy of Philip II and the revolt of the Netherlands

Fernando González de León and Geoffrey Parker

In responding to insurgent heresy, perhaps the most serious challenge that confronted central governments in the early modern era, Philip II faced a particularly difficult problem. Unlike any other early modern ruler, the king of Spain had to coordinate his response with the needs of a huge global empire. The royal response to events in the Netherlands was, therefore, shaped and determined to a very considerable degree by Philip II's imperial strategy and, in turn, the challenge of the Dutch Revolt helped the Spanish monarchy to clarify and organise its foreign policy goals.

This essay seeks to test the controversial thesis that Philip II did indeed possess a grand strategy, a 'blueprint for empire', an idea still widely questioned by scholars.[1] From H. G. Koenigsberger's 1971 article, 'The Statecraft of Philip II', to Paul M. Kennedy's more recent *The Rise and Fall of the Great Powers*, historians have frequently denied the existence of a set of geopolitical principles and priorities underlying Spanish imperialism and informing the decisions of its rulers.[2] Some have even denied that Philip possessed an overall strategy. Instead, discrete explanations for the individual policies of the king of Spain (for example in the Netherlands) abound. Some, like Pierre Chaunu, have stressed economic factors (especially the fluctuations of incoming American treasure to the port of Seville).[3] Others, like David Lago-marsino, have focused on the role of Spanish court politics, particularly the conflicts over patronage, power and policy between the factions led by Fernando Alvarez de Toledo, duke of Alba and by Ruy Gómez de Silva, prince of Eboli.[4] Fernand Braudel and Paul Kennedy, although they placed the Spanish response to the Dutch Revolt within the context of Spain's imperial politics, concentrated on structural issues such as the problems posed by distance, or by lack of resources.[5] All these explanations offer brilliant insights into their particular area of analysis, but all coincide in assigning a minimal or non-existent role to a critical factor in

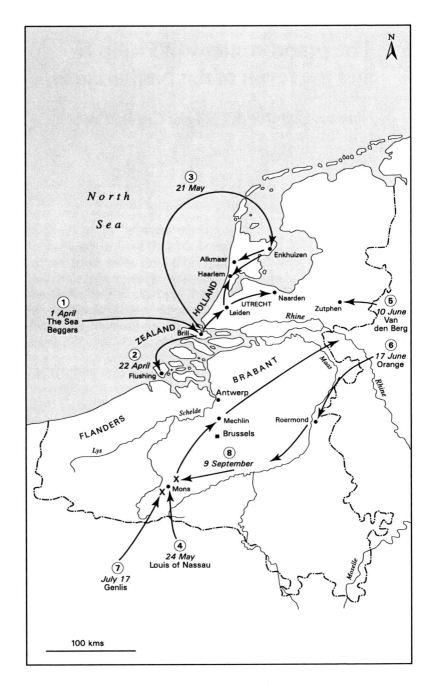

Map 5 The 1572 campaign.

the formation and execution of Spanish policy, namely the coherent set of strategic principles that underlay it. This is not, of course, to deny the importance of other factors in shaping the government's response to the revolt, but merely to recall how strategic considerations affected the choice of one or another course of action at several crucial moments.

Those who deny that Philip II possessed an imperial strategy sometimes point to the absence of a written master plan and to the apparently haphazard way in which the king and his ministers chose their policies. They portray the king as a timid and passive character conducting a primarily reactive (and reactionary), confused and vacillating foreign policy whose day-to-day purpose was to respond to crises only at the last possible moment and only with the most obvious and expedient means at hand. Leaving aside the glaring discrepancy between the popular image of Philip as a bigoted and inflexible king, and that of a ruler who based his policy on the morning mail, it is clear that the absence of a publicly stated aggressive grand design to dominate Europe (if not the world) did not necessarily preclude the existence of a set of underlying political principles. Even some of Spain's enemies realised that, although Philip and his ministers did not publicise the strategic rationale for their decisions, they none the less possessed a number of geopolitical principles that helped the monarchy to maintain its position in Europe and the world and to coordinate its policies and actions.

Close examination of the lengthy debates in Madrid over European policy, and most particularly the response to the troubles in the Netherlands in the 1560s and 1570s, reveals a recurrent group of consensual foreign policy goals. These goals, not simply a list of desiderata but a series of interrelated principles forming a coherent system, can be roughly divided into two broad categories, religious and political, and placed in an approximate rank order:

Religious or ideological principles

1   Defence of Catholicism. The major goal of the empire was the defence of the Catholic faith against foreign armed attack or internal subversion. Alliances with heretics or infidels must be avoided at all costs.
2   Theological and ethical justification. Deeply concerned about his role in history and aware of the importance of public opinion, Philip keenly felt the need for theological and ethical justification for his foreign policy.[6] Consequently he frequently consulted and relied upon the views of theological experts and committees on the ideological and propagandistic implications of strategy.[7]

3   Providentialism. A king and an empire that practised the two previously stated principles saw a historical mission destined to achieve victory and expected supernatural help from God in the form of more or less subtle miracles. They also attributed incidental reverses to the inscrutable or punitive will of the Deity.[8] Providentialism thus allowed Spanish planners to leave room for the role of unforeseen circumstances in the execution of strategy. Their vision formed an early modern Catholic version of what Renaissance military theorists called 'fortune' and modern strategists like Carl von Clausewitz termed 'friction'.

4   Reputation. The king and the empire must strive, at all costs, to keep not only honour, but all public appearances of honour. This was also a matter of religious principle, for as a royal councillor put it, 'Christian obligation requires the preservation of one's reputation inviolate'.[9]

Political and military principles

1   Defensive stance. The king of Spain frequently stated that he already possessed enough territories; he needed only to defend them against aggression. As in the case of religion, defence not conquest or gain formed the ultimate goal.[10]

2   The inalienable nature of patrimonial lands. Inherited kingdoms and domains had to remain, whatever the cost, within the Spanish branch of the family and should not be yielded, especially not to heretics or infidels, for each loss would strengthen Spain's enemies. A firm defence, again, seemed of the essence.

3   The hierarchy of territorial priorities. Not all royal possessions were equally important. In policy-making, the interests of Iberia and the Indies would come first, Italy and the Mediterranean second, the Netherlands and the North Sea third. In time of war, however, the defence of these far-flung possessions must be coordinated into a coherent military effort.[11]

4   The 'domino theory' or 'escalation of possible disasters'. The loss of one possession would eventually lead to the gradual folding of the empire. This element was linked directly with the notions of the epidemic nature of loss of reputation as well as the territorial primacy of Spain, for it allowed for the argument, effectively made in 1566–7, that the loss of a distant possession such as the Netherlands would ultimately entail the loss of Spain through a gradual erosion of respect for the king.

5   The inevitability and even desirability of war somewhere in the

empire, especially in the interest of peace in Spain. The goal was to keep conflict as far away as possible from the heartland of the empire, i.e. the Iberian peninsula.

6 Dynastic ties and solidarity with the Austrian branch of the Habsburgs, as long as they did not conflict with any of the other principles of policy.

These principles could and sometimes did come into conflict with each other, but a consistent direction for royal foreign policy almost always emerged from the debate.

Philip II did not build his imperial strategy from scratch, however. In 1548, his father, Emperor Charles V, composed a set of instructions that later came to be known as his 'political testament'.[12] In this instrument the emperor took stock of his possessions and explained to his son their assets and weaknesses, as well as the challenges he would be likely to face. He advised Philip that God had appointed him to continue the sacred mission of defending Catholicism against all its enemies, for which he could expect providential assistance. Although he must always maintain good relations with his Habsburg cousins in the Holy Roman Empire, he needed to understand that war somewhere would be inevitable and that it was essential to safeguard his reputation, for its loss would inexorably lead to a general collapse of his rule. Finally, Charles warned his son to remain especially vigilant in the Netherlands, for they could play a crucial role in conflicts with France.

Charles's advice, though both perceptive and persuasive, could not entirely determine his son's policies. Above all, Philip's dominions differed significantly from those of his father. To be sure, the Turkish war continued, but France, which had constantly sought to thwart Charles, disintegrated into civil war in the 1560s and could do little to undermine Philip's designs, while England's Queen Elizabeth, although astute and unpredictable, had no obvious heir, ruled a religiously divided country and lacked powerful allies abroad. Portugal too, which had maintained a fierce independence towards Charles V, became dependent on Spain during the minority and troubled adolescence of King Sebastian I, whose closest male relative (and ultimate successor) was none other than Philip II.

The ideology of the central government also shifted in the 1550s.[13] The projects of universal empire advanced by some of Charles's advisers disappeared (at least for a while) and, especially after 1559, Spain became the focus of all policy-making. As Fernand Braudel pointed out, Philip II's 1559 journey from Flushing to Laredo marked a turning point in European history. Although Braudel criticised this decision for having created an 'unfavourable arithmetic of distances' by exiling the court 'outside the centre of Europe', at the time it made eminent sense.[14] Whereas a northern-focused empire had seemed perfectly possible while Philip was both king of England and likely to succeed as Holy Roman Emperor, by 1559 such a strategic orientation had become unrealistic, and Philip's decision to locate his capital in Spain was understandable. Castile supported the royal budget with the largest tax revenues and the Spanish colonies in the Indies provided the second largest share. In addition, Spanish soldiers formed the core of the royal army (the famous and redoubtable *tercios*), and Spanish ships the mainstay of the royal fleets; the major port of the empire was Castilian (Seville), as were its financial centres (Valladolid and Medina del Campo); Spanish *letrados* ran the bureaucracy and Castilian was the language of the majority of the king's subjects.

Had Philip's capital remained in Brussels, other equally serious problems caused by distance would have ailed the empire, especially in its relations with Spain and the Indies, as indeed Charles V had experienced several times during his reign. Furthermore, one might ask whether Philip would have been able to integrate Portugal and its global empire had he made Brussels his capital. Spain was clearly at the geographic centre, if not of Europe, at least of the lands Philip inherited, and so the move to Spain actually reduced the problems of distance. Consequently, it was not inaccurate to say, as the royal secretary Francisco de Eraso told the Cortes of Castile in 1570, that:

> His Majesty [knows] how necessary and convenient his presence is in these kingdoms, not only for their own good and advantage, but also to act and provide for [the needs of] the other states, since these kingdoms are the centre, the head and principal part of all his dominions.[15]

In other words, Philip made Spain not only his capital but also his foremost strategic priority. His empire was much more Spanish than his father's had ever been.[16]

The rank accorded to other possessions and geographical areas in the king's order of priorities reflected their proximity to Spain, and their capacity to protect or harm Spanish interests. Philip and his court therefore rated the importance of Italy, North Africa, the Mediterranean and later Portugal far above that of the Netherlands, which were geographically distant and seemed from a cultural and even a climatological perspective rather alien and remote.[17] Their major importance, aside from tax revenues, was that, as Philip once put it, 'it is from [there] that the king of France can be best attacked and forced into peace'.[18] The Low Countries, instead of forming the heart of a hegemonic northern European (and international) empire, now became a distant appendage to an Iberian one focused on the Mediterranean and the Atlantic. As if to advertise the new status of his northern possessions at his departure in 1559, Philip left behind two *tercios* or regiments of Spanish veterans.[19]

Although the transfer of power from Charles V to Philip II in 1555–6 was widely regarded as a defining moment for Habsburg imperialism, the new hierarchy of territorial priorities was none the less far from firmly established in the early years of the reign.[20] Within policy-making circles rival perspectives on this issue existed. The Portuguese-born Ruy Gómez de Silva, prince of Eboli, and his political allies advocated a strategy based on a decentralised and less hispanocentric model of hegemony founded upon alliances with (supposedly pro-Catholic) foreign elites, such as the French Catholic leaders and the Netherlands nobility. The rival view, propounded by the duke of Alba and his followers, was much more hispanocentric, with a deep-seated distrust of 'foreign' (i.e. non-Spanish) connections and a markedly chauvinist perspective, contemptuous even on ethnic grounds of non-Spaniards and eager to make Spain the spearhead of a Counter-Reformation crusade.[21] Although strategy probably did not constitute the major source of enmity between Eboli and Alba, their policy differences suggest that the Eboli faction represented a transitional imperial ideal, based on the medieval legacy of Burgundy and the Holy Roman Empire, with a vast dominion controlled by a multinational elite, as well as on the universalist and tolerant ideals of Erasmus and his Spanish disciples, while the Alba project related much more closely to the modern notion of the hegemonic nation-state. Unfortunately, the Spanish political theories evolved in response to the Dutch Revolt have not yet received sufficient scholarly attention. Nevertheless in Spain, as in France and England, the challenge of insurgent heresy provoked serious reflection upon the nature of political action and authority. The debate over policy towards the Netherlands also formed part of a much larger controversy on the nature of empire taking place in sixteenth-century Spain.[22]

The consequences of Philip's departure for the Netherlands soon became evident. Philip left his half-sister Margaret of Parma as regent, but she found herself surrounded by a local elite with a political agenda rather different from Philip's. In Spain the king quickly became concerned with the traditional strategic objectives of the Iberian monarchies – especially the old crusading ideal, now transformed into a modern war against the Ottoman Turks.[23] Over the next two decades he would place the defence of the Mediterranean above all other foreign obligations, and not even the outbreak of rebellion in the Netherlands, followed by the shrill calls of the duke of Alba and others to concentrate on the 'enemy at home' rather than a challenge abroad, would make him change his policy.

The Low Countries elite saw Philip's strategic reorientation as a golden opportunity to press their traditional claims for a greater role in government and for local autonomy. Acting through the local States or provincial assemblies, they refused to provide the royal government with any tax revenue until the Spanish troops had left. In 1561, after considerable deliberations, the king yielded to this demand and the troops sailed home. This concession, construed by the Netherlands opposition as a sign of the king's willingness to compromise, actually formed part of Philip's imperial strategy, since it stemmed in part from the need to reinforce Spanish garrisons in the Mediterranean against Turkish attack after a major defeat at Djerba the previous year.

The road to the Dutch Revolt was paved with many other similar misunderstandings. The Netherlands nobility, frequently out of touch with the principles of imperial policy (and sometimes even with the agenda of their own allies in the Spanish court), managed to convince itself that Philip was flexible on crucial issues of religion and policy. The king, on the other hand, could not understand why his actions and dispatches were sometimes misread in the Netherlands, and came to believe that his subjects there feigned confusion in order to avoid complying with his wishes. Consequently, dissatisfaction and mistrust between the two parties grew steadily between 1560 and 1566.[24]

Contributing to the increasing alienation between the king of Spain and the Netherlands elite was Philip's preoccupation with the defence of the Mediterranean against the Turks, a staple of his grand strategy inherited from Charles V. He focused all his resources and attention on breaking the Turkish blockade of Oran (1563), mounting an expedition to capture the Peñón de Vélez, near Tetuan (1564), and ensuring the relief of Malta in the teeth of a massive Turkish siege (1565).

This constant preoccupation with the Mediterranean soon became known in the Low Countries. Margaret of Parma's Council of State, on which the count of Egmont and Prince William of Orange sat, received regular reports on developments in the Mediterranean from Netherlanders at the court of Spain and its members drew the obvious conclusions. In addition, the public 'media' in the Low Countries, through published newsletters and broadsides made much, perhaps too much, of the Mediterranean campaigns, leading a magistrate of Ghent to state that, in view of the siege of Malta, Philip could not but concede all the claims and demands put to him.[25] The Netherlands opposition apparently came to believe that events in the Mediterranean and the tacit collaboration of the Eboli faction would lead slowly to a weakening of royal control over the Low Countries and, by default, to greater local autonomy.

This construction of future Spanish policy was based on a grave – indeed, as it turned out, fatal – misunderstanding of the royal grand strategy. Although Philip was deeply concerned with stopping the Muslim offensive in the Mediterranean, he never wavered in his commitment to defend the Catholic faith against Protestants too. In 1565, Philip sent his envoys to meet with the French regent at Bayonne to propose a common front against heresy, but the conference did not lead to an agreement. The failure of the Bayonne summit, coupled with continued religious unrest in the Netherlands, discredited the Eboli faction in Madrid. Their internationalist programme of alliance and détentes with foreigners appeared to have failed. In reality, the foreign policy alternatives that Eboli and his group offered the king had never been particularly coherent. For instance, the nobility of the Netherlands, hoping for plunder and advancement, favoured a renewal of war with France, a project obviously at odds with the French alliance sought by their allies in Madrid. Philip now turned for advice to their rivals, gathered around the duke of Alba, who advocated a much more intransigent programme of government.[26] Thus when the count of Egmont visited the court in 1565, among other things to propose another war with France, Philip had already decided to resist further concessions. However, he delayed responding and engaged in a game of equivocation, leading the count to believe he would be flexible, in order to gain time to deal with the Turkish challenge to the south.[27] Spurred by the theological advice of a charismatic Augustinian monk, Fray Lorenzo de Villavicencio, and believing that the conciliatory policy towards heresy pursued by the French monarchy had encouraged revolt, the king could not reconcile his conscience to any ideological compromise.[28] Consequently, as soon as he learnt of the relief of Malta, he wrote to Margaret of Parma reaffirming his earlier policies: no toleration for Protestants, and the expansion of the Inquisition.[29]

By now, the mistaken perception in the Netherlands of Philip's ultimate intentions had led to more dramatic demonstrations of defiance, including the presentation of a petition for political and religious freedom (the 'Request') to Margaret of Parma in April 1566, followed shortly thereafter by increasingly public Calvinist services. When Philip learned of these events he began to make preparations to return to the Netherlands, but then, once more, the Turks mounted a naval offensive in the Mediterranean, and the king, again making the preservation of the empire's southern flank his top priority, postponed his journey and gave the local elite a further (false) impression of weakness and willingness to compromise. For a second time, the Netherlands elite convinced themselves that Philip would cave in to their demands and, for a time, events appeared to support this thesis.[30] In July the king agreed to remove the papal Inquisition (albeit in exchange for a return of the episcopal Inquisition), somewhat softened the heresy laws, and issued a pardon for political offences to the leaders of the incipient revolt. David Lagomarsino has argued that these were minor, almost symbolic concessions: but they greatly troubled Philip. In a private demonstration of determination, the king declared before a notary that he had made them under duress and therefore regarded them as not binding. A week later he ordered the recruitment of thousands of German soldiers for service in the Low Countries and sent a bill of exchange for 300,000 ducats to pay for them. The future army of Flanders was born.[31]

At this point events in the Netherlands again outstripped Philip's efforts to gain control of the situation. In August 1566, iconoclastic disorders 'purified' hundreds of churches for Calvinist worship by destroying their images, paintings, stained glass and statues.[32] Shocked by such massive defiance, Philip could no longer postpone decisive intervention. After learning that the Turks had concentrated their yearly offensive against the eastern borders of Christendom (Hungary and the Adriatic), Philip deliberated with his ministers on a forceful solution to the troubles in his northern possessions. The records of the Spanish Council of State's deliberations in September and October 1566 provide valuable insight into the major principles of Spanish foreign policy and royal grand strategy. His councillors used the argument of the 'escalation of potential disasters', or 'domino theory' to goad the king into action, warning him that 'if the Netherlands situation is not remedied, it will bring about the loss of Spain and all the rest'.[33] Others cautioned that any appearance of weakness would imperil 'reputation', and asserted that French and Protestant interests would prevail in Europe if not stopped in the Low Countries.[34] Fray Lorenzo de Villavicencio reminded Philip that the Spanish monarchy could not shrink from its historical mission to defend the faith, because 'it is for this that God has given Your Majesty a sceptre, a sword, a crown, power, riches, grandeur, kingdoms, states, nobles, soldiers, and brilliant victories'.[35] Villavicencio also appealed to the king's own conscience and to the strategic legacy of Charles V, arguments that could not fail to register with the king who had long considered himself entrusted with a religious mission.[36] Though Villavicencio and Alba disagreed on the use of military force and on the role of Spain within the monarchy, both concurred that the challenge of the Netherlands represented a sort of Armageddon: a major moment of decision and definition for the Spanish monarchy, with profound international and historical consequences. Evidence that the Dutch Calvinists had allied themselves with those in France and Germany lent credibility to these arguments and further undermined the position of Eboli and his supporters, who still advocated a peaceful solution to the troubles that would respect the traditional liberties and prerogatives of the Low Countries.[37]

The duke of Alba had clearly won the day. Whereas his rivals could only advocate vague compromises, the Alba faction, equipped with a potent political, historical and military vocabulary, proposed a clearer imperial strategy rooted in the legacy of Charles V and in Philip's own ideological inclinations. In addition, whereas the Alba faction coordinated its projects with supporters in the Netherlands, the Eboli party continued to favour a foreign policy essentially at odds with the preferences of their friends in Brussels. They therefore found themselves undermined by their allies' independent agenda. On the other hand, the coherence of the Alba option doubtless appealed to Philip who reiterated his resolve to go back to the Netherlands – although, in view of the doubtful loyalty of the coastal provinces and the international ramifications of the crisis, he decided to send a powerful army commanded by the duke himself to pacify the country before his arrival and make it safe for his presence.[38] Even at this point, Philip II made his journey dependent on a stable military situation in the Mediterranean, and probably held Alba back while he kept an eye on the south.[39] However, despite this caution, over the winter of 1566–7 Philip II put his grand strategy into action and involved his monarchy in a policy of military commitment on all fronts. The empire would only enjoy complete peace for six more months of his entire reign (in 1577). The same costly, inflexible policy would, with relatively brief intermissions, remain in force at least until the reign of his grandson Philip IV and would become a major factor in the ultimate decline of Spain from hegemonic status in Europe.[40]

Alba arrived in Brussels only on 22 August 1567, and he soon realised that the long royal absence, coupled with the government's lack of troops, had fostered a very dangerous political and military situation: large numbers of those involved in the disorders had fled abroad and were said to be preparing, with French and German help, an armed invasion.[41]

The king had already reached the same conclusion. Two weeks before Alba arrived in Brussels, Philip resolved to remain in Spain until the following spring. His desire to keep the decision entirely secret led him to encode personally much of his eight-page letter of explanation to Alba. 'Nobody knows that I am writing to you', he claimed, as he reviewed in detail the implications of his drastic change of plan. Margaret of Parma would need to be replaced as regent in the Netherlands and Philip raised the possibility of sending his young brother Don Juan, whom Alba could train so that he would be ready to take over after the king's visit. More funds would be required to maintain all Spanish troops for the additional months, and the duke must find ways to secure them locally. The punishment of those implicated in the troubles, which Alba had been instructed to carry out at once, could now be delayed until the winter, in the hope that:

> This might offer reassurance to the Prince of Orange, so that he will want to return to those provinces (although I doubt it). It would be a great thing to be able to deal with him as he deserves, because if we punish the others first it would rule out dealing with him forever. Nevertheless, [the king concluded] I remit all this to you, as the person who will be on the spot, with a better understanding of the advantages and disadvantages which might arise in all this, and of whether to act swiftly or slowly in the matter of punishments, on which so much depends.[42]

Although these suggestions contained much wisdom, the king's decision to put off his departure and to leave Alba to take all the essential decisions in the meantime proved fatal errors. On the one hand, the duke wasted no time in pressing ahead with 'the punishments'. Only five days after entering Brussels he set up a secret tribunal to try those accused of heresy and rebellion; early in September he had Egmont and other Netherlands leaders arrested. Margaret of Parma, outraged by the detention of her former advisers, resigned almost immediately, forcing Alba to take over the civil government of the provinces himself. Orange, just as the king had feared, remained in Germany. On the other hand, Philip had lost his last opportunity to revisit the Netherlands.

The year 1568 proved to be one of the worst of the reign. Although the Mediterranean remained at peace, in the Low Countries the rebels, led by William of Orange, launched a serious invasion which Alba only defeated by mobilising almost 70,000 troops and campaigning for several months. Meanwhile, in Spain, the behaviour of Don Carlos, heir to the Spanish throne, became so erratic and intemperate that the king had to arrest him. By the time Alba had triumphed, Don Carlos was dead, and so was Philip's queen, Elizabeth de Valois, whom he had intended to leave as his regent while he revisited Brussels. Finally, after a period of relative quiet, serious trouble erupted on the southern front. At the end of 1568, a major rebellion broke out among the Moriscos (Muslim converts to Christianity) of Granada, which spread rapidly the following year. In 1569, the Turks resumed their attacks on Christian outposts in the Mediterranean, invading the Venetian island of Cyprus. In keeping with his hierarchy of policy priorities, the king chose to stay in Spain and concentrate his resources on restoring order in the peninsula and defending the Mediterranean.

With typical tenacity, however, Philip remained committed to an uncompromising religious and political course in the Low Countries. He rejected out of hand all pleas from his cousin, Emperor Maximilian II, to moderate his policies and compromise in matters of religion, declaring that:

> Neither human regard nor reason of state, nor anything else in all the world would make him deviate nor stray in a single point from the road that in this matter of religion and its conduct within his kingdoms and states . . . he has followed and means to follow and maintain forever. And [he will do so] with such firmness and constancy, that in this matter he will not only reject advice and arguments that contradict this, but also cannot in any fashion listen to them nor think it proper that such advice should be offered.[43]

He also forcefully rejected Maximilian's argument that, since most of the provinces of the Low Countries were fiefs of the empire (a claim endorsed by many in the Netherlands), he had a right as Holy Roman Emperor to intervene in the dispute.[44] Bitter disagreements over the Netherlands thus prompted Philip to deviate from his father's advice to maintain close relations with his Habsburg relatives in Vienna. It was one of the few principles of Charles V's 'political testament' that Philip abandoned. Consequently, relations between the two branches of the family remained cool for decades.

Meanwhile, in the Netherlands Alba's administration succeeded at least temporarily in paying for itself with new and highly unpopular taxes, leaving Philip free to send a massive fleet (maintained jointly by himself, Venice and the papacy) into the eastern Mediterranean where, in October 1571, it inflicted a crushing defeat on the Ottoman navy at the battle of Lepanto. Although the duke remained characteristically pessimistic about his master's long-term prospects for victory, in reality, Philip II's grand strategy was never more successful than during these years. After all, his forces had managed to hold their own in the Mediterranean and at the same time reconquer all rebellious areas in the

Netherlands. Without leaving Castile, the king of Spain had ordered and supervised the creation of the largest army and the largest navy in Christendom, which then conducted two brilliantly successful military campaigns by land and sea, in the farthest reaches of his European empire. Government by remote control had worked, despite Braudel's 'unfavourable arithmetic of distances'. The question was: for how long?

The Turks made good their naval losses remarkably swiftly, forcing Philip to allocate an even larger share of his resources to the Mediterranean theatre in 1572, and to pressure the duke of Alba to raise more revenues locally to support his unpopular regime.[45] In April of that year, a force of about 1100 Dutch exiles loyal to William of Orange and popularly known as the Sea Beggars, captured Brill in South Holland and were later welcomed into Flushing. The following month, with the help of French Protestants, Louis of Nassau took by surprise the city of Mons in the southern province of Hainault. Then, in June, another rebel force crossed from Germany and seized several strategic towns in the eastern province of Gelderland. Finally, in July, William of Orange brought another army from Germany and began to capture towns in Limburg, also in the east. At the same time, it appeared as if King Charles IX of France, influenced by his Protestant advisers, would shortly declare war on Spain.[46]

Alba's response to these threats was quite consistent with the Spanish monarchy's overall strategic priorities. In view of the manifest danger of a French declaration of war, he decided to give absolute precedence to the southern frontier. Despite the steady progress of the rebels in the north, Alba not only refused to reinforce his subordinates there, but instead withdrew their best troops southwards. Alba's strategic choice would not only contribute to the independence of the northern Netherlands, just as his subordinates then predicted, but would also guide the Spanish military effort in the Low Countries for decades to come. At least since Charles V's 'political testament', Spanish strategists had viewed the Netherlands primarily as a platform to launch attacks against Spain's enemies in northern Europe, and the duke of Alba, who had long been in favour of a belligerent stance against France, could not be expected to act otherwise.[47]

Alba's gamble paid off. In July, Spanish troops destroyed a French Protestant attempt to reinforce Mons. Then in August the massacre of Huguenots, first in Paris and then in other cities, temporarily ruled out further French intervention in the Netherlands. Alba also repulsed Orange's attempt to relieve Mons and the city surrendered. Within a month, William's army had disintegrated in the face of the duke's relentless skirmishing.[48]

In the intervening time, however, the Calvinist rebels had become entrenched in dozens of towns in the north. Alba, desperate for money to replenish his depleted army and resolved to conduct a methodical campaign of siege and attrition against the northern rebels, pleaded with Philip II to alter his grand strategy:

> Everything spent on the League [against the Ottomans] is wasted . . . I beat my head against the wall when I hear talk about what we are spending here, since it is not the Turks who are disturbing Christendom but the heretics, and they are already within the gates.[49]

However, even after Venice's defection from the Holy League in February 1573, the king refused to change course, but instead continued to pour millions of ducats (at least as much as he spent on the army of Flanders) into the Mediterranean theatre. His refusal stemmed not only from the traditional commitment to defend Christendom, but also from his conviction that to seek peace from the sultan would damage his reputation.[50]

Without resources to conduct a traditional campaign against the fifty or so Netherlands towns in revolt, Alba decided to practise a policy of selective brutality designed to intimidate the Dutch into surrender. At first this policy worked. The savage sack of Mechelen, Zutphen and Naarden late in 1572 produced the unconditional capitulation of many towns in the south and east. The following year, however, the massacre of the garrison of Haarlem after a surprisingly long siege, as well as Alkmaar's successful resistance, greatly stiffened Dutch resolve. In addition, the Spanish army mutinied for pay and the Dutch scored an important naval victory in October. The revolt therefore continued. The king now concluded that Alba was a spent force and he ordered Don Luis de Requesens to take over. The new captain general assumed office in December 1573.[51]

Success still proved elusive, however, despite the remittance of unprecedented sums from Spain, which allowed Requesens to increase the size of the army of Flanders to its highest level ever: 86,000 men. After the Spanish attempt to capture Leiden failed for the second time in October 1574, Requesens and his advisers concluded that, given Philip II's strategic dilemma, traditional military tactics would not succeed against the Dutch.[52] The most imaginative and potentially deadly of the alternatives they presented to the Spanish monarch was the systematic inundation of Holland and Zeeland, that is, literally to drown the Dutch. From a military standpoint, the operation was entirely feasible but, to the disgust of the high command in Brussels, Philip vetoed the operation.[53]

Requesens had run up against another major principle of royal policy: the need to preserve his reputation. Philip, who had once toured Dutch lands drowned by an earlier collapse of the dikes, knew very well how effective this tactic could be but feared its impact on European public opinion.[54] 'Even though their guilt is notorious and the punishment is justified', he wrote, 'we should also recognize that it would earn for us a reputation for cruelty, especially against our vassals, which would be better avoided'.[55] On both moral and political grounds the king rejected a military solution that, in spite of the problems of distance and money, might have ended the Dutch Revolt in a matter of weeks.

Another alternative for ending the rebellion involved creating a royal fleet in the North Sea. Several defeats in late 1573 and early 1574 had all but eliminated the king's navy in the Netherlands, and everyone recognised that, in view of William of Orange's powerful fleet and his control of major ports in Holland and Zeeland, unless Spain gained command of the seas the revolt could last for decades.[56] The king had long appreciated the value of sea power to defend his Mediterranean and Atlantic possessions.[57] In February 1574 Philip signed orders to create a fleet based on Santander both to clear 'the Channel [of Dutch vessels] and to recapture some ports in the Netherlands occupied by the rebels'.[58] At the same time, he appointed one of Spain's most successful and experienced admirals, Pedro Menéndez de Avilés, to command this force.[59] However, in the end, despite great efforts, Philip cancelled the expedition due to the death of its leader, an epidemic in the ranks and (perhaps most importantly) a renewed Turkish threat in the Mediterranean. Again, the monarchy's grand strategy had got in the way of military success in the Netherlands.[60]

This fiasco, coupled with major reverses in both the Mediterranean and the Low Countries, led the king and his advisers to consider yet another alternative: a negotiated settlement with the Dutch. His decision to recall Alba stemmed primarily from his growing conviction that force must henceforth be tempered by concessions to save the Netherlands for God and its sovereign. Even before the duke departed, in July 1573 Philip urged him to moderate his policy and try to reach a settlement with the rebels. Alba strenuously objected, and it fell to Requesens to try his hand at securing a compromise.[61]

Even before official parleys could begin, however, each side adopted principles of negotiation thoroughly unacceptable to the other. Philip II expressly forbade Requesens to make religious concessions or to pardon the rebel leaders, and William of Orange insisted on toleration for all Calvinists, the restoration of the antebellum government structure, and the withdrawal of all foreign troops.[62] Philip nevertheless showed considerable flexibility and by July 1575 agreement had been reached on almost all political issues. When this did not suffice, Requesens reluctantly accepted Alba's vision of the revolt: religion constituted the real cause of the continuing resistance of the Dutch. Although a military victory had become extremely difficult, to Philip and his Spanish advisers a settlement involving the toleration of Protestantism remained absolutely unacceptable.[63] The same dilemma undermined peace talks in 1577, 1579, 1589 and 1598.[64] Eventually the very idea of negotiation with the rebels would become unpalatable to Philip II's advisers, for fear that it would damage the king's reputation. Yet again, the ideological foundations of Spanish imperial policy contributed to the continuation of the military stalemate in the Netherlands.[65]

The strain of fighting on two fronts (or, as Paul Kennedy would put it, 'imperial overstretch') led in September 1575 to an official decree of bankruptcy suspending all payments from the Spanish Treasury. As Requesens wrote in despair, 'short of a miracle the whole military machine will fall apart'.[66] Since no miracle occurred, Requesens' pessimism proved prophetic: in March 1576 he himself died of the plague and in July the unpaid Spanish field army mutinied and abandoned Holland and Zeeland at a time when their offensive again seemed about to succeed. Another power vacuum occurred. Requesens' successor, the king's half-brother Don Juan of Austria, did not arrive in the Netherlands until November 1576 and in the meantime the Spanish high command, acting on their own initiative, pursued a hard line against both the rebels and the government in Brussels. The abuses that their troops committed, particularly the sack of Antwerp, alienated almost the entire country. The States of the 'loyal' provinces began talks with the rebels and, early in 1577, forced Philip II to withdraw all foreign troops from the Netherlands.[67] The entire country thus slipped out of royal control.

Although the king appeared to have abandoned his northern possessions, in reality, as in 1565, royal policy in the Netherlands responded not just to local events but also to global strategy. Despite Lepanto, the Ottoman navy seemed more dangerous than ever. Fear of a Muslim offensive in 1576, after the decree of bankruptcy had destroyed his ability to raise loans, probably explains Philip's uncharacteristic willingness to allow the Low Countries to go their own way, at least for a time.[68] However, no sooner did Philip receive news that the sultan had agreed to a suspension of hostilities than in August 1577 he ordered the return of the *tercios* to help restore the authority of Don Juan of Austria.

By this time, the Spaniards held the province of Luxemburg and little else. In order to woo prominent members of the local nobility back to the royal camp, Don Juan's successor, Alexander Farnese, prince of Parma, agreed to a second withdrawal of foreign troops from the country in 1579.[69] Philip II gave his approval to this measure only because, once more, his strategic principles urged him to refocus his attention on problems closer to 'home': on the neighbouring kingdom of Portugal, whose crown he seemed likely to inherit. As in 1561, the troops went directly from the Low Countries to the southern theatre of operations and in 1580–3 participated in one of Philip's greatest achievements, the annexation of Portugal, followed by the conquest of the Azores. As one councillor starkly observed, 'in terms of the utility, the good and the strength of Spain, and of the grandeur and power of Your Majesty, uniting the crowns of Portugal and Castile matters more than the reconquest of the Netherlands'.[70] During these years, the funds sent from Spain to the Netherlands plummeted, but as soon as the neighbouring kingdom was secure, Philip sent the *tercios* back to the Low Countries.[71]

Before long, the king's attention turned to yet another challenge: the emergence of England as a major Atlantic naval power. Consequently, despite substantial expenditure, the Low Countries remained a secondary priority within Spanish imperial strategy. Nevertheless, Parma's considerable military skills allowed him to put to tremendous advantage the window of opportunity he now enjoyed. In the three years following the annexation of Portugal he more than doubled the area under the king of Spain's obedience and brought the army of Flanders before the gates of Antwerp, the rebels' capital.[72] Ironically, his rapid success turned out to be counterproductive for it provoked England's Queen Elizabeth (already at odds with Spain over religion, trade with the Indies and several Spanish plots against her life) to offer the Dutch a treaty of military cooperation. The Treaty of Nonsuch, signed in August 1585, though it failed to save Antwerp, led to increased English naval activity against the Spanish Indies and prompted Philip II to begin serious consideration of 'the enterprise of England'.[73]

In this planned naval invasion, which occupied Philip and his advisers for three years, the interests of the royal cause in the Netherlands took a back seat to the defence of Spain's Atlantic empire. As Don Juan de Zúñiga the king's major adviser on foreign strategy effectively argued in 1585, the Dutch problem affected only the Netherlands and was thus much less important than the English one, which threatened the entire empire.[74] In fact, Spain's oceanic reorientation had begun much earlier, after the absorption of Portugal gave Philip a magnificent Atlantic seaport at Lisbon which could serve as a naval *plaza de armas* or headquarters for the *Armada del Mar Océano* (High Seas Fleet).[75] The failure of his fleet to land in England, which Philip attributed to the negative intervention of Providence, did not shake his determination to fight Elizabeth, and the Netherlands sank further still in his list of priorities when the last bout of religious civil war in France began in 1589. Spanish intervention during the last decade of Philip's reign in an attempt to keep France Catholic, though ultimately successful, was fought and financed with men and money from the army of Flanders, thus providing the rebels with the opportunity to secure the independence of the northern Netherlands.

The history of Philip II's initial response to the Dutch Revolt thus offers partial support for the explanations advanced by Fernand Braudel and Paul Kennedy for Spain's failure to secure long-lasting European and global mastery. The long distance (1000 kilometres) separating Spain from the Netherlands first contributed to mutual misunderstandings that led to the outbreak and the continuation of the revolt, and thereafter made it difficult for the king to apply political solutions and to support the military effort needed to crush the uprising. Eventually Philip found that his domains lacked sufficient resources with which to offer adequate support to a huge and distant army, especially when he remained heavily committed to the defence of the Mediterranean and the Atlantic as well.

Yet this neat 'materialistic model' of military and economic determinism for the survival of the Dutch Revolt, although accurate as far as it goes, remains insufficient in four major respects. First, it overlooks the fact that Spain, thanks to its relatively efficient military system and its enviable range of resources, came several times within a hair's breadth of victory on all fronts, especially in 1568, 1572, 1575 and 1585. Second, it leaves no room for the numerous factors unconnected with economics or distance that thwarted the royal efforts and thereby prolonged the war, such as Philip's refusal to visit the Netherlands in 1567, Alba's overuse of selective brutality against the rebels in 1572, or the hard-line policies of the Spanish high command in 1576–7. These incidents, which the king, like his opponents, attributed to providential intervention, were only remotely connected to issues of distance and resources. Third, the 'materialistic model' leaves no room for intriguing counterfactual possibilities, all of them perfectly plausible even within the context of royal strategy. The outcome of the troubles in the Netherlands could easily have been different had Alba in 1567 delayed his programme of repression (as Philip II suggested) until after Orange had returned to Brussels, or had he in 1572 offered clemency to rebel cities and thus avoided a protracted siege. Finally, and most importantly, the materialistic explanations completely ignore the existence and application of a global strategy which conditioned and limited the king's choices just as much as (if not more than) distance and limited resources. The 'materialistic model' does not explain Philip's consistent preference for the Mediterranean, Atlantic and Iberian theatres over and above the Netherlands in the allocation of resources, attention and manpower, nor his rejection of tactical inundation, his failure to gain naval mastery in the North Sea, and, above all, his refusal to negotiate a compromise settlement. All of these decisions and delays, failures and triumphs, sprang from political and ideological considerations, not from economic or military factors.

The Dutch Revolt constituted, in Philip II's own words, 'the greatest and most important enterprise with which I have had, or could have, to deal', since it stood at the intersection of religious, dynastic, political and military issues of major contemporary relevance and of vital interest to the survival of his complex monarchy.[76] Unlike his counterparts in France in the late sixteenth century or in the Holy Roman Empire in the seventeenth, who also faced armed Protestant rebellion, Philip had to take into account a much wider geopolitical scenario. Formulating a satisfactory response to the challenge of insurgent heresy thus led the Spanish court both to a clearer understanding of a grand strategy for the entire empire and to its practical application in the determination and enforcement of policy. Thus in 1573, when a group of cardinals pressed Philip either to reside in Italy to campaign against the Turks, or in the Netherlands to supervise the conduct of war there, his ambassador in Rome (Don Juan de Zúñiga) reminded them that:

> Since Your Majesty rules so many kingdoms and states, and since in their conservation and in the life and well-being of Your Majesty reposes the entire welfare of Christendom, it is not enough to believe that the journey should be of benefit to the affairs of either Italy or the Netherlands if it is not of benefit to the entire global empire which depends on Your Majesty.

Such broad considerations continued to serve as a crucial catalyst in the developing of a global stance that remained more or less unaltered until the reign of Philip IV.[77]

Contrary to standard scholarly opinion on the Netherlands conflict, this was not 'a war [Philip II] could not win'.[78] From 1559 to the end of his reign, the king's ideological and strategic principles shaped the fate of the Netherlands. Within his grand strategy, the Low Countries seldom constituted the highest priority and, as a result, he never applied to the Revolt the single-minded attention and resources that would have been necessary to suppress it. Though Philip did possess the means to defeat the rebels, his grand strategy consistently diverted his efforts elsewhere: that is, if Philip became 'trapped' in the Low Countries, the trap was primarily of his own making, and its nature was ideological and strategic, not material. To be sure, imperial Spain was both challenged by distance and lacked sufficient resources to impose its will everywhere, but this has been the plight of most hegemonic powers in the history of the world. Under such circumstances, the Dutch Revolt became a conflict that exposed the tensions inherent in Philip II's ambitious global strategy: the defence of Christianity in the south versus the protection of Catholicism in the north. The king did well to retain control of the largest portion of the country (ten of the seventeen provinces) and bequeath it to his heirs.

Notes

Abbreviations used in the notes:

AA: Archivo de la Casa de los Duques de Alba, Madrid. Manuscript Collection (with 'caja' and folio).

AGRB: Archives Générales du Royaume/Algemeeen Rijksarchief, Brussels.

AGS: Archivo General de Simancas, Spain.

BL: British Library, London, Department of Western Manuscripts.

BNM: Biblioteca Nacional, Madrid. Manuscript Section.

BPU Favre: Bibliothèque Publique et Universitaire, Geneva, Collection Manuscrite Edouard Favre.

BZ: Biblioteca de Zabálburu, Madrid (with 'caja' and folio).

Codoin and *Nueva Codoin: Colección de documentos inéditos para la historia de España* (112 vols, Madrid, 1842–95); *Nueva colección de documentos inéditos para la historia de España* (5 vols, Madrid, 1892–4).

IVDJ: Instituto de Valencia de Don Juan, Madrid, Manuscript Collection (with 'envío' and folio).

1 For the earlier period, see the recent study, dealing primarily with naval strategy, by Fernando de Bordejé y Morencos, *El escenario estratégico español en el siglo XVI (1492–1556)* (Madrid, 1990).

2 H. G. Koenigsberger, 'The Statecraft of Philip II', *European Studies Review*, I (1), (1971), pp. 1–21; Paul Kennedy, *The Rise and Fall of the Great Powers* (New York: Random House, 1987).

3 Pierre Chaunu, 'Seville et la "Belgique", 1555–1648', *Revue du Nord*, XLII (1960), pp. 259–92 criticised by Geoffrey Parker in his 'Spain, Her Enemies and the Revolt of the Netherlands, 1559–1648', in *Spain and the Netherlands* (2nd edition, London: Fontana, 1990), pp. 17–42.

4 David Lagomarsino, 'Court Factions and the Formulation of Spanish Policy Towards the Netherlands (1559–1567)' (unpublished doctoral dissertation, Cambridge University, 1973).

5   Fernand Braudel, *The Mediterranean and the Mediterranean World in the Age of Philip II* (2 vols, New York: Harper and Row, 1973).

6   For instance, before giving his approval to the planned invasion of England, Philip consulted with the Pope on how to justify the operation to the world: Jorge Calvar Gross, *Batalla del Mar Océano* (3 vols, Madrid, 1988–93), vol. I, pp. 553–4, Philip II to the count of Olivares, 2 January 1586. He did the same before invading Portugal in 1580.

7   This is, of course, rather ironic for a monarch with such a consistently negative image in the historiography. For a dated, though still interesting sample of historical views, see John Rule and J. J. TePaske, *The Character of Philip II. The Problem of Moral Judgements in History* (Boston, 1963).

8   For example, when the annual Indies fleet arrived safely at Seville, the king proudly informed his ministers that 'God has done this'. BZ 166/92 and 100, Hernando de Vega to Philip II and reply, 9 and 11 November 1586.

9   AGS Estado 2851, unfol., opinion of the marquis of Almazán, 22 November 1588, and Estado 2855, unfol., 'Lo que parecio sobre los quatro papeles principales', November 1589.

10 'God is my witness', wrote Philip near the end of his reign, 'that I have never made war to gain more kingdoms, but only to maintain them in the [Catholic] faith and peace'. In L. Pereña Vicente, *Teoría de la guerra en Francisco Suárez* (Madrid, 1954), vol. I, p. 62, from a funeral oration in 1598 quoting a letter from Philip II to the *corregidor* of Toro.

11 Historians sometimes deny that such a hierarchy of priorities existed. See, for instance, John Lynch, *Spain Under the Habsburgs* (2 vols, Oxford: Blackwell, 1965–9), vol. I, p. 347.

12 See the entire text in Manuel Fernández Alvarez, *Corpus documental Carlos V* (5 vols, Salamanca, 1974–81), pp. 569–601, as well as some recent interpretations by B. Beinert, 'El testamento político de Carlos V de 1548. Estudio crítico', in *Carlos V. Homenaje de la Universidad de Granada* (Granada, 1958) and Manuel Fernández Alvarez, 'Las instrucciones políticas de los austrias mayores. Problemas e interpretaciones', in *Gesammelte Aufsätze zur Kulturgeschichte Spaniens*, XXIII (1967), pp. 171–88.

13 See M. J. Rodríguez-Salgado, *The Changing Face of Empire. Charles V, Philip II and Habsburg Authority, 1551–1559* (Cambridge: Cambridge University Press, 1988), pp. 76, 78.

14 Braudel, *The Mediterranean*, vol. II, p. 950. For a detailed discussion of the origins and background of Philip's decision see Rodríguez-Salgado, *Changing Face of Empire*, pp. 297–8 and 339–56.

15 *Actas de las Cortes de Castilla*, vol. III (Madrid, 1863), p. 16. The capital of the empire would (after 1559) remain in Castile forever, though there were, of course, some long royal absences, most of them prompted by rebellion and/or war in the periphery, such as Philip II's stay in Lisbon from 1580 to 1583, and Philip IV's visits to Aragon in the 1640s.

16 The Spanish Habsburg empire underwent another similar change in its 'centre of gravity' in the later half of the seventeenth century when, according to John Lynch, a 'shift of power' took place from the peninsula to the American colonies. See John Lynch, *The Hispanic World in Crisis and Change 1598–1700* (Oxford: Blackwell, 1992), pp. 287–98.

17 Braudel, *The Mediterranean*, vol. II, pp. 951–2.

18 Quoted in L. P. Gachard, *Retraite et mort de Charles-Quint* (2 vols, Brussels, 1854–5), vol. II, p. 43, from Philip II's instructions to Bartolomé de Carranza, 5 June 1558.

19 Geoffrey Parker, *The Dutch Revolt* (2nd edition, New York: Penguin, 1984), p. 46.

20 For contemporary Spanish reaction to the accession of Philip II to the crown see Lagomarsino, 'Court Factions', p. 317; for the changing priorities, see Geoffrey Parker, *The Grand Strategy of Philip II* (London and New Haven: Yale University Press, 1998), p. 91.

21 For the duke of Alba's views of non-Spaniards see Fernando González de León, 'The Road to Rocroi: The Duke of Alba, the Count-Duke of Olivares and the High Command of the Spanish Army of Flanders in the Eighty Years War' (unpublished doctoral dissertation, Johns Hopkins University, 1991), ch. I.

22 For the Dutch side there is the splendid recent study, Martin Van Gelderen, *The Political Thought of the Dutch Revolt, 1555–1590* (Cambridge: Cambridge University Press, 1992). For the Spanish side, see Lagomarsino, 'Court Factions', ch. 8, pp. 289–319. For the wider debate in Spain, see Anthony Pagden, *Spanish Imperialism and the Political Imagination*, and *Lords of All the World. Ideologies of Empire in Spain, Britain and France c. 1500–c. 1800* (London and New Haven: Yale University Press, 1995).

23 For a summary of Spain's long preoccupation with the Muslim south, see Rodríguez-Salgado, *Changing Face of Empire*, pp. 253–88.

24 Lagomarsino, 'Court Factions', p. 123. Ironically, historians of these events, often working from one or the other side of the divide, have been prone to similar misunderstandings.

25 Ibid., pp. 65–6 and 286, note 46.

26 Ibid., pp. 149–70, 192–3.

27 Ibid., pp. 123–5.

28 Ibid., pp. 110–12, 163–76, 181.

29 Parker, *Dutch Revolt*, pp. 66–7.

30 Lagomarsino, 'Court Factions', pp. 214–15.

31 Ibid., pp. 238–44.

32 Parker, *Dutch Revolt*, pp. 74–81.

33 Ibid., p. 88.

34 Lagomarsino, 'Court Factions', p. 297.

35 Ibid., p. 297.

36 See Rodríguez-Salgado, *Changing Face of Empire*, pp. 160–1.

37 Lagomarsino, 'Court Factions', pp. 254–9.

38 Ibid., pp. 265–88.

39 For the suggestion that Mediterranean affairs might have held Alba back, see Fourquevaux's letters in C. Douais, *Dépêches de M. de Fourquevaux, Ambassadeur du Roi Charles IX en Espagne, 1565–72* (3 vols, Paris, 1896–1904), vol. I, pp. 147–8, Letter to Charles IX 9 December 1566 and pp. 172–9, letter to Catherine de Medici, 18 January 1567.

40 On the persistence of these priorities, see J. Israel, *Conflicts of Empires. Spain, the Low Countries and the Struggle for World Supremacy* (London: Hambledon Press, 1997), chs 2–4 and 6.

41 Parker, *Dutch Revolt*, pp. 91–2.

42 AA 5/69 Philip II to Alba, 7 August 1567.

43 *Codoin*, vol. CIII, Documento de S. M. al Archiduque su primo, January 1569.

44 Ibid., Respuesta que S. M. dio al Archiduque Carlos, 20 January 1569. See also Lagomarsino, 'Court Factions', p. 214.

45 For details on the Turks' rapid recovery after Lepanto see the exciting new evidence in C. Imber, *Studies in Ottoman History*. Analecta Isiniana XX (Istanbul, 1996), pp. 85–101. For the Hispano-Turkish struggle in the Mediterranean see R. Cerezo Martínez, *Años cruciales en la historia del Mediterraneo (1570–1574)* (Barcelona, 1971).

46 AGRB Audience 340/31, Alba to the count of Bossu, 13 February 1572; AGS Estado 551/94, Relación de lo que se trató en consejo; BL Additional Ms 28, 702/261–4, Relación sobre los abusos; AGRB Audience 404/139, Zweveghem to Alba, London 25 March 1572; Audience 340/70, Alba to Wacken, 4 April 1572; Audience 340/72, 79, 81 and 105, Bossu to Alba, 2, 3, 4 and 7 April 1572; Audience 344/21 and 29, Bossu to Alba, 23 May 1572. See the standard account of the Nassau brothers' negotiations with the Huguenots in P. J. van Herwerden, *Het verblijf van Lodewijk van Nassau in Frankrijk. Huguenoten en geuzen, 1568–1572* (Assen, 1932), with a few additional data in A. Jouanna, *Le devoir de révolte. La noblesse française et la gestation de l'état moderne (1559–1661)* (Paris, 1989), pp. 154–6. For fears that France would declare war, see the pessimistic letters in J. M. March, *El comendador mayor de Castilla, Don Luis de Requeséns en el gobierno de Milán (1571–3)* (2nd edition, Madrid, 1946), pp. 153–5. In Madrid, ambassador Sauli of Genoa believed that France would soon declare war: Archivio di Stato, Genoa, Archivio Segreto 2414, unfol., letters to Genoa of 25 May, 27 June and 2 July 1572.

47 C. Piot and E. Poullet, *Correspondance du Cardenal de Granvelle* (12 vols, Brussels, 1877–96), vol. IV, p. 351, Morillon to Granvelle, 10 August 1572; AGRB Audience 344/83, Alba to Bossu, 15 June 1572; Audience 313/303–4, Council of Gelderland to Alba, 28 June 1572, protesting against his order of the 25th to recall royal troops south. The governor of Friesland refused to release any troops to Holland: Audience 297/162, baron Billy to Alba 16 June 1572. Audience 344/88, 135, 169, Bossu to Alba 17 June, 5 and 18 July 1572; ibid. fo. 164, Alba to Bossu, 17 July 1572. Bossu finally complied a week later, reporting that the rebels had immediately occupied all places abandoned by the Spaniards: ibid., fo. 174, Bossu to Alba, 26 July 1572. For Alba's long-standing views on France, see Lagomarsino, 'Court Factions', p. 28.

48 *Epistolario del III duque de Alba* (3 vols, Madrid, 1952), vol. III, p. 169, Alba to Philip II 19 July 1572 describing the defeat of the French column; J. Estèbe, *Tocsin pour un massacre: La saison de St Barthélemy* (Paris, 1968), analyses the events before, during and after 24 August; see also G. Groen Van Prinsterer, *Archives ou correspondence inédite de la maison d'Orange-Nassau, 1552–1789* (1st series, 8 vols, and supplement, Leiden, 1835–47), vol. III, p. 505 and vol. IV, p. cii, Orange to Count John, 21 September 1572, lamenting the impact of Saint Bartholomew on his cause.

49 *Codoin*, vol. LXXV, p. 190, Alba to Gabriel de Zayas, 12 February 1573.

50 AGS Estado 554/89, Philip II to Alba 18 March 1573.

51 Parker, *Dutch Revolt*, pp. 141–2, 156–63.

52 *Nueva Codoin*, vol. V, p. 368, Requesens to Philip II, 6 October 1574.

53 AGS Estado 560/91, Francisco de Valdés to Requesens 18 September 1574. See also M. C. Waxman, 'Strategic Terror: Philip II and Sixteenth Century Warfare', *War in History*, IV (1997), pp. 339–47.

54 For Philip's visit in 1549, see Parker, *Dutch Revolt*, p. 28.

55 AGS Estado 561/122, Philip II to Requesens, 22 October 1574.

56 BNM Ms 1749/361–79, memorial of Alonso Gutiérrez, 23 October 1577. For some other Spanish appreciations of the need to achieve naval mastery at this time, see AGS Estado 1236/24, Requesens to Philip II, 23 February 1573; IVDJ 67/203, Requesens to Zúñiga, 14 December 1573; *Nueva Codoin*, vol. I, pp. 31–2, Zúñiga to Requesens, 9 January 1574; IVDJ 76/505–6, anonymous memorandum on the need to control the North Sea, 1575; AGS Estado 578/119–21, opinions voiced at the Council of State 14/23 June 1578; Piot, *Correspondance du Cardenal de Granvelle*, vol. X, p. 239, Granvelle to Broissia, 7 June 1583; and vol. XII, p. 169, Granvelle to Charles of Mansfeld, 18 April 1586. Even poets advocated creating a navy, because conquering the Dutch by land 'would be to confront the impossible'. See Francisco de Aldana's 'Octavas' in his *Obras completas* (Madrid, 1953), pp. 17–56, and especially 33–4 and 40–1.

57 In the Mediterranean, thanks to a massive programme of construction, Philip managed to triple the size of his galley fleet, and throughout his administration he issued a stream of orders designed to raise the quality and quantity of ships meant for convoy duty in the Americas and other purposes. See M. Pi Corrales, *Felipe II y la lucha por el dominio del mar* (Madrid, 1989), and David Goodman, *Spanish Naval Power, 1589–1665. Reconstruction and Defeat* (Cambridge: Cambridge University Press, 1997).

58 M. Pi Corrales, *España y las potencias nórdicas. 'La otra invencible', 1574* (Madrid, 1983), p. 182.

59 On his career, see C. Vigil, *Pedro Menéndez de Avilés, primer adelantado y conquistador de la Florida* (Avilés, 1892), and Eugene Lyon, *The Enterprise of Florida. Pedro Menéndez de Avilés and the Spanish Conquest of 1565–8* (Gainesville, 1976).

60 It would be decades before Spanish planners would return to this project. See R. A. Stradling, *The Armada of Flanders. Spanish Maritime Policy and European War, 1568–1668* (Cambridge: Cambridge University Press, 1992).

61 AA 8/45, Philip II to Alba, 8 July 1573; AGS Estado 554/146, Requesens to Philip II, 30 December 1573 (citing Alba's intransigent views).

62 For the Dutch position, see L. P. Gachard, *Correspondance de Guillaume le Taciturne* (6 vols, Brussels, 1849–57), vol. III, pp. 81–7, copies of four letters from Orange to Julián Romero (Spanish commander who had served with the prince in 1559–60), 7–10 November 1573. Orange had made his terms clear several months earlier: see H. H. Rowen, *The Low Countries in Early Modern Times* (New York: Macmillan, 1972), pp. 45–6, Orange to his brothers, 5 February 1573. For the Spanish position, see BPU Favre 30/71–4, Philip II to Requesens, 20 October 1573; *Codoin*, vol. CII, p. 323, Philip II to Alba, 21 October 1573; ibid., pp. 277–306, the instructions for Requesens; and AGS Estado 554/146, Requesens to Philip II, 30 December 1573, regretting the prohibitions they contained.

63 AGS Estado 561/25, Consulta de negocios de Flandes, 24 February 1574; IVDJ 67/287a, Vázquez to Philip II and reply, 28 June 1574; AGS Estado 568/38 and 49, consultas of 23 and 27 January 1575; IVDJ 67/106,

Requesens to Zúñiga, 9 July 1575 and ibid., fo. 271, Requesens to the count of Monteagudo (Spanish ambassador to Vienna), 6 March 1575. *AGS* Estado K 153/23, Requeséns to Don Juan de Zúñiga, 23 March 1575 gives a good overview of his negotiating position at Breda.

64   Parker, *Dutch Revolt*, pp. 182, 195–7, 223–4.

65   AGS Estado 2843/7, consulta of the Council of State, 5 September 1577; ibid., 2851, unfol., opinion of the marquis of Almazán, 22 November 1588 and Estado 2855, unfol., 'Lo que parecio sobre los quatro papeles principales', November 1589.

66   IVDJ 37/72, Requesens to Zúñiga, 12 November 1575.

67   See F. González de León, 'The Spanish Fury at Antwerp: A Military Coup d'Etat in the Sixteenth Century' (forthcoming).

68   Parker, *Dutch Revolt*, pp. 187–8.

69   Ibid., p. 208.

70   See Fernando Bouza Alvarez, 'Portugal en la monarquía hispánica 1580–1640. Felipe II, las cortes de Tomar y la génesis del Portugal católico' (doctoral thesis, Universidad Complutense de Madrid, 1987), p. 70.

71   Geoffrey Parker, *The Army of Flanders and the Spanish Road 1567–1659* (2nd edition, Cambridge: Cambridge University Press, 1990), p. 293.

72   Parker, *Army of Flanders*, pp. 209–21.

73   On the strategic aspects of the Armada plan, see Geoffrey Parker, *Grand Strategy*, ch. 6.

74   Ibid., pp. 180–1.

75   In September 1580 Philip approved the shipment of hundreds of troops to Smerwick in Ireland. See Parker, *Grand Strategy*, pp. 164–7.

76   BPU Favre 30/30, Philip II to Requesens, 30 January 1573.

77   *Codoin*, vol. CII, p. 68, Don Juan de Zúñiga to Philip II, 2 April 1573. See also Israel, *Conflicts of Empires*, chs 2–4 and 6.

78   Lagomarsino, 'Court Factions', p. 224.

7 Keeping the wheels of war turning

Revenues of the province of Holland, 1572–1619

James D. Tracy

Already in Roman times it was commonly said that 'money is the sinews of war' (*pecunia nervus belli*). This ancient maxim applies with particular force to the long struggle of the seven United Provinces against the mighty Spanish empire. Spain's seasoned troops had a clear edge in land warfare (if not at sea), but the spectacular economic growth of the rebel provinces after about 1590[1] proved more than a match for the stream of silver that flowed into Spain from the mines of Spanish America. The direct relationship between economic strength and revenue-raising capacity is shown by the fact that the single province of Holland – centre of the region's prosperity – contributed between 55 per cent and 65 per cent of the funds needed for the Eighty Years War. As an illustration of this one province's importance, Table 7.1 gives Holland's share in the annual war budget of the States General for the years 1586–98 (all sums given in this chapter are in Holland pounds).

It should also be noted that, over a period of thirteen years, Holland's actual payments on behalf of the States General fell short of its assigned quotas by only 239,649 Holland pounds or 0.79 per cent. In light of the fact that other provinces were often substantially in arrears on their quotas, Holland's reliability is even more impressive than its ability to carry, at this time, nearly two-thirds of the total burden. One would thus expect Holland's finances to have attracted the interest of historians. In fact, however, little has been done. There is an excellent analysis of the finances of the republic as a whole, starting from 1625, and a promising new project on the finances of the province of Zeeland.[2] But for Holland in particular there is not even one study that may be pointed to, certainly not for the difficult early decades of the revolt, when each of the rebel provinces accumulated debts that were far in excess of its annual revenues.

One need not spend a great deal of time in the National Archives of the Netherlands[3] to find an explanation for this puzzling gap in studies

Table 7.1 Holland's contributions to the States General war budget, 1586–1598
(Holland pounds)

	Total consent by States General	Amount consented by Holland (%)	Sum credited as paid by Holland
1586	2,900,000	1,863,291 (64.25)	1,863,734
1587	3,490,956	2,042,034 (58.45)	–
1588	3,000,000	1,939,142 (64.64)	1,944,191
1589	3,000,000	1,927,542 (64.25)	890,504
1590	2,900,000	1,863,291 (62.10)	2,098,531
1591	3,200,000	2,056,045 (64.25)	1,992,497
1592	3,300,000	2,120,296 (64.25)	2,195,719
1593	3,300,000	2,120,296 (64.25)	2,195,719
1594	3,800,000	2,441,553 (64.25)	2,605,802
1595	4,000,000	2,570,056 (64.25)	2,164,505
1596	4,100,000	2,629,825 (64.14)	2,820,299
1597	5,350,000	3,578,973 (70.26)	3,018,830
1598	4,950,000	3,119,908 (63.02)	2,939,941
Totals	47,290,956	30,272,252 (64.01)	30,032,603

Table 7.1 is based on ARA (Algemeen Rijksarchief, The Hague) 3.01.134, no. 187.
During the era of the revolt the Holland pound was a unit of account (not an actual
coin) equivalent to twenty silver stuivers or forty silver groats.

of the revolt: the pertinent fiscal records are largely missing. Under its
Habsburg counts[4] (1482–1572) the county or province of Holland had a
receiver of the subsidies to collect and disburse the ruler's taxes, a
receiver general for the common territory to collect and disburse
revenues for purposes decreed by the States of Holland, and district
receivers to collect certain other revenues employed either by the ruler
or by the States. After 1572 there was no more need for an official to
collect subsidies for the ruler. The receiver general for the common
territory now rendered accounts to the States General for all sums
supporting the annual war budget, but some of the more important
revenues were actually collected and disbursed by the district receivers,
who now took their instructions not just from the States of Holland, but
also from the magistrates of each revenue district's main town. For
almost every year of the Habsburg period, the annual accounts of fiscal
officials at all levels are faithfully preserved in the National Archives.
But for the era of the revolt, in which both receivers general and district
receivers usually held office for many years, one finds (at best) only the
first in a long series of accounts a given receiver would have rendered
during the course of his career. By way of illustration, for Cornelis van
Mierop, who served as Holland's receiver general from 1581 until his

death in 1612, the only extant account is his first one, for the period October 1581–February 1583.[5] For the accounts of the district receivers one might hope for better luck in Holland's many town archives, but I have not found any such records, save for a partial summary of the Gouda District Receiver's receipts and expenditures for the years 1594–1606.[6]

Yet the National Archives do preserve other materials that at least help to make up for the missing accounts. Contemporary or nearly contemporary summaries of accounts no longer extant, which once guided deliberations in the States of Holland, may now serve to guide the historian. Supplemented by town fiscal records that are better preserved, these documents permit one to piece together an approximate picture of how Holland's fiscal managers raised the vital revenues that kept the wheels of war turning. This essay attempts a step in that direction. The following discussion will first describe the major elements of the fiscal strategy adopted by the States of Holland in order to meet the province's wartime obligations, and then present an overview of how the different kinds of provincial revenue developed over time, from the beginning of the revolt until the onset of the Twelve-Year Truce in 1609.

Fiscal strategy of the States of Holland

In 1572 the immediate problem was how to find money to pay, and pay reliably, the garrisons that were the only hope of thwarting the duke of Alba's plans to conquer rebel towns one by one. The only thing to do was to seize Holland's most reliable stream of revenue and dedicate it to this purpose. Since the 1540s, district receivers for Holland's various revenue districts had been collecting province-wide excise taxes in order to make annual interest payments on bonds (in Dutch, *renten*) that were backed by the full faith and credit of the province. These instruments of debt had been sold on the open market to raise money for subsidies granted by the States of Holland to Emperor Charles V, who was (among his many titles) count of Holland from 1515 until 1555. When subsidies were raised in this fashion (instead of by the more traditional method of levying taxes on property), Charles's government in Brussels was assured of getting its hands quickly on the cash it desperately needed to fight the emperor's wars (mainly against France). Deputies of the States, assembled in Holland's capital, The Hague, had the satisfaction of knowing that the province's precious credit was protected: f o r the revenues by which the *renten* debt was funded – that is, the excise taxes – the district receivers were answerable to the States of Holland, not (as for other revenues they collected) to officials of the central government.[7] With the onset of the revolt, however, the excises that had been created to fund the debt became, by authority of the States, the 'common revenues' (in Dutch, *gemene middelen*), so-called because these excises, unlike those that each city had long collected within its own territory, were collected throughout the province. As before, district receivers farmed out each of the excises to the highest bidder, usually for a six-month term. The only difference was that each district receiver made payments on his receipts not to local holders of pre-1572 *renten*, but to the captains of local garrisons and their men.

This decision was pregnant with implications. First, it soon became apparent that the common revenues by themselves were not sufficient to meet the costs of war. Receipts were disappointing in the early years, no doubt because Hollanders were still deciding whether they had to meet their obligations to a government whose authority was not yet secure. More importantly, Holland could not be adequately defended by town garrisons; there had to be garrisons in frontier fortresses and in friendly towns beyond the border, as well as cavalry to carry the war to the foe. At least by 1574, the States hit on the idea of bridging this gap by raising contributions from each of the cities adhering to the revolt, according to a quota based on rough estimates of their relative wealth. For that year the common revenues brought in only 111,000 Holland pounds, but 320,000 were raised by a series of what would henceforth be known as allotments (in Dutch, *repartitien*). If it was up to each town to raise the sums called for as it wished, in fact there was little room for flexibility. Town revenues, like those of the province, were dwarfed by debts already outstanding. Hence magistrates depended on the voluntary cooperation of their citizens. But Holland's burghers, like their counterparts in other late medieval or early modern cities,[8] were not amenable to the idea of direct taxes on their wealth. Instead, they insisted that their contributions be treated as loans, to be repaid at the going rate of interest (from 12 per cent to as high as 18 per cent). The result was that the allotments, proceeds of which were always urgently needed at the moment, quickly became just another form of debt looking for repayment. Had it not been for the respite Holland was afforded by the temporary collapse of Spain's war effort occasioned by the Spanish fury in Antwerp (1576) and the ensuing Pacification of Ghent, it is not at all clear how the province could have maintained its credit.

During this short breathing space, the States made two important decisions aimed at managing the various kinds of debt by which Holland was burdened. First, the States created a new kind of revenue to which unpaid military obligations[9] as well as debts arising from the allotments could be assigned. For several reasons the States chose to seek added revenue by taxing real property. First, most kinds of commercial trans-actions within the borders of the province of Holland were already struck by one or another of the excise taxes that made up the common revenues. Second, while the gentlemen deputies from the eighteen cities with voting rights in the States were determined to keep taxes on the vital export trade to a minimum, they saw no reason why landowners and their tenants should not pay a bit more.[10] Finally, Holland's rural economy had a full share in the growing prosperity that, from the 1590s, radiated outwards from Amsterdam.

Hence the States levied a 1 per cent tax on the estimated value of houses in the cities and land in the countryside for each of the years between 1577 and 1580.[11] From 1581 the so-called 'hundredth penny' was largely superseded by a new annual levy known as the assessment (in Dutch, *verponding*). By 1584 there was an agreed-on quota for the so-called 'ordinary assessment', set at a level expected to yield 667,036 pounds per year. Summaries of the assessment accounts indicate that the proceeds were indeed employed for loans by burghers (the allot-ments) as well as for old debts to military commanders and for loans taken out by the district receivers responsible for collecting the common revenues. More often than not, however, payments were only for the annual interest due; principal sums had to be continued from year to year.[12] The assessments were thus a way not of paying off Holland's unsecured war debt, but of managing it.

Interest on *renten* issued by the States of Holland in the decades before the revolt represented a different kind of debt. The negative side of the States' decision to divert excise tax revenue to the needs of war was that no interest was paid on this old debt during the years 1572 to 1576 – a failure by which Holland's unofficial credit rating, carefully nurtured during the Habsburg era, was gravely imperilled. In the years immedi-ately following the Pacification of Ghent, the States took the first steps towards repairing provincial credit by decreeing that all unpaid interest for the years 1572–6 would be capitalised at a rate of 1:16, or 6.25 per cent, and by creating additional excise taxes specifically dedicated to the old *renten* debt.[13] Deputies also reduced the amount of debt outstanding by decreeing (in October 1579) that all *renten* payable to persons 'holding to the King of Spain' were henceforth forfeit. In what may be con-sidered a stroke of genius, some of these confiscated *renten* were subsequently brought back to life, by persuading military commanders to accept them as part payment for long-standing arrears. Old *renten* that no longer had a lawful owner were a convenient substitute for new *renten* that, as yet, no one would buy.[14]

For debt that could not be paid off, but had to be serviced over a long period, the best strategy was to reduce carrying costs by persuading creditors to accept conversion of their unsecured 'obligations' to funded or consolidated debt at a lower rate of interest. But this well-trodden path of fiscal wisdom was foreclosed to the States of Holland, at least for a time, owing to Holland's failure to keep up payments during the 1570s on funded debt created before the revolt, that is, the old *renten*. When 'buyers' for new Holland *renten* did appear on the scene, they were not exactly voluntary. Beginning in 1588, burghers were persuaded to accept conversion of their still outstanding allotment loans to Holland *renten,* backed by subsidiary guarantees from their own town governments. Only in 1594, it seems, did Holland's receiver general begin selling new *renten* on the open market, as his predecessors of the Habsburg era had done. From this time forward, the sale of *renten* increasingly became Holland's preferred way of raising credit. New *renten* were an improvement on the assessments not because they made it possible to cleanse the ledgers of war debt, but because they made it possible to service the debt more cheaply. The great success of Holland's fiscal regime lay in carrying an ever-rising war debt at increasingly lower rates of interest.

Overview of Holland's revenues, 1572–1609

Table 7.2 draws on information from the aforementioned account summaries preserved in the National Archives, as well as town archives in Amsterdam and Gouda. Amsterdam's 'extraordinary treasurers', whose annual accounts are preserved for all but three of the years between 1585 and 1609, collected and/or oversaw disbursement of the sums for which Amsterdam was responsible to the States of Holland.[15] Like the accounts and account summaries on which it is based, Table 7.2 represents sums that were due to be collected, not sums actually collected. In the accounting practice of the era, 'income' meant all sums that were due the receiver, and 'expenses' meant every form of documentation that acquitted him of responsibility for some portion of the income due, such as quittances for payments made by order of the proper authorities. For example, Holland's receiver general counted as assessment income the quotas for every town and village, regardless of whether or not these sums were in fact paid; under expenditures he listed not only receipts for payment of interest or principal on loans charged to the assessments, but also the 'graces' granted by the States in partial remission of the quotas for towns or villages deemed afflicted. A series of such accounts can give a reasonable picture of overall trends, if not a reliable year-by-year indication of actual cash flow.

Sources used in constructing Table 7.2 are given in the Appendix.

Table 7.2 States of Holland income, 1572–1609

	A	B	C	D
	Common revenues[a]	Allotments[b]	Assessments[c]	Sales of renten[d]
1572	31,051			
1573	66,261			
1574	111,498	320,000		
1575	158,000			
1576				
1577				
1578	818,397	50,000		
1579	663,787			
1580	[836,575]	175,000		
1581	833,970	67,000	119,285	
1582	867,693	85,000	220,000	
1583	950,487	31,000	354,000	
1584	960,207	462,200	887,159	
1585	1,058,885	780,406	667,036	
1586	1,190,424	132,906	1,589,505	
1587		760,000		
1588		440,000	1,556,461	1,500,000
1589		87,000	2,031,726	
1590		30,000	1,334,072	130,000
1591			1,334,072	130,000
1592			1,334,072	
1593			[1,436,956]	
1594	[1,960,205]		1,334,072	250,048
1595	[1,621,487]		1,334,072	100,000
1596	1,726,710		1,486,957	45,000
1597	[1,896,256]		1,486,957	
1598				80,328
1599			1,586,957	172,280
1600			1,586,957	142,933
1601			1,686,957	
1602			1,786,957	
1603			1,714,957	184,388
1604	[2,567,324]		1,756,182	230,775
1605			1,786,957	
1606		200,000	1,786,957	339,058
1607			1,786,957	[1,426,956]
1608				[1,622,472]
1609			1,786,957	

Notes
[a] *gemene middelen* or excise taxes.
[b] *repartitien* or loans by burghers.
[c] *verpondingen* or taxes on property.
[d] funded debt.

Figures in brackets represent my extrapolations, the arithmetic for which is also explained in the Appendix.

Table 7.2 follows sixteenth-century practice in counting as 'income' the receipts from loans, not just the receipts from taxes. Columns A and C – the common revenues and the assessments – represent tax receipts, but columns B and D – the allotments and the *renten* – represent loans. The justification for this practice, then and now, is that the money Holland used to meet its obligations to the States General came as much from loans as from taxes. Once again, it becomes clear that the great problem to be met in paying for a war was the management of debt.

In one respect Table 7.2 departs from sixteenth-century usage. Holland's incomes were classified by contemporaries in terms of the quota system by which Holland's revenue districts were made to pay, not in terms of the kind of income involved. To give but one telling example of how quota systems differed, Amsterdam's share in the assessment agreed upon in 1584 – a tax on the value of houses and farm land – was only 5.65 per cent of the total. But in the allotments (burgher loans) based on the estimated wealth of the cities, Amsterdam's share was 18 per cent. Hence in the clash of interests represented in the States of Holland, wealthy Amsterdam sometimes had to give way to the smaller cities by agreeing to an 'assessment' raised according to the allotment quota. Beginning in 1594, it could also happen that part of the sums needed for an assessment or an allotment were actually raised by having Holland's receiver general sell *renten* on the open market; what mattered most was the sum for which each revenue district was responsible, not the means by which money was raised. Where the sources permit such distinctions to be made, Table 7.2 classifies incomes according to the type of revenue involved, so that (for example) *renten* sold for an allotment or an assessment are entered under column D, not column B or C.

Column A: The district receivers[16] who collected the common revenues were at first accountable to Holland's receiver general, as their predecessors had been in the pre-revolt era. But during Jacob Muys' tenure as receiver general, from the last half of 1574 through the first half of 1578, the ruling elites of Holland's towns, through their deputies in the States, decided that no one except themselves needed to know exactly how much income local collectors of the common excise taxes had at their disposal. Subsequent receivers general, beginning with Cornelis van Mierop (1581–1616), received quittances for the garrison wages each local excise tax collector was obliged to pay from his receipts, but there is no information on what a receiver's total income was, or what he had done with any sums he might have collected over and above what was due for the garrisons.[17]

Discussions leading up to the 1579 Union of Utrecht envisaged that other provinces in the Union would establish excises on the same basis as Holland. Holland's common revenues were formally made over to the Union by act of the States in June 1581, when monthly receipts were estimated at 71,711 Holland pounds.[18] In practice, this meant that Holland's receiver general forwarded to the receiver general for the States General the documents which certified that the garrisons and regiments 'standing to Holland's charge' (according to the war budgets agreed to by the States General) had been duly paid by the collectors of Holland's common revenues.

In the early years of the revolt, the expected receipts for a given revenue district were often not adequate to cover the monthly wage and salary[19] bill for the garrisons assigned to it. Hence collectors had to engage their personal credit to raise funds to meet the insistent demands of the troops for payment on time. As Holland prospered, especially from the 1590s, the receipts of the common revenues began to exceed what was needed to meet standing payment orders.[20] Even so, the collectors continued their borrowing,[21] in part because the actual flow of money through a collector's office was retarded by the slow pace at which Holland's ordinary folk made their payments to the excise tax farmers.

There were also two important forms of common revenues which are not included in column A, owing to scarce documentation. First, certain new excise revenues were set aside (as mentioned above) for the purpose of paying the annual interest due on still outstanding *renten* issued by the States of Holland prior to the revolt. Second, the so-called 'reserved common revenues' were usually kept back to cover operating expenses for the States of Holland and its small army of officials. In 1586, excises for the old *renten* and for the reserved Common Revenues were estimated to have annual yields of 123,000 and 120,000 Holland pounds respectively.[22] If Gouda's[23] records are a reliable guide for Holland as a whole, receipts for these two kinds of excises amount to approximately one-fourth of all common revenue income collected, or one-third of the sums reported in column A.

Column B: Because the allotments here were based on attempts to gauge the general wealth of each city and its surrounding district, the quotas assigned by the States (or sometimes by Prince William of Orange) might differ significantly from what each city paid in levies based on a census of their houses, as noted above for Amsterdam.[24] The parts of Holland[25] which, with Zeeland, stood alone against the might of Spain during the earliest years of the revolt could not have survived without these levies on wealth. Pro-rata taxes on the wealth-holders were not unknown in Holland, and would no doubt have been a fairer way of sharing the burden. But the States seldom mustered agreement for the direct taxation of private wealth (even the hundredth or fiftieth pennies that city governments levied for their own purposes on the esti- mated total wealth of burghers usually took the form of loans, not taxes).

With rare exceptions,[26] burghers whose loans to their city made up the city's share in an allotment expected to receive the going rate of interest. At least from the 1580s it became common to add to the carrying costs of such loans a further 1 per cent for brokerage fees, indicating that it was easier for magistrates to let the money men find investors than it was to constrain their burghers to join in patriotic loans. These loans were continued from year to year, since there were always more pressing demands on the allotments to which repayment had been assigned. The 1 per cent brokerage fee carried forward as well, since it was often necessary to find replacement creditors for burghers who demanded repayment according to the original terms of the loan.

Column C: In an assembly dominated by representatives of the eighteen towns with voting rights, it was to be expected that taxes based on real property – that is, on land and houses, not on the personal property held by burghers – would provide the main remedy for Holland's continuing fiscal distress. The allotment levied for the first time in 1581 was intended, like the hundredth and fiftieth pennies it largely replaced, to pay off loans charged to the receipts of the common revenues. Yet money was also needed to repay loans by burghers, and to cover unplanned-for military expenses made necessary by Alexander Farnese's advances in the southern Low Countries. By 1584, the assess- ment was set for 667,000 Holland pounds, roughly six times the sum raised in 1581. Bitter disputes concerning the quotas of various cities – Amsterdam in particular – led to a revision of the assessment in 1584/5. The new calculation became the basis for the so-called 'ordinary' assessment of 667,000 Holland pounds per annum.

Already in 1584, 667,000 Holland pounds a year were not enough. Each year, the States consented to 'extraordinary' assessments, and by the early 1590s a second levy equivalent in amount to the ordinary assessment had become routine.[27] Beginning in 1599 there were still further levies, which stabilised at a level of 300,000 pounds per year. Unlike the other assessments, these added sums were raised not accord- ing to a valuation of real property, which of course fell heaviest on the countryside, but on the valuation of urban wealth used for the allot- ments.[28] Column C lumps all the different kinds of assessment income together, without regard to these distinctions.

Column D: Before they could expect investors to have confidence in new *renten* issued by the States, Holland's fiscal managers first had to restore confidence in the province's ability to meet its outstanding obligations. The re-funding of the pre-revolt *renten* debt, mentioned above, was a first step in this direction. A memorandum of 3 September 1587 suggested what proved to be a further milestone.[29] As the authors pointed out, the assessments of future years (1590, 1591) could be set aside for 'cleansing' the common revenues of debt only if the charges for allotment loans, payable from the same assessments, could be met in some other way. Toward this end, the States in 1588 agreed, as the memorandum had proposed, that a capital sum of the order of 1,500,000 pounds, representing unpaid burgher loans currently running at 12 per cent interest plus 1 per cent for brokerage fees, would be 'converted' to *renten* having either a lower interest rate, or a limited life expectancy.[30]

Only in 1594 did Cornelis van Mierop, Holland's receiver general, begin issuing new *renten* charged against his 'office', that is, against the full faith and credit of the province. Like the old *renten*, interest on these new obligations was paid from the excise taxes set aside for this purpose. By 1616, some years beyond the period covered in this essay, the receiver general's 'office' supported[31] annual *renten* interest in the amount of 1,204,906 pounds,[32] 309,201 of which represented the interest on *renten* sold between 1610 and 1614 to pay off loans charged to the accounts of the collectors for the common revenues.

Conclusion

The figures in Table 7.2 give a rough idea of how Holland was able to continue meeting its share in the growing demands of the States General's war budget, as shown in Table 7.1. For example, in the twelve-year span represented in Table 7.1 (1586–98), the total of the sums Holland agreed to raise for the States General increased by 67 per cent. For a similar twelve-year span for which figures are available from Table 7.2 (1584–96), total revenues raised by the province increased 41 per cent. For the years in which total revenues can be compared with total payments to the States General, it is clear that the gentlemen deputies of the States of Holland had money left over to apply to purposes of their own devising.[33]

Columns A and C of Table 7.2, representing tax receipts as distinct from loan receipts, show a steady growth over the entire period covered in this essay, representing a rising prosperity that was visible in the rural economy (column C) as well as in the commercial transactions struck by the excise taxes (column A). Columns B and D show a shift from reliance on unsecured burgher loans (column B) to funded debt in the form of States of Holland *renten* (column D), with sums raised by burgher loans reaching a peak in the mid-1580s, just before the greater part of this debt was converted to *renten* in 1588. One may summarise by saying that ordinary folk bore the cost of the common revenues (column A) in their daily business, while landowners and their tenants bore the cost of the assessments (column C), and wealthy Hollanders entrusted a portion of their fortunes to the province, not as taxes, but as investments (columns B and D).

Yet although sales of new *renten* on the open market are detectable from 1594 on, it seems Holland's credit had not entirely regained the lustre of former times. The account of Amsterdam's extraordinary treasurers for 1599 reports 101,262 pounds in income from a sale of *renten* 'for which the city of Amsterdam interposed its credit, and the States of Holland gave letters of indemnity, taking the capital sum to Holland's charge'.[34] In other words, Amsterdam's burghers were as of this date still not willing to entrust their hard cash to provincial officials without a back-up guarantee from the guardians of their own city's rock-solid reputation. Holland's fiscal system, presented here, catered to the interests of wealthy burghers. But it also ultimately depended on a fiscal credibility that belonged more to the cities (especially Amsterdam) and their burghers than to the province itself.

Notes

1 Jan de Vries and Aert van der Woude, *The First Modern Economy: Success, Failure and Perserverance of the Dutch Economy, 1500–1815* (Cambridge: Cambridge University Press, 1997).
2 Marjolein 't Hart, *The Making of a Bourgeois State. War, Politics and Finance during the Dutch Revolt* (Manchester: Manchester University Press, 1993); Michiel de Jong, 'Dutch Public Finance during the Eighty Years War: The Case of the Province of Zeeland, 1585–1621', in Marco van der Hoeven (ed.), *Exercise of Arms. Warfare in the Netherlands, 1568–1648* (Leiden, 1998), pp. 133–52; for Zeeland's considerable arrears, see figure 2, p. 139.
3 Now officially known as the Rijksarchief van Zuid-Holland (National Archives for the Province of South Holland) in the Hague, but still referred to by its old name, Algemeen Rijksarchief (General National Archives), and abbreviated here as ARA.
4 Habsburg rulers, like Emperor Charles V (ruled 1515–55), governed by separate titles in each of their Low Countries provinces; there was no princely title for the region as a whole.
5 ARA 3.01.28 no. 352. Mierop received his commission as receiver general on 19 September 1581. It is possible that many of the accounts no longer extant were discarded in the early years of the nineteenth century, when the capital value of Holland's 'old debt', tracing from *renten* issued by the States during the Habsburg period and the era of the revolt, was reduced by two-thirds.

6 Streekarchief Gouda, *Inventaris* by Geselschap, nos. 3708–15. This unusual survival of fiscal information which (one may infer) town magistrates did not want bruited about may be related to the fact that the district receiver who compiled the summary had to declare bankruptcy in 1607.

7 See my *A Financial Revolution in the Habsburg Netherlands. 'Renten' and 'Renteniers' in the County of Holland, 1515–1566* (Berkeley and Los Angeles: University of California Press, 1985). The lesson of long experience was that debts assigned to revenues controlled by officials of the central government could be and usually were diverted to more pressing military needs, leaving debt-holders in the lurch. But the penalties for not making timely interest payments on *renten* charged to the province were immediate and severe: creditors in other provinces could and did have local officials distrain wayfaring Hollanders and their goods as a way of claiming satisfaction for unpaid debts. This practice continued during the decades of the revolt.

8 For example, the famous *catasto* of 1427 served as a basis not for taxing the wealth of Florentines, but for assessing the forced loans the city carried at interest. See David Herlihy and Christiane Klapisch-Zuber, *Tuscans and their Families: The Florentine Catasto of 1427* (New Haven, 1985).

9 The largest of many such debts was an 'obligation' or promissory note for 500,000 Holland pounds owing to Ernst von Manderslo and other German cavalry commanders who had participated in an abortive effort to relieve the duke of Alba's siege of Mons (1572), temporarily occupied by French forces allied with the revolt. Manderslo's share of the debt was calculated at 184,517 Holland pounds, of which he was still owed 136,974 in 1584. See the essay cited in note 15.

10 The countryside had no representation in the States save through the College of Nobles, which had only one vote, as did each of the eighteen cities.

11 ARA 3.01.29, no. 797, an essay on the finances of the early republic dating from 1755: for purposes of the hundredth penny, houses were capitalised at a 1:14 income:capital ratio, and land at 1:18 (1:16 in the alluvial districts of Voorne and Putte). I have not found any summary of actual income for the hundredth penny levies.

12 ARA 3.01.14, no. 91, budget summaries for the assessments of 1583, 1590, 1594, 1596 and 1598.

13 *Resolutions of the States of Holland*, 8 May, 11 June, 3 July, 13 August, and 22 August 1577; and 29 August, 11 September, 19 December 1578, 6 March, 16 September 1579.

14 Part of the debt owed to Ernst von Manderslo (above, note 9) was paid in this fashion, the rest by a transfer of properties confiscated from the Catholic church and from wealthy loyalists who had emigrated from Holland to regions still controlled by Spain. See my 'Confiscated Property in the Dutch Revolt: The *Sacra Anchora* of Holland Finance, 1572–1585', in a collection of essays on the Dutch Revolt and the French Wars of Religion edited by Philip Benedict and Henk van Nierop. See note 3 on page 46 of this book.

15 Accounts for 1593, 1598 and 1608 are missing. There are separate annual accounts for the ordinary treasurers, who collected and disbursed revenues expended by order of Amsterdam's magistrates.

16 What the receivers actually collected were the sums contracted for by those who farmed each of the excises, usually for terms of six months or a year.

17 See ARA 3.01.13, no. 21, a summary of Muys' first account as receiver general, for the period beginning July 1574, and 3.01.14, no. 44, a portfolio of documents relating to Muys' lawsuit against the States in 1586/1588.

18 ARA 3.01.14, no. 99B.

19 The accounts always have separate entries for wages for the troops and salaries for the officers.

20 Gemeentearchief Amsterdam (GAA) 5044, no. 81: as early as 1585, Jan Pieterszoon Reael, collector of the common revenues for the Amsterdam district, was able to transfer money from his receipts to help the extra-ordinary treasurers meet the city's other obligations to the States General.

21 ARA 3.01.14, no. 339: according to a summary drawn up for the year 1596, the eight common revenue collectors for Holland south of the IJ had a total of 1,726,710 pounds in 'income due', and 1,171,019 in outstanding loans.

22 ARA 3.01.14, no. 99D, estimates for the excises for the old *renten*: eight stuivers per barrel of beer (72,000), an excise on the consumption and shipment of turf (36,000), and taxes on the income due for Holland *renten* (15,000); and estimates for the reserved common revenues (handed over for that year to the earl of Leicester), a doubling of the excise on the slaughter of horned animals (one-half was used for paying garrisons, the other, normally, for the expenses of the States), and a new excise on linen cloth.

23 Gemeentearchief Gouda, *Inventaris* of Geselschap, nos. 1708–15. For 1596, total receipts were 130,719, of which 32,036 (25.5 per cent) were set aside for the payment of old *renten* or the reserved common revenues.

24 To give another example, in an Allotment for 55,000 in October 1575, Dordrecht owed 13,177 (24 per cent) and Rotterdam 7018 (12.8 per cent): ARA 3.01.13, no. 21. In the ordinary assessment for 1584, expected to yield 667,036 pounds for all of Holland, Dordrecht's houses were assessed for 3856 pounds (0.56 per cent) and Rotterdam's for 1500 pounds (0.22 per cent). Thus Rotterdam owed 39 per cent of Dordrecht's dues in the assessment, but 53 per cent of the older city's quota in the allotment. Such differences in proportion suggest that the allotments were taking some account of Rotterdam's advance as a port, partly at the expense of its upstream rival, Dordrecht.

25 Haarlem, reconquered by Spanish troops, adhered definitively to the revolt only in 1576, wealthy Amsterdam only in 1578.

26 ARA 3.01.14, no. 99B: a 'capital loan' of 150,000 for 1585 (one of many allotments for that year), of which 125,000 was to be raised from the cities and 25,000 from wealthy peasants, was to be repaid without interest.

27 GAA 5044, nos. 88 and 89: the accounts of Amsterdam's extraordinary treasurers still distinguish between what the city owes for ordinary and extraordinary assessments, but from 1594 they report a single lump sum (the account for 1593 is missing).

28 GAA 5044, nos. 96–102: from 1602 to 1609 Amsterdam's quota for this 300,000 pounds was 63,000 pounds, or 21 per cent, a rate even higher than the 18 per cent at which Amsterdam contributed to the allotments.

29 ARA 3.01.14, no. 84.

30 Such 'conversion' required the consent of the creditor, who had the right to

cash in his or her loans rather than accept the new terms. *Renten* were of two kinds. Heritable *renten* carried low rates of interest (in this case, 8.33 per cent), but they lasted from generation to generation, until the issuer (in this case, the States of Holland) redeemed the original capital sum. Life *renten* carried higher rates (16.66 per cent for the lifespan of one named beneficiary, 12.5 per cent for the one beneficiary as well as his or her heir), but were sooner or later extinguished altogether by the death of the beneficiary.

31 It should be noted that these figures come from a summary of payments that had not been made for the years 1616 and 1617: ARA 3.01.14, no. 145G.

32 Since interest rates had by this time been reduced to 1:16 for heritable *renten* and 1:12 for life *renten,* one may assume that the capital sum involved was on the order of fourteen times higher than the annual interest due, or 16,868,684 pounds.

33 For example, in 1586 Holland made payments on behalf of the States General totalling 1,863,774 pounds, but had income totalling 2,912,835. Much of the difference went to pay interest charges (with some redemption of principal) on Holland's outstanding debts.

34 GAA 5044, no. 93.

Appendix: Sources for Table 7.2 (by year and column)

1572A–1574A: Totals for 1572/1574 from ARA 3.01.13, nos. 20–2.

1574B: ARA 3.01.13, no. 21: assessments of 45,000 per month for six months beginning July 1574, plus a further 50,000 pounds (60,000 crowns) for the relief of besieged Leiden.

1575B: ARA 3.01.14, no. 79.

1578–1586A: ARA 3.01.14, no. 99A, contains a summary of common revenue receipts for the period January 1578–March 1586.

1578B: ARA 3.01.13, no. 13: the States borrowed 100,000 to cleanse the Common Revenues of debt, with repayment assigned on receipts of the hundredth penny tax for this year. To repay half the money immediately, cities were to borrow 50,000 on their own credit, at 12 per cent, 15 per cent or even 18 per cent.

1580A: see source cited for 1578A. The document quoted does not give an income figure for the first quarter of 1580, but I have assumed that income for this quarter is the same as for the last quarter of the previous year, as is true for other years.

1580B: ARA 3.01.14, nos. 79, 99B.

1581A: ARA 3.01.14, no. 99B.

1581B: ARA 3.01.14, no. 99B, and 3.01.28, no. 352.

1581C: ARA 3.01.13, nos. 24, 25; 3.01.28, no. 352, gives a figure of 110,000.

1582A: ARA 3.01.14, no. 99A.

1582B: ARA 3.01.14, no. 99B, and 3.01.28, no. 352.

1582C: ARA 3.01.28, no. 352.

1583A: ARA 3.01.14, no. 99A.

1583B: ARA 3.01.14, no. 99B.

1583C: ARA 3.01.14, no. 91.

1584A: this figure, from ARA 3.01.14, no. 99A, is corroborated by an estimate in 3.01.14, no. 99B, that Holland's common revenue receipts for this year amounted to 80,000 per month.

1584B: ARA 3.01.14, no. 99B, listing allotments for this year of 75,000, 46,000, 52,200, 150,000 and 75,000.

1584C: ARA 3.01.13, no. 25, gives a total of 667,036 for the sixfold ordinary Assessment (i.e. six times the amount raised in 1581) levied in 1584; 3.01.28, no. 352, estimates a yield of 200,000 pounds for the extraordinary assessment of the same year.

1585A: this figure, from ARA 3.01.14, no. 99B, is corroborated by 3.01.28, no. 352, estimating 95,000 in monthly *gemene middelen* receipts for 1585.

1585B: GAA 5044, no. 81, lists allotments of 75,000, 67,000, 50,000, 112,000, 33,500 (for sailors on Dutch ships before Antwerp), 150,000 and 150,000 again. ARA 3.01.14, no. 99B, which does not include the levy for the sailors, gives a figure of 729,000.

1585C: GAA 5044, no. 85, indicates that only the ordinary assessment, in which Amsterdam's share was 37,695, or 5.65 per cent of 667,036 was levied this year.

1586A: ARA 3.01.14, no. 99D, estimates common revenue income for 1586 at 99,206 per month; 3.01.14, no. 99B, gives 1,048,821 as the income for the first three quarters of 1586.

1586B: ARA 3.01.14, no. 99B. GAA 5044, no. 86, gives a figure of 133,000.

1586C: according to GAA 5044, no. 86, in addition to the ordinary assessment for 1586, the States consented to raise the ordinary assessment for 1587 a year early, and to levy a further sum equal to two-ninths of the ordinary assessment for fortifications. Assuming that Amsterdam's quota in all of these levies was 5.65 per cent, the grand total would be 1,589,505.

1587B: GAA 5044, no. 83, lists allotments for this year of 200,000, 100,000, 50,000, 150,000, 150,000 again and 110,000; Amsterdam's quota for each was 18 per cent.

1587C: there was no assessment for this year, since the ordinary assessment for 1587 had already been raised in 1586.

1588B: ARA 5044, no. 84.

1588C: GAA 5044, no. 84: an ordinary assessment, an extraordinary assessment yielding the same amount and a smaller levy for fortifications.

1588D: the estimate of the capital value of burgher loans charged against the assessment that were to be converted to *renten* comes from ARA 3.01.14, no. 84, a memorandum of September 1587 proposing this step. ARA 5044, no. 84, the capital sum for outstanding loans of Amsterdam burghers (dating from allotments for the years 1584–7) that were converted to *renten* in 1588 was 154,800. This is less than 18 per cent of the total, but many burgher loans dated from before Amsterdam's adhesion to the revolt (1578).

1589B: GAA 5044, no. 85.

1589C: GAA 5044, no. 85. The figure I give assumes that Amsterdam's quota for the three extraordinary assessments (in which it contributed a total of 77,105) was 5.65 per cent, as for the ordinary assessment.

1589D: GAA 5044, no. 85: this year Amsterdam converted still more burgher loans into *renten* charged against the States of Holland, with an annual interest rate of 7790. Assuming the same ratio between capital value and annual interest rate as obtained in 1589, the capital value of the Amsterdam loans converted in 1589 would be 56,367. I have no figures for Holland overall for this year.

1590B: GAA 5044, no. 86.

1590C: GAA 5044, no. 86.

1590D: according to GAA 5044, no. 86, this sum represents not the conversion of old allotment loans into *renten,* but a new allotment in the form of a sale of *renten,* in which Amsterdam's share was the 18 per cent customary for allotments.

1591C: GAA 5044, no. 87.

1590D: GAA 5044, no. 87 – again, an allotment in the form of a sale of *renten.*

1592C: GAA 5044, no. 88.

1593C: ARA 3.01.14, no. 343, gives a figure of 1,020,064, which seems to represent the total of all assessments for Holland south of the IJ. Assuming that this represents 73.12 per cent of the total for all of Holland (as in ARA 3.01.14, no. 91, where figures are given for both North and South Holland in an ordinary assessment), the total for all of Holland in 1593 would be as reported above.

1594A, also 1595A, 1597A, 1604A: the figures in column A for 1594, 1595, 1597 and 1604 are extrapolations based on Streekarchief Gouda, nos. 3708–15, and ARA 3.01.14, nos. 339–41. The latter source gives a sum total of 1,726,710 for 'income due' in 1596 for all of the common revenues (including those not counted here in column A), but only for the eight district receivers for Holland south of the IJ. The former gives summaries of the actual common revenue income and expenditures for the Gouda District for the years 1594–1606 (though complete only for some of these years). For the Gouda district in 1596, income due was 144,945, but actual income was 130,719. Thus the actual income for Gouda in that year represents 7.57 per cent of the 'income due' for the eight revenue districts. Assuming that the same proportions apply for other years, I have calculated estimates of common revenues' 'income due' for 1594, 1595, 1597 and 1604, of which actual income as reported in Gouda would have represented 7.57 per cent.

1594C: GAA 5044, no. 89.

1594D: ARA 3.01.14, nos. 139–41, 278 and 280, summaries of annual interest paid on various categories of States of Holland *renten* by Joachim van Mierop, Cornelis van Mierop's kinsman and successor as Holland's receiver general. ARA 3.01.14, no. 139, gives 250,048 as the capital sum for *renten* sold in 1594 and 1595 to pay off loans charged against the receipts of collectors for the common revenues.

1595C: GAA 5044, no. 90.

1595D: GAA 5044, no. 90, an allotment of 100,000 to be raised by a sale of *renten,* in order to assist France's King Henri IV.

1596A: ARA 3.01.14, nos. 339–41, gives accounts for total receipts of the eight district collectors of the common revenues for Holland south of the IJ from autumn 1595 to spring 1597; thus 1596 is the only year for which full figures are given. Since these figures apparently include the revenues dedicated to the funding of *renten* and the 'reserved' revenues for the States, but nothing for Holland north of the IJ, the total seems a good approximation for the roughly 75 per cent of the common revenues for all of Holland that were devoted to the States General's war budget.

1596C: GAA 5044, no. 91.

1596D: ARA 3.01.14, nos. 278, 280.

1597C: GAA 5044, no. 92.

1598D: ARA 3.01.14, nos. 278, 280.

1599C: GAA 5044, no. 93: an assessment (apparently 100,000) in excess of the usual assessments, in which Amsterdam's quota was 22,000.

1600C: GAA 5044, no. 94.
1600D: see 1594D.
1601C: GAA 5044, no. 95.
1602C: GAA 5044, no. 96.
1602C: GAA 5044, no. 97. For this year I have deducted 68,000 from the assessments and added a like sum to the *renten* total, because Amsterdam raised this much of its assessment quota through a sale of *renten* charged against Holland: see also 1604D.
1603C: GAA 5044, no. 97.
1603D: see the sources cited for 1594D; *renten* were sold this year as part of the levy of a 200th penny.
1604C: GAA 5044, no. 98.
1604D: GAA 5044, no. 98. The same account indicates that a further 108,750 were raised by selling States of Holland *renten* to Amsterdam burghers as a means of raising the city's portion of a 300,000 pound levy in excess of the usual ordinary and extraordinary assessments, 68,000 in 1603 and 30,775 in 1604.
1605C: GAA 5044, no. 99. There was also a provincial chimney tax this year, but I have figures only for Amsterdam (20,730).
1606B: GAA 5044, no. 100.
1606C: GAA 5044, no. 100.
1606D: see the sources cited for 1594D. Cornelis van Mierop sold 416,220 in *renten* this year charged to his office, to which were added a further 139,058 in *renten* sold by François Kegeling, the collector of the common revenues for Gouda, apparently because of Kegeling's bankruptcy. GAA 5044, no 100, Amsterdam's share in a 200,000 Allotment raised by a sale of Holland *renten* was 42,500. I assume that the *renten* sold 'on Mierop' should be charged to 1607, not 1605, but that the 200,000 mentioned in the Amsterdam account were not part of the sales reported by Mierop.
1607C: GAA 5044, no. 101; there was also a provincial chimney tax, netting 37,300 in Amsterdam.
1607D: see the sources cited for 1594D. I assume a rate of 1:12 for *renten* sold 'on Mierop' in 1607, with an annual interest charge of 118,913.
1609C: GAA 5044, no. 102.

8 From Domingo de Soto to Hugo Grotius

Theories of monarchy and civil power in Spanish and Dutch political thought, 1555–1609[1]

Martin van Gelderen

Introduction

As he meditates the causes of the Dutch Revolt in the concluding chapters of the *Relatione delle Provincie Unite,* written in 1611, the Bolognese Cardinal Guido Bentivoglio considers the importance of 'l'amor della libertà'. In the hearts of all men, ponders Bentivoglio, the love of liberty is a major force, 'ma sopra tutte le altre nationi del mondo, hanno mostrata sempre grandissima inclinatione al goderla i popoli Settentrionale d'Europa, e frà loro particolarmente quei della Fiandra'.[2] Bentivoglio reminds his readers of the celebrated Batavian revolt against the Romans, 'ch'è descritta sì nobilmente nelle historie di Tacito'. In its confrontation with the Spanish monarchy the Dutch rebellion is the renaissance of Batavian liberty. And so Bentivoglio concludes: 'Quindi esser finalmente risorti gli antichi Batavi, e contra la Monarchia Spagnuola haver prese le armi, come i loro maggiori le presero contro l'Imperio Romano.'[3]

The importance of 'l'amor della libertà' as the key motive of the Dutch rebels features prominently in the recent historiography of the Dutch Revolt.[4] In political terms liberty was the central issue in the conflicts about the independence and self-government of the Dutch towns and provinces. In religious terms liberty referred to the discussions about freedom of conscience, freedom of worship and the acceptance of religious pluriformity. In the conflict about the persecution of heresy, religious and political dimensions of liberty came together. The question of how to deal with Protestant heretics involved issues of political, legal and juridical autonomy, matters of faith, toleration and the links between political and religious unity, between ecclesiastical and secular authority. All of these issues raised important questions concerning the office of government in the commonwealth. The conflicts between Philip II and the Dutch rebels about political and religious liberty entailed crucial differences in the conceptions of monarchy and civil power.

Dutch authors recognised the political and intellectual connections between liberty and civil power from the beginning of their protest against the policies of Philip II. In 1570 a *Libellus Supplex*, presented to the Imperial Diet of the old German Empire, argued that 'idle men' under the leadership of Cardinal Granvelle and the duke of Alba were conspiring to subject the Low Countries 'to one form of laws and jurisdiction', to bring them 'to the name and title of kingdom', so that the Dutch provinces could be governed 'with new laws by discretion as the kingdoms of Sicily and Naples are, that have been acquired by conquest'.[5] In 1570 Granvelle and Alba were the main villains. Throughout the 1560s Dutch authors did not hold Philip directly responsible for the policy of the central government. The picture of the cruelly misled, yet *au fond* virtuous prince was dropped by the *Libellus Supplex*. The reputation of Philip II crashed in the 1570s. In the Dutch view Philip II wanted to rule the Low Countries 'freely and absolutely' with absolute power, just as he was doing in the kingdoms of Naples and Sicily, in Milan and in the Indies. The *Apology* of William of Orange was the most powerful blast in a long series of pamphlets. William presented Philip II as the tyrant of all tyrants, 'an incestuous king, the slayer of his sonne, and the murtherer of his wife'.[6] As these words reverberated through Europe, the *Apology* destroyed the reputation of Philip II. For future generations in the Netherlands, England and other European countries the Dutch Revolt was in its essence the clash between Spanish tyranny and Dutch liberty.

This chapter explores the relationship between Dutch and Spanish conceptions of civil power and monarchy. The focus is not only on the clashes, which have featured so prominently in European historiography,[7] but also on the surprising connections between Spanish and Dutch political thought in the time of Philip II.

The Castilian idea of monarchy

The Dutch rebels imputed a Spanish conception of monarchy to Philip II as being founded on the claim to absolute power. In conformity with trends elsewhere in Europe, Castilian authors had started during the late medieval period to include the concept of absolute power in their theories of monarchy. Castilian theorists were at the forefront of the revival of the maxims of Roman laws which strengthened monarchical claims to power and legislative authority.[8] Ulpian's phrase *princeps legibus solutus est* (Digest 1.3.31) was used to argue that the prince was not bound by human law but that the will of the king was the supreme source of civil law.[9] In the fifteenth century the idea of the king as law-giver was enriched with the notion of the king as supreme temporal authority, the *rex qui superiorem non recognoscit*. The union between the concepts of 'poder absoluto' and 'señor sobrano' provided the juristic foundations for the claims to sovereignty and absolute power under Charles V and Philip II.

This juristic idea of monarchy was intertwined with the theological conceptions of kingship, which dominated monarchical theory until the late sixteenth century. Castilian theories of monarchy were imbued with the notion of the king as God's vicar, *vicarius Dei*, who received his authority directly from God. The divine origin endowed kingship with celestial 'grandeza', which imposed supreme authority and moral obligations on the king and also entailed stories about the sacred powers and virtues of kings, including their amazing powers of healing.[10] In their personal convictions Charles V and Philip II were greatly indebted to this conception of divine monarchy. They accepted not only the political but also the intellectual legacy of the Catholic monarchs and applied it to their own circumstances. In his various instructions to his son, including those of 1543 and the political testament of 1548, Charles insisted on the divine origin of monarchy, spelling out the religious, moral and political duties of the office. As God's vicar the principal duties of the prince were the protection of religion and the administration of justice. Charles urged his son to stamp out heresy and to administer justice with mercy, enlightened by the virtue of clemency.[11] Philip accepted the burden. In the public representation of his policy the protection of the true religion featured prominently. In 1566 Philip promised Pius V 'rather than suffer the least damage to the Catholic church and God's service I will lose all my states, and a hundred lives if I had them'. The promise was repeated frequently, acquiring messianic proportions during the final decades of Philip's reign.[12] Poets such as Fernando de Herrera celebrated Spain as the *Civitas Dei,* where the finest virtues of the Hebrews and Romans were united.[13]

The 'confesionalismo' of the Spanish monarchy was not just the result of the personal religious convictions of Charles V and Philip II and the enthusiasm of Spanish poets and priests. The representation of Spain as the most Catholic monarchy on earth was related to crucial external affairs, including the policy to establish Spain's independence, if not superiority *vis-à-vis* Rome, and to enforce practical control over the church in Spain itself. In addition, the debate on the Catholic monarchy and its relationship with Rome played a major role in the internal conflicts at Philip's court, where factions used these issues to strengthen their membership, internal cohesion and power.[14]

As far as the Dutch Revolt was concerned Philip's messianic state-ments were also related to profound political worries. Philip was not the scourge of Dutch heretics only because he thought it was his duty as a Catholic monarch to protect the Roman Catholic church but also, and maybe principally, because he thought that maintaining religious unity within the empire was a precondition for maintaining the empire itself. Throughout the vast territories of the monarchy Philip pursued a cautious policy of centralisation. Philip's proverbial prudence was bolstered by conceptions of universal monarchy. The idea of universal monarchy had been extremely popular in the Erasmian circles around Charles V and his chancellor Gattinara, where humanists – though not Erasmus himself – hailed the emperor as the modern Renaissance replica of Marcus Aurelius, the philosopher–king who as universal monarch would be the keeper of peace and concord.[15] The continuity with the Roman Empire was also emphasised by the poets and philo-sophers who justified the conquest of Mexico and Peru and heralded Charles as 'lord of the world'.[16]

The painters, poets and pamphleteers of Philip II glorified 'el rey prudente' along the lines of the Habsburg tradition. In the 1580s ideas of universal monarchy were employed to support the annexation of Portugal, the continuing war in the Low Countries, and the plans for the conquest of England with the expensive – but not so invincible – Armada. The triumphal entry into Lisbon was a magnificent celebration of Philip II as *senhor do mundo* ('lord of the world'). As Philip arrived, one of the arches depicted Janus surrendering the keys of his temple to the king who governed the four parts of the world, Asia, Africa, Europe and America. The medals of the 1580s commemorated Philip's new universal monarchy. Some medals went as far as to claim that 'the world is not enough' for the Spanish monarch: 'Non sufficit orbis'.[17]

The Dutch idea of self-government

The Dutch were not amused. Spanish claims to universal monarchy were contested throughout the political literature of the Dutch Revolt. William of Orange and a host of other authors insisted that Philip's kingship did not extend to the Low Countries:

> Let him be a King in Castile, in Arragon, at Naples, amongst the Indians, and in every place where he commaundeth at his pleasure: yea let him be a king if he will, in Ierusalem, and a peaceable gover-nour in Asia and Africa, yet for all that I will not acknowledge him in this countrey, for any more than a Duke and a Countie, whose

power is limited according to our privileges, which he sware to observe, at his gladsome entraunce.[18]

From the very beginning of the protest against the policies of Philip's government, Dutch authors built their conceptions of good government on the constitutional legacy of their provinces and cities, which, as elsewhere, consisted of the great charters of the late medieval period. Principal examples were the charters of 1477 and the famous Joyous Entry of Brabant, to which, from 1356, every duke of Brabant had to take a solemn oath on the occasion of his inauguration by the States of the duchy. Philip himself took the oath in 1549. The charters had played a major role in the formulation and codification of political rights and duties. In their cumulation they began to form a sort of 'implicit constitution',[19] which, in combination with other written and unwritten customs and rules, restricted the power of the prince, codified participatory claims, guaranteed civic rights and, in so doing, secured the rule of law in the Burgundian Netherlands.

The charters were the expressions of a long-lasting, powerful ideological current in the Low Countries. Being extorted at moments of weakness of the central government, they reflected the political views of the most important towns and provinces of the Low Countries. During the late medieval period the powerful towns in the Burgundian Netherlands, and those of Brabant and Flanders in particular, tried to create a political order marked by a weak but efficient central government and dominated by self-governing city-republics.[20] The charters of 1477 and the Joyous Entry were the expression of this ideal of self-government.

In legitimating their resistance against the government of Philip II, Dutch authors represented the charters as an essential part of the 'ancient constitution' which had been created by wise ancestors to safeguard Dutch liberty. Within the 'ancient constitution' the charters functioned as constitutional guarantees of liberty. As pointed out by many treatises, under special reference to the Joyous Entry of Brabant, to become lord of the country, Philip II had to take a solemn oath to uphold and respect the charters. They were the fundamental laws of the country, which no prince was allowed to violate or change; they were the bridles of the prince and they contained the conditions on which the prince had been accepted by the States on behalf of the people. Whilst the charters were the constitutional and legal guarantees of liberty, the States assemblies and the citizens of the Netherlands were presented as its virtuous guardians. In the course of the 1570s the Dutch rebels formulated an interpretation of the Dutch political order as based on liberty, constitutional charters, representative assemblies and civic virtue.

A delicate and elaborate synthesis of the legitimation of the revolt was offered by Aggaeus van Albada in his annotations to the *Acts of the Peace Negotiations* which took place in Cologne in 1579. Albada was a gifted Frisian jurist who had received a thorough humanist education in Paris, Orleans, Bourges and Italy. In Cologne he acted as the principal spokesman on behalf of the States General.[21] Albada's political thought is based on the premise that the essence of political authority is to foster and protect the common good of the community. Albada argues that God has created men 'free and equal'. The sole purpose for the creation of princes is, to the profit of the people, to enlighten the maintenance of 'human and civil society or citizenhood' and to make it easier for people to help each other with 'mutual benefactions'. The *bene et beate vivere*, or, as the authors of the Italian Renaissance called it, the *vivere civile* is the principal aim of politics.

Albada emphasises that princes have been made by the people, and not the people by princes. He rejects the argument that all men have been created for the sake of 'a hundred' princes as absurd and he wonders who, 'since a king is made by the people and because of the people, and without the people could not remain king, will be surprised that we conclude that the people is above the king?'[22] Albada maintains that this principle applies to all magistrates, amongst whom the prince hold but 'the first place'. He concludes that 'the right of ruling' is 'nothing but a right of the common people'.[23] The authority of all magistrates, including both prince and States, rests on the 'supreme rule of the common people'.[24]

On the basis of these fundamental principles Albada offers an elaborate analysis of the position and authority of prince and States in the Netherlands. Realising that the position of Philip II was, as Albada himself points out during the negotiations, next to religion the principal point of conflict, the Frisian humanist emphasises that the prince is but a 'custodian, servant and executor' of the law, 'a servant of the ship'. In the ship of the community the prince holds the place of the 'steersman'; the *populus* is the master of the ship.

The States assemblies have been created for the same purpose as the prince: it is their bounden duty to serve the 'fatherland', 'to foster the common welfare and good, yes, to consider their own welfare inferior to the common'.[25] The States are the representatives of the community. They are elected officers of the community, not of the prince. Albada emphasises that the States have been fully entitled to 'take up arms to the defence of their life and freedom'. On the basis of the principle of popular sovereignty he concluded that the States, being those who have established a prince in his authority, retain the power to take the latter's authority back, if he violates the conditions on which he is appointed.

Albada was the first Dutch author to give a full account of popular sovereignty as an active force in the Dutch constitution. The abjuration of Philip II in 1581 merely intensified the debates on the optimal state of the Dutch commonwealth and on the location of sovereignty in the peculiar Dutch interplay of towns, provincial States and States General.[26] The most influential interpretation was developed by François Vranck, who responded to the argument of the English councillor Thomas Wilkes that the States of Holland were mere delegates who acted on order and instruction of their principals, the sovereign community.

Vranck admitted that the States were representative institutions whose work had to be seen in terms of delegation. A delegate, participating in the States, could only act 'in conformity with his instruction and commission'. The delegates received their instruction from their principals, the estates of nobles and towns. In Vranck's view the towns of Holland were important self-governing political entities. Together with 'the corporation of the Nobles', the 'Colleges of Magistrates and Town Councils' represented 'the whole state and the entire body of the inhabitants'. Thus Vranck accepted the notion of popular sovereignty, with the term 'popular' referring to the 'nobles and towns' of Holland. He also accepted that members of the States were delegates, acting on the instructions of their 'principals'. According to Vranck this did not diminish the importance of the States. For although sovereignty resided with the people, it was administered by their delegates, the States. Employing the distinction between the location and the administration of sovereignty, Vranck concluded 'that the sovereignty of the country is with the States in all matters'.[27]

For decades theorists continued to discuss the issues of sovereignty, representation and participation in the Dutch Republic. Hugo Grotius was a major contributor to these debates. In a series of manuscripts and publications Grotius glorified the new republic of Holland in elaborate comparisons with Athens, republican Rome and the Hebrew republic. In the *Treatise on the Antiquity of the Batavian Republic*, Grotius explained that Holland had always been a virtuous republic of optimates. In Grotius's hands the old constitution of Holland was traced back to the age of antiquity with amazing ease. The Batavian resistance against the Romans was presented as 'the just beginning of a free republic, constituted in liberty by a people of free origin'.[28] Celebrating the Batavians as 'the authors of liberty' Grotius drew a sharp contrast between *libertas* and *regnum* and he argued that Tacitus had described the people, assemblies and citizenship of the Batavians in terms of 'what we nowadays call a free *respublica*, what Caesar called the *civitas* of the Helvetians, a republic'.[29]

The Spanish–Dutch connection

In the clarity and forcefulness of Grotius's argument the distinction between Spanish tyranny and Dutch liberty, which had dominated Dutch political thought since the 1560s, evolved into an opposition between kingship and republic. Although this overt anti-monarchism was relatively rare, the opposition between the Castilian idea of monarchy and the Dutch *respublica mixta* was one of the driving forces of the Dutch Revolt. It was impossible to reconcile the Castilian plea for a monarchy where the king as *vicarius Dei* has the fullness of power and the Habsburg dream of universal monarchy with the Dutch passion for a *respublica mixta* based on liberty, ancient constitution, popular sovereignty, representation and civic virtue.

In terms of intellectual history the battles did not run along a neat line of Spanish–Dutch division. Monarchism was not the only trademark of Spanish political and intellectual traditions; liberty was not the patent of Flanders, Brabant and Holland. The political union between Spain and the Burgundian Netherlands had contributed to the intensification of economic and cultural contacts. Erasmus was the towering figure of Dutch and Spanish humanism. When Philip II visited Rotterdam in September 1549 during his grand tour of the Low Countries he and his Spanish entourage paid homage to the prince of humanism.[30] Spanish humanists were integrated into the humanist circles of Antwerp, the economic and cultural metropolis and the place of publication of studies such as Furió Ceriol's *Concejo y consejeros del príncipe* and Sebastian Fox Morcillo's *De regni regisque institutione*, both of which appeared in 1556. The university of Louvain was another centre for the exchange of ideas. Louvain was a stronghold not only of humanist studies, but also of neo-scholasticism, which manifested itself in theology, law and political theory. The Frisian humanist Joachim Hopperus was one of the Louvain jurists who made their careers in the government of councils that characterised the reign of Charles V and Philip II. Between 1566 and 1576 Hopperus was *presidente de Flandes* in Spain. His works included *Ferdinandus, sive de institutione principes*, a mirror-for-princes in the form of a dialogue featuring two of the most prominent members of Philip's government, Granvelle and Viglius, and Hopperus himself. Fully in line with the Castilian idea of monarchy, Hopperus celebrated the king as *vicarius Dei* who was to protect and promote the *bonum commune* of his subjects through rightful and merciful administration of justice and through excellence in the virtues.[31] Hopperus elaborated his views in the unfinished commentary on Psalm 119, *Doctrina y officio del rey*,[32] which is mainly devoted to the study of the duties and moral obligations of royal office. In the second and third chapter of the *Doctrina* Hopperus explains how the king is tied through his office to the *bonum commune* of the *respublica*, to justice and to the law of God. This insistence on the moral duty of kingship to serve *bonum commune* and *iustitia* and on the subjection of the *princeps* to eternal, natural and divine law was common-place in theories of monarchy in the Low Countries, in Spain and elsewhere in Europe. The implications of this commonplace were, however, the subject of intense controversy. It was one of the themes which dominated the political thought of the school of Salamanca of Francisco de Vitoria and his pupils such as Domingo de Soto.

The political language with which the theologians of the school of Salamanca discussed the political issues of their times was shaped to an important extent by Thomas Aquinas and his appropriation of Aristot-elian thought.[33] This did not mean that the neo-Thomists of the school of Salamanca were slavish followers of Aristotle and Aquinas. On the contrary, they were fully aware of the novelties of humanism in general and the renaissance of stoic thought in particular.

Following Aquinas, Vitoria and his pupils wanted to deal with political problems in rationalist terms, which meant that the neo-Thomists placed their full weight on natural law theory. Endorsing Aquinas' definition of natural law as the 'participation by rational creatures in the eternal law',[34] neo-Thomists regarded natural law as the foundation for the analysis of such political issues as the origins, scope and limits of civil power. The 'first principles' (*prima praecepta*) of this foundation consisted of those self-evident rules which every man by virtue of his reason recognised as his natural inclinations. Neo-Thomists assumed that these first principles were 'implanted' in each and every man. As Soto put it in the fourth book of his masterpiece *De iustitia et iure*, which he dedicated to Charles and Philip, 'the law of nature . . . is promulgated by the light of natural reason and instinct . . . so that, as far as the first principles of natural reason are concerned, no human being can plead ignorance as excuse'.[35]

Being derived from the law of nature, civil power is a divine ordina-tion. Accounting for the origins of the commonwealth and civil power, Soto argues that 'God through nature gives to individual things the faculty of conserving themselves and resisting their contraries': God endows human nature with the faculty of conserving not only their temporal but also their spiritual well-being. He 'adds to them', as Soto phrases it, 'the instinct of sociability because man is simply unfit for solitary life'.[36]

The congregation of the *respublica* leads to the institution of *civilis potestas*. As the commonwealth is unable to defend itself and to administer justice – indeed to govern itself, in the words of Soto – it selects 'magistrates, to whom it grants its faculty'. As Soto explains, civil power is instituted by the people: 'Kings and monarchs are not created proximately, and, as they say, immediately, by God . . . but, as the law "quod placuit" has it, kings and princes are created by the people.'[37] This act of creation consists of the total transfer of 'imperium et potestatem' from people to king, establishing him as the principal source of civil law. The transfer of 'imperium et potestatem' entails duties on both sides. Having ceded their faculty to the king by natural reason and instinct – and therefore by divine ordination – the members of the common-wealth are obliged to obey him. The transfer turns them into subjects. Whilst civil laws are binding in conscience, the king cannot wield his 'imperium et potestatem' at will. Soto insists throughout *De iustitia et iure* that the purpose of the law is the protection and prosperity of the *bonum commune*: 'lex est regula dirigens in commune bonum'.[38]

Soto's account of the origins and duties of civil power and monarchy represented the mainstream of the political thought of Spain's neo-scholastics. It was taken up by jurists such as Fernando Vázquez de Menchaca, who served Philip II in the 1560s. In 1564 Vázquez dedi-cated his main study, *Controversarium illustrium aliarumque usu frequentium*, to the king.

The foundation of Vázquez's account of civil power is the pre-sumption that before the establishment of the first acts of human law all *res* are in a state of natural liberty. In the case of some *res*, most famously the sea, this natural liberty can never be relinquished. In the case of human beings 'the natural appetite for society, the *naturalis apetitus socialis*, and the necessity of human beings to protect themselves against wrongdoers leads to the formation of society and civil power'.[39] In strong contrast with Soto, Vázquez draws a sharp line between the natural movement to society and the artificial establishment of civil power.[40] Natural sociability leads to the congregation of free citizens in society. But men do not naturally live at peace with each other, and so society will suffer from discord and dissent. For their own protection free citizens will then decide to establish civil power. As Vázquez puts it, all kings 'are understood as created, elected or given not for their own sake or that of their own utility, but for the sake of the citizens and the utility of the citizens'.[41] In Vázquez's theory *civilis potestas* is power conceded by free citizens to the king, who should govern them for their own good.

Even more than Soto's account of civil power and monarchy Vázquez's theory raised the question of the legitimacy of resistance in situations where the king abused his 'imperium et potestatem' and turned into a tyrant. In the case of Vázquez the radical answer was that if the jurisdiction of the king is based on the consent of the citizens, 'then that consent is of its nature revocable, since they are seen to have subjected themselves for their own utility, not that of their prince'.[42]

The theories of civil power and monarchy, as developed by Vitoria, Soto and other members of the school of Salamanca and then radicalised by Vázquez, were taken up by Dutch authors in the course of the revolt. The principal example is Aggeaus van Albada, who bolsters his theory of popular sovereignty and the civil power of the Dutch States with references not only to the classical works of Plato, Aristotle, and Cicero's *De officiis*, but also to the medieval commentators on Roman law such as Bartolus and Baldus, and to the more recent studies of Soto, Vázquez, Mario Salomonio, and the *Vindiciae contra tyrannos*.

Albada's main sources are Vázquez's *Controversies* and Salomonio's *De principatu*. Albada refers to Vázquez at almost all stages of his legitimation of the Dutch Revolt and of the civil power of the States assemblies. The basic premise of Albada's argument, 'that all forms of government, kingdoms, empires and legitimate authorities are founded for the common utility of the citizens, and not of the rulers' is quoted from the *Controversies*,[43] and is followed by a long reflection on Salomonio's *De principatu* which leads to Albada's endorsement of popular sovereignty. The argument that all princes are bound by the laws and that Philip II in particular is tied to the charters of the Low Countries is supported with references to both Soto and Vázquez.[44] The defence of the active policy of intervention by the States is based on Vázquez's theory of jurisdiction and 'natural protection'. The legitimacy of Dutch resistance against Philip II is supported with the argument 'that if a community is oppressed by its Prince or Stadtholder, it shall take recourse to its overlord; but if there is no overlord, the community is entitled to take up arms'. According to Albada this argument was first formulated by Soto and then endorsed by Vázquez.[45]

The peace negotiations at Cologne failed, marking the final rupture between Philip II and the Dutch rebels. In terms of political history the Cologne negotiations can be described as the ultimate clash between 'Spanish tyranny' and 'Dutch liberty'. However, as Albada's annotations to his own arguments show, in terms of intellectual history such a juxtaposition makes no sense. Monarchism did not monopolise Spanish political thought in the sixteenth century. In the tradition of Aragonese constitutionalism the celebration of ancient liberties and political liberty was as dominant as it was in the political thought of the Dutch Revolt.[46] However, from the point of view of intellectual history, the outright

Aragonese rejection of Castilian monarchism was perhaps less threatening to claims of absolute power and universal monarchy than the subtle theories coming from Salamanca. Vitoria, Soto and Vázquez were no anti-monarchists. Their theories of civil power were to an important extent the result of the exploration of the links between divine ordination, natural law and the authority of the prince. Vitoria, Soto and Vázquez tried to clarify themes which had been part of the Castilian conception of monarchy for centuries. In the hands of Albada and other Dutch authors the arguments of Soto and Vázquez were brought to a radical conclusion. To an important extent the intellectual foundation of the Dutch rejection of Philip II was provided by a theory of civil power advanced by two of Philip's own counsellors.

Climax: Vázquez and Grotius

The political rupture between Spain and the Netherlands in the time of Philip II did not lead to a breakdown of intellectual connections. The best was yet to come. The political theory of Hugo Grotius was the culmination of the close link between Spanish and Dutch political thought. Grotius had no qualms about his admiration for Spanish thinkers. When, in 1615, the ambassador of France in The Hague, Aubéry du Maurier, asked Grotius's advice on the proper education for a *politicus*, Grotius included a section on law. He recommended the study not only of Plato, Cicero and Thomas Aquinas but also of the three outstanding 'jurists' of his own days: François Hotman, Alberico Gentili and Fernando Vázquez.[47] The recommendation was repeated in the prolegomena of *De iure belli ac pacis*, where Grotius praised Vázquez for 'treating the controversies of peoples and kings . . . with great freedom'.[48]

Grotius's engagement with Vázquez started at an early age. In 1603 the seizure of a Portuguese vessel by ships of the Dutch East India Company prompted a number of Mennonite shareholders to question the right to wage war against the Portuguese and to take prizes. Between 1604 and 1606 Grotius wrote the work which is now known as *De iure praedae*, and which he himself called *De rebus Indicis opusculum*.[49] Grotius's defence of Dutch colonial enterprises was greatly inspired by the works of Spanish theorists. *De iure praedae* contains sixty-eight references to Vitoria and seventy-four to Vázquez.

From the very beginning of *De iure praedae* Vázquez is a guiding author for Grotius.[50] Grotius praises him as 'the pride of Spain, who in no instance leaves anything to be desired in the subtlety with which he explores the law, nor in the liberty with which he teaches it'.[51] The turn to Vázquez begins in the *prolegomena* as Grotius establishes the nine axiomatic rules and thirteen fundamental laws underlying his political theory. He starts with the famous argument that self-preservation (*sui-amor*) and friendship (*amicitia*) are the main characteristics of individuals in the state of natural liberty, where each is 'free and *sui iuris*'. At this point Grotius, following Vázquez, elucidates the move from natural liberty to human society and the establishment of civil power. For reasons of demographic growth, better protection and greater economic convenience individuals create smaller societies, which are 'formed by general consent for the sake of the common good'.[52] Thus Grotius endorses Vázquez's view that whilst 'human society does indeed have its origin in nature, civil society as such is based on deliberate institution'.[53] Grotius uses the concept of *respublica* to refer to a multitude of private persons who have come together to increase their protection through mutual aid and to assist each other in acquiring the necessities of life. Referring to Vázquez, Grotius emphasises the 'will of individuals' (*singulorum voluntas*) as the constitutive force for their union by way of civil contract – Grotius uses the term *foedus* – in a 'unified and permanent body' with its own set of laws. From *singuli* the individuals taking this seminal decision are turning themselves into *cives*, citizens.

The laws of the commonwealth emanate from its will as a unified body based on consent. With references to Vázquez, Vitoria and Covarruvias, Grotius argues that 'civil power, manifesting itself in laws and judgements, resides primarily and essentially in the bosom of the commonwealth itself'.[54] Of course not everybody has the time to devote himself to the administration of civil affairs. The exercise of lawful power is therefore entrusted to a number of magistrates, who act for the common good. By mandate the magistrates have the authority to make laws for the *respublica*, which bind all citizens.

The introduction of the concept of *magistratus* represents a subtle and important shift in political language. Grotius's account of the origins of civil power follows Vitoria and especially Vázquez. At crucial moments, including the emphasis on natural liberty and the definition of *respublica* and civil power, Grotius acknowledges his agreement with Vitoria and Vázquez. With the introduction of the concept of *magistratus*, Grotius follows the example of Aggaeus van Albada, and merges Vázquez's theory of civil power with the language of the Dutch and French theories of resistance. As with Albada this merger leads to the distinct rejection of theories of absolute power. The explicit use of the concept of *magistratus* emphasises that those who exercise civil power, be they king, princes, counts, States assemblies or town councils, are administrators. Arguing that 'just as every right of the magistrate comes from the commonwealth, so every right of the commonwealth comes from private persons', Grotius reaffirms in *De iure praedae* that 'public power is constituted by collective consent'.[55] As Peter Borschberg has observed, throughout the unpublished works of the first decade of the seventeenth century Grotius maintains this preference for the concept of civil or public power, and carefully avoids concepts such as *maiestas* or *summum imperium*. Whilst Bodin defines sovereignty as 'la puissance absolue & perpetuelle d'une Republique, que les Latins appellent *maiestatem*',[56] Grotius sticks to the term *summa potestas* in explicit contravention of the old and new theories of absolute power. In the *Commentarius* Grotius adopts the old definition of Bartolus and describes *summa potestas* in terms of 'the right to govern the commonwealth which recognises no superior authority among humans'.[57] But the power to govern is neither absolute nor eternal. When Grotius discusses the most important element of *summa potestas*, the right to declare war, he reaffirms Vitoria's position that 'all civil power resides in the commonwealth, which by its very nature is competent to govern and administer itself, and to order all its faculties for the common good'. Grotius then repeats that the power of princes is derived from the power of the commonwealth, and he points out that 'the right to undertake a war pertains to the prince only in the sense that he is acting for the commonwealth and has received a mandate from it'. According to Grotius, 'the greater and prior power to declare war lies within the commonwealth itself'. Generalising this point Grotius endorses the position of Vázquez that 'the power of the commonwealth remains intact even after the establishment of the principate'. Going back to Vitoria, Grotius accepts the argument of 'the Spanish theologian . . . that the commonwealth may change one prince for another or transfer the principate from one dynasty to another'.[58]

And so the theory of civil power forms the foundation for the discussion of a wide range of issues in *De iure praedae*, including the authority of the States assemblies and the justification of the Dutch Revolt. In line with the political thought of his rebellious Dutch predecessors, Grotius defends the authority of the States assemblies with reference to the old Dutch charters. He characterises the assembly of the States as the 'supreme magistrate which maintains the law of the commonwealth and the citizenry'. Faced with the 'foreign arms' of the duke of Alba it was their duty to defend the commonwealth and to uphold 'the pacts which had been sanctified by the oath of the prince, and which gave continuity to the form of government (*formam imperii*)'. It was the duty of the States assembly to 'liberate the commonwealth and the individual citizens from exactions, which directly contravened not only the law but also the common liberty of mankind because, as the Spanish Doctor argues, these exactions lead to immediate pillage and to future servitude'.[59]

As Grotius moves on to justify the abjuration of Philip II, he appeals to Vázquez not only as the 'Spanish Doctor' but also as one of Philip's own 'senators'. Grotius endorses Vázquez's view that when 'superiors' such as Philip 'refuse justice to the subjects, they are not only deprived *ipso jure* of supreme jurisdiction, but also become forever incapacitated from recovering that jurisdiction'.[60] Grotius puts the full weight of his justification of the Dutch Revolt on the basic principles that the commonwealth is the source of civil power and that government is based on contractual consent. He upholds the 'doctrine which has maximum support among the Spaniards themselves that the power which has been given to the prince can be revoked, particularly when the prince exceeds his bounds, because then *ipso facto* he ceases to be regarded as a prince'. With a final blow Grotius reiterates – with a further reference to Vázquez – that 'he who abuses supreme power renders himself unworthy of it, and ceases to be a prince in consequence of what he does to make himself a tyrant'.[61]

Conclusion

As Grotius unfolds his analysis of just war and international law he continues to appeal for support to the members of the school of Salamanca, from the founding father Vitoria to the radical Vázquez. Most famously Grotius supports his defence of the freedom of the seas in chapter 12 of *De iure praedae* with elaborate references to both Vitoria and Vázquez. The freedom of the seas was a key issue in the peace negotiations between Spain and the Dutch Republic which led to the truce of 1609. To substantiate the Dutch claim to freedom of trade and freedom of the seas Grotius published chapter 12 as a separate work, his famous *Mare liberum*.[62]

Grotius undoubtedly used his Spanish sources partly for political reasons, just as Albada had done in 1581. Both Albada and Grotius must have been delighted to be able to answer the claims of Philip II and Philip III with the theories of their own counsellors. These were fine moments of political embarrassment. It would, however, be wrong to reduce the close link between the Spanish theories of Vitoria, Soto and Vázquez and the Dutch works of Albada and Grotius to a mere matter of political convenience. *De iure praedae* was much more than a meticulous political defence of the activities of the Dutch East India Company. It was Grotius's first major attempt to formulate a new humanist theory of natural law.[63] Elucidating the *methodus* and *ordo* of his approach Grotius argues that the problems of war and peace cannot be solved 'solely on the basis of written laws'. A proper enquiry requires a turn to the *ratio naturae*, 'to the ordered plan of nature'. Dutch colonial adventures prompt Grotius to formulate a theory of natural law inspired by those 'jurists of antiquity', who, as Grotius puts it, 'refer the art of civil government back to the very fount of nature'.[64] He argues that the 'discipline of law' should be derived 'from the inmost heart of philosophy'. The problems of war and peace should be tackled with a *methodus* based on persuasion by 'natural reason'. Grotius underpins his new *methodus* with references to Cicero, Baldus and the *Controversies* of Fernando Vázquez.

Grotius and Vázquez have more in common than a couple of legal and political arguments. They are the seminal figures of an intellectual tradition of humanists, who combine the languages of jurisprudence and neo-Scholasticism, of Roman law and the school of Salamanca, with the Renaissance vocabulary of civic humanism and republicanism.[65] Aggaeus van Albada and his main Italian source, Mario Salomonio, belong to the same tradition of legal humanism. In *De principatu* Salomonio offers a smooth integration of Roman law and Italian republicanism, which in combination with Vázquez's *Controversies* shape Albada's theory in structure and substance.[66] In *De iure praedae* Grotius incorporates the heart of Vitoria's and Vázquez's theories to develop a new comprehensive system of legal and political theory, which covers the central issues of Grotius's days, from the origins and limits of civil power to the legal questions concerning international trade.

The connections between the Spanish works of Vitoria, Soto and Vázquez and the Dutch works of Albada and Grotius show that in terms of intellectual history the Dutch revolt cannot be reduced to a simple clash between Spanish tyranny and Dutch liberty. Decades of war led to a profound political rupture between Spain and the Netherlands which tainted Spanish–Dutch relations for centuries. For decades Dutch and Spanish families were haunted by the cruelties of war, by death and destruction, by the plundering of cities and by thousands of helpless refugees. As Guido Bentivoglio recognised in 1611, the Dutch Revolt had been long and grim. For forty years 'la Fiandra' had been turned into 'una scena militare in Europa', which had shown 'al theatro dell'Universo tutte le novità, e spettacoli più memorabili, che mai si vedessero in alcun' altra guerra delle passate, e che mai sian per vedersi in alcuna delle future'.[67]

Among the ashes Spanish and Dutch legal humanists, struggling with the issues of universal monarchy, civil power, and war and peace, shaped a rich intellectual tradition which in the hands of Grotius led to the modern theory of natural law and human rights. This was the cruel irony of early modern Spanish–Dutch history.

Notes

1 An earlier version of this paper was presented at the conference *Europa divida: La monarquia catolica de Felipe II*, 20–23 April 1998, organised by José Martínez Millán and his colleagues at the Universidad Autonoma de Madrid. I would like to thank Xavier Gil, Alfred Kohler and Blair Worden for their help, comments and suggestions. This paper was previously published in *Il Pensiero Politico*, XXXII (2) (1999).

2 Guido Bentivoglio, *Relatione delle Provincie Unite* (1632), ed. S. Mastellone and E.O.G. Haitsma Mulier (Florence, 1983), p. 121: 'But of all the nations in the world, it is the people from northern Europe, and particularly those from Flanders, who have always been most keen to enjoy it – i.e. "the love of liberty"'.

3 Ibid., p. 123: 'Therefore they rose again to fight against the Spanish Monarchy just as their ancestors, the ancient Batavians, fought against the Roman Empire.'

4 For a fine recent overview, see Henk van Nierop, 'De troon van Alva. Over de interpretatie van de Nederlandse Opstand', *Bijdragen en mededelingen betreffende de Geschiedenis der Nederlanden*, 110 (1995), pp. 205–23 (now published in English as Chapter 2 in this volume).

5 *Libellus Supplex Imperatoriae Maiestati caeterisque sacri Imperii Electoribus, Principibus, atque ordinibus, nomine Berlgarum ex inferiori Germania, Evangelicae Religionis causa per ALBANI Ducis tyrannidem eiectorum, in comitijs Spirensibus exhibitus* (1570), p. 17. For the English translation, 'A Defence and True Declaration', see Martin van Gelderen (ed.), *The Dutch Revolt*, Cambridge Texts in the History of Political Thought (Cambridge: Cambridge University Press, 1993), p. 20.

6 William of Orange, *The Apologie of Prince William of Orange against the proclamation of the King of Spaine* [1581] (Leiden, 1969), p. 44.

7 This includes my own work. This paper is an attempt to refine the analysis of my book, *The Political Thought of the Dutch Revolt, 1555–1590* (Cambridge: Cambridge University Press, 1992).

8 See José Manuel Nieto Soria, *Fundamentos ideológicos del poder real en Castilla (siglo XIII–XVI)* (Madrid, 1988), pp. 111–34; José Antonio Maravall, *Estado moderno y mentalidad social*, vol. I (Madrid, 1972), pp. 278–83; J. H. Burns, *Lordship, Kingship, and Empire. The Idea of Monarchy, 1400–1525* (Oxford: Clarendon Press, 1992), pp. 71–96.

9 See Digest 1.4.1: *Quod princeps placuit.*

10 See Nieto Soria, *Fundamentos ideológicos del poder real en Castilla*, pp. 49–107.

11 For Charles's instructions see J. A. Fernandez-Santamaria, *The State, War and Peace. Spanish Political Thought in the Renaissance, 1516–1559* (Cambridge: Cambridge University Press, 1977), pp. 237–47.

12 See Geoffrey Parker, 'David or Goliath? Philip II and his World in the 1580s', in Richard L. Kagan and Geoffrey Parker (eds), *Spain, Europe and the Atlantic World. Essays in Honour of John H. Elliott* (Cambridge: Cambridge University Press, 1995), pp. 245–66.

13 See Arthur Terry, 'War and Literature in Sixteenth-Century Spain', in J. R. Mulryne and Margaret Shewring (eds), *War, Literature and the Arts in Sixteenth-Century Europe* (Basingstoke, 1989), pp. 101–18 and Fernando J. Bouza-Álvarez, 'Monarchie en lettres d'imprimerie. Typographie et

propagande au temps de Philippe II', *Revue d'Histoire Moderne et Contemporaine*, 41 (1994), pp. 214–17.

14 See José Martínez Millán, 'Introducción. Los estudios sobre la corte. Interpretación de la corte de Felipe II', in José Martínez Millán (ed.), *La corte de Felipe II* (Madrid, 1994), pp. 22–35 and Agostino Borromeo, 'Felipe II y el absolutismo confesional', in *Felipe II: Un monarca y su época. La monarquía hispánica* (Madrid, 1998), pp. 185–95.

15 See Terry, 'War and Literature in Sixteenth-Century Spain', pp. 102–3; Fernandez-Santamaria, *The State, War and Peace. Spanish Political Thought in the Renaissance, 1516–1559*, pp. 35–57; Xavier Gil, *Imperio, monarquía universal, equilibrio: Europa y la política exterior en el pensamiento político español de los siglos XVI y XVII* (Perugia, 1996). For Charles and Gattinara see Frances A. Yates, 'Charles V and the Idea of Empire', in Frances A. Yates, *Astraea. The Imperial Theme in the Sixteenth Century* (London, 1975), pp. 1–28 and John M. Headley, 'Gattinara, Erasmus, and the Imperial Configurations of Humanism', *Archiv für Reformationsgeschichte*, 71 (1980), pp. 64–98.

16 Anthony Pagden, *Lords of All the World. Ideologies of Empire in Spain, Britain and France c. 1500–c. 1850* (New Haven and London: Yale University Press, 1995), pp. 29–46.

17 See Fernando Checa, *Felipe II: mecenas de las artes* (third edition, Madrid, 1997), pp. 268–82 and the recent studies of Geoffrey Parker, including Geoffrey Parker, *The Grand Strategy of Philip II* (New Haven and London: Yale University Press, 1998), pp. 1–6.

18 William of Orange, *Apology*, p. 48.

19 Wim Blockmans, 'La signification constitutionelle des privilèges de Marie de Bourgogne (1477)', in Wim Blockmans (ed.), *1477. Le privilège général et les privilèges regionaux de Marie de Bourgogne pour les Pays-Bas*, in the series *Ancien Pays et Assemblées d'états*, vol. LXXX (Kortrijk-Heule, 1985), p. 507.

20 See W. P. Blockmans, 'Alternatives to Monarchical Centralization: the Great Tradition of Revolt in Flanders and Brabant', in H. G. Koenigsberger (ed.), *Republiken und Republikanismus im Europa der frühen Neuzeit* (Munich: Oldenbourg, 1988), pp. 145–54.

21 For Albada, see Wiebe Bergsma, *Aggaeus van Albada (c. 1525–1587), schwenckfeldiaan, staatsman en strijder voor verdraagzaamheid* (Meppel, 1985).

22 Aggaeus van Albada, *Acten van den vredehandel geschiet te Colen* (Antwerp, 1581), p. 101.

23 Ibid., p. 144.

24 Ibid., p. 26.

25 Ibid., p. 123.

26 See Van Gelderen, *The Political Thought of the Dutch Revolt*, pp. 166–212 for the debates of the 1580s.

27 François Vranck, 'Short Exposition of the right exercised from all old times by the knighthood, nobles and towns of Holland and Westvriesland for the maintenance of the liberties, rights, privileges and laudable customs of the country', in Van Gelderen (ed.), *The Dutch Revolt*, pp. 227–38.

28 Hugo Grotius, *Liber de antiquitate reipublicae batavicae* (Leiden, 1610), p. v.

29 Ibid., p. 18.

30 Henry Kamen, *Philip of Spain* (New Haven and London: Yale University Press, 1997), p. 43.

31 For Hopperus's ideas see Paul David Lagomarsino, 'Court Faction and the

Formulation of Spanish Policy towards the Netherlands (1559–1567)', (unpublished doctoral dissertation, Cambridge, 1973), pp. 290–319 and G. Janssens, 'Barmhartig en rechtvaardig. Visies van L. de Villavencio en J. Hopperus op de taak van de koning', in W. P. Blockmans and H. van Nuffel (eds), *Etat et religion aux XVe et XVIe siècles* (Brussels, 1986), pp. 25–42.

32 I have used the edition in Gustaaf Janssens, 'Brabant in het verweer. Absolute monarchie of staat bewind van Alva tot Farnese, 1567–1578', (doctoral dissertation, Leuven, 1981), pp. 353–71.

33 For the exceptional revival of Thomism in the sixteenth century, see Quentin Skinner, *The Foundations of Modern Political Thought* (2 vols, Cambridge: Cambridge University Press, 1978), vol. 2: *The Reformation*, pp. 135–73; Bernice Hamilton, *Political Thought in Sixteenth-Century Spain* (Oxford: Oxford University Press, 1963); Michel Villey, *La formation de la pensée juridique moderne* (4th edition, Paris, 1975), pp. 338–95; Anthony Pagden, *The Fall of Natural Man. The American Indian and the Origins of Comparative Ethnology* (2nd edition, Cambridge: Cambridge University Press, 1986), and most recently Annabel S. Brett, *Liberty, Right and Nature. Individual Rights in Later Scholastic Thought* (Cambridge: Cambridge University Press, 1997). For the following discussion of Vitoria, Soto and Vázquez, I am particularly indebted to this important and innovative study.

34 Thomas Aquinas, *Summa theologiae*, I–II, question 91, article 2 .

35 Domingo de Soto, *De iustitia et iure*, book iv, question iii, article 1. I have used the edition published in Lyon (1569). For Soto's theory of political society and civil power, see in particular Brett, *Liberty, Right and Nature*, pp. 154–64.

36 Soto, *De iustitia et iure*, book iv, question iv, article 1 (fol 107v).

37 Ibid., book i, question i, article 3 (fol 4r).

38 Ibid., book i, question i, article 4 (fol 4r).

39 Fernando Vázquez de Menchaca, *Controversiarum illustrium aliarumque usu frequentium libri tres* (Venice, 1564), Preface, nos. 121–2. I have used the edition by Fidel Rodriguez Alcalde, which also has a Spanish translation (Valladolid, 1931).

40 See for this point in particular Brett, *Liberty, Right and Nature*, p. 173, whose analysis I am following.

41 Vázquez, *Controversiarum*, Preface, no. 119.

42 Ibid., book ii, ch. lxxxii, no. 6.

43 Albada, *Acten*, p. 166 referring to Vázquez, *Controversarium*, book 1, ch. I, no. 40.

44 Albada, *Acten*, pp. 16, 106 and 121.

45 Ibid., p. 122 referring to Soto, *De iustitia et iure*, book v, question i, article 3 and Vázquez, *Controversarium*, book 1, ch. VIII, no. 33.

46 See Xavier Gil, 'Aragonese Constitutionalism and Habsburg Rule: The Varying Meanings of Liberty', in Kagan and Parker, *Spain, Europe and the Atlantic World*, pp. 160–87.

47 P. C. Molhuysen (ed.), *Briefwisseling van Hugo Grotius. Eerste deel, 1597–17 Augustus 1618* (The Hague, 1928), p. 386.

48 Hugo Grotius, *De iure belli ac pacis*, ed. Jean Barbeyrac (Amsterdam, 1725), prolegomena 55, p. xxxviii.

49 Molhuysen, *Briefwisseling van Hugo Grotius. Eerste deel*, p. 72.

50 Hugo Grotius, *De iure praedae commentarius*, ed. H. G. Hamaker (The Hague,

1868). I will also give references to the English translation – Hugo Grotius, *De iure praedae commentarius. Commentary on the Law of Prize and Booty*, vol. 1, ed. Gwladys L. Williams and Walther H. Zeydel (Oxford/London, 1950), but I have sometimes changed the translation for reasons of historical accuracy.

51 Grotius, *De iure praedae*, p. 236; *Commentary*, pp. 249–50.
52 Grotius, *De iure praedae*, pp. 19–20; *Commentary*, p. 20.
53 Grotius, *De iure praedae*, p. 92; *Commentary*, p. 92.
54 Grotius, *De iure praedae*, p. 25; *Commentary*, p. 25.
55 Grotius, *De iure praedae*, p. 91; *Commentary*, p. 92.
56 Jean Bodin, *Les six livres de la republique* (Paris, 1583; reprinted Aalen, 1961), p. 122.
57 Hugo Grotius, 'Commentarius in theses XI', in Peter Borschberg, *Hugo Grotius 'Commentarius in theses XI': An Early Treatise on Sovereignty, the Just War, and the Legitimacy of the Dutch Revolt* (Bern, 1994), p. 215.
58 Grotius, *De iure praedae*, p. 269; *Commentary*, p. 284.
59 Grotius, *De iure praedae*, p. 271; *Commentary*, p. 286.
60 Grotius, *De iure praedae*, p. 272; *Commentary*, p. 286.
61 Grotius, *De iure praedae*, p. 274; *Commentary*, p. 289.
62 Hugo Grotius, *Mare liberum sive de iure quod Batavis competit ad Indicana commercia dissertatio* (Leiden, 1609). For the historical context of the publication of *Mare liberum*, see C. G. Roelofsen, 'Grotius and the International Politics of the Seventeenth Century', in Hedley Bull, Benedict Kingsbury and Adam Roberts (eds), *Hugo Grotius and International Relations* (Oxford, 1990), pp. 108–12 and Frans de Pauw, *Grotius and the Law of the Sea* (Brussels, 1965), pp. 14–22.
63 For this point see especially the work of Richard Tuck, including Richard Tuck, *Philosophy and Government, 1572–1651* (Cambridge: Cambridge University Press, 1993), pp. 154–201 and Richard Tuck, 'Grotius and Selden', in J. H. Burns (ed.), *The Cambridge History of Political Thought, 1450–1700* (Cambridge: Cambridge University Press, 1991), pp. 499–522.
64 Hugo Grotius, *De iure praedae commentarius*, ed. H. G. Hamaker (The Hague, 1868), p. 6. For the English translation see Hugo Grotius, *De iure praedae commentarius. Commentary on the Law of Prize and Booty*, vol. 1 (Oxford, 1950), p. 7.
65 For Vázquez see Annabel Brett, *Liberty, Right and Nature*, p. 175; for Grotius see – in addition to Richard Tuck's works – Martin van Gelderen, 'The Challenge of Colonialism: Grotius and Vitoria on Natural Law and International Relations', *Grotiana*, new series, 14–15 (1993–4), pp. 3–37.
66 For Salomonio see Skinner, *Foundations*, vol. 1, pp. 148–52 and vol. 2, pp. 132–4 and Anthony Black, 'The Juristic Origins of Social Contract Theory', *History of Political Thought*, XIV (1993), pp. 57–76.
67 Bentivoglio, *Relatione delle Provincie Unite*, p. 94: 'the world's stage all the novelties and most memorable sights that have never been seen in any past war and will never be seen in any future one'.

Index

Lightning Source UK Ltd.
Milton Keynes UK
UKOW050641230212

187790UK00001B/21/P

9 780415 253796